CINEMA AT THE EDGES

Cinema at the Edges

New Encounters with
Julio Medem, Bigas Luna and José Luis Guerín

Abigail Loxham

berghahn
NEW YORK · OXFORD
www.berghahnbooks.com

Published in 2014 by
Berghahn Books
www.berghahnbooks.com

Library of Congress Cataloging-in-Publication Data

Loxham, Abigail.
  Cinema at the edges : new encounters with Julio Medem, Bigas Luna and
José Luis Guerín / Abigail Loxham.
    p. cm.
  Includes index.
  ISBN 978-1-78238-304-8 (hardback : alk. paper) —
ISBN 978-1-78238-305-5 (ebook)
1. Medem, Julio, 1958—Criticism and interpretation. 2. Bigas Luna, José Juan,
1946–2013—Criticism and interpretation. 3. Guerin, José Luis—Criticism and
interpretation. 4. Motion pictures—Spain—History and criticism. I. Title.
  PN1998.3.M399L69 2014
  791.4302'330922—dc23

2013033613

British Library Cataloguing in Publication Data

A catalogue record for this book is available from the British Library

Printed on acid-free paper

ISBN: 978-1-78238-304-8 hardback
ISBN: 978-1-78238-305-5 ebook

Contents

Acknowledgements

This book began as a research project funded by the Arts and Humanities Research Council, UK, and so my first thanks must be to them. Additional support during this time was provided by Fitzwilliam College Cambridge, from its Graduate Scholarship scheme, and the Department of Modern and Medieval Languages at the University of Cambridge. A postdoctoral fellowship from the University of Queensland has enabled me to complete this book.

At Berghahn I wish to acknowledge Mark Stanton for his help in the early stages and Adam Capitanio for his patience and support in latter stages. I would also like to thank the anonymous reviewers of a first draft whose comments were invaluable.

A number of people provided feedback for this project in its earlier stages and particular thanks must go to Paul Julian Smith, Emma Wilson, Rosemary Clark, Jenny Chamarette, Debbie Martin, Steve Joy and Jo Evans. Dominic Keown provided patient and unfaltering intellectual and personal support to the project. Previous versions of work in Chapters Two and Four were originally published as 'Barcelona under Construction: The Democratic Potential of Touch and Vision in City Cinema as Depicted in *En Construcción* (2001),' in *Studies in Hispanic Cinemas* 3, no. 1 (2006): 35–48, and 'Veo, Veo; Leo, Leo?: A (Re-)Viewing of Haptic and Visual Discourse in Bigas Luna's *Bilbao* (1978),' in *Studies in European Cinema* 4, no. 3 (2007): 211–221. I thank both journals for their generous permission to reprint this work. I am also indebted to my former colleagues at the University of Hull and my current colleagues at the Centre for Critical and Cultural Studies at the University of Queensland, in particular Graeme Turner. Morgan Richards deserves a special thank you for technical assistance with the images. The Dorothy Sherman Severin Award from the AHGBI and WISPS provided financial support for work on the final chapter and funded a trip to Barcelona where the staff at the Filmoteca de Catalunya were very accommodating.

I must also thank my family, my parents Eddie and Ruth Loxham and my sisters, Naomi, Hannah, Miriam and Esther for their bemused but unconditional support. Finally this wouldn't have been possible with the emotional and practical support of Tim Keenan. And although his arrival has considerably slowed the process of writing and research it has enriched my life in other ways, so for that I must thank Isaac and dedicate this book to him.

Figures

INTRODUCTION
Defining the Edge

In 2007 José Luis Guerín was invited to show his film *En la ciudad de Sylvia* at the Venice biennale, alongside an exhibition of photographs that were conceived as a separate project to the film but also in dialogue with it, expanding the mode of display, and cementing the intermediality of the work that this talented director is involved in. This journey to Venice and the cinematic journey that it initiated became the material for Guerín's next film. Hiding behind his camera, in his own words, he decided to accept every invitation issued to him during a period of twelve months to exhibit, discuss, present and expand upon his audio-visual works. The result of this endeavour is the film *Guest,* a cinematic journey through the cities to which he was invited during the twelve months of the recording. It is a cinematic essay that encompasses the richness of an exploration of subjectivity that positions itself at many edges. It challenges generic boundaries, as it is part fiction, part road movie, and part eulogy to cinema's beginnings (a tendency that unites his films), part biography. Guerín inscribes his own subjectivity within the film from the outset but this is never an explicitly biographical/autobiographical project. The self is present in fragments – his spectacles on a table, the shadow cast by the man behind the camera on the building that he records, or the sketch made of the director by a street artist in Colombia as the cineaste employs his camera to facilitate encounters with the people that he meets on his travels. His subjectivity is inseparable from the recordings and the moment of the recording; his hand-held mobile camera for the course of the recording is a point of contact, of encounter and, as an extension of the director's body, is what transmits to the spectator (after the fact) this embodied encounter with time and space.

This film epitomizes the peripheral, corporeal, embodied subjectivities that, to my mind, unite the approach to these directors that take shape in my new readings of them in this book. Descriptions of film and its appreciation tend to be couched in the vocabulary of vision: we 'see' or 'watch' films and respond according to this optically centred universe with its intrinsic aural accompaniment.[1] This book began because of an interest in the way in which vision and, by inference, perspective appeared to be manipulated, distorted, but also extended, in a selection of films from Spain. These were a selection of films directed by Bigas Luna (1946–2013), José Luis Guerín (1960–) and Julio Medem (1958–).

These disparate works are unified by an identifiable preoccupation with perspective and with the place of the marginal subject in the cinematic landscape. If vision has constituted power for so long in the critical discourse that surrounds cinema then this new perspective subverts, undercuts and, more positively, expands, representations of vision and its primacy. This is not a new approach to cinema but it is a new way to read these works, which combines their aesthetic approach with a social, cultural and national context. Thus, what I attempt here is a tentative exploration of a cinematic response to intricate questions of identity and subjectivity in this European context. That is the marginality of the Iberian peninsula, the exteriority of Spain and Spanish culture and the minority nationalities/regionalities within the Spanish nation state (Catalonia, the Basque country and Galicia). Although I argue that their position at the edges of the Spanish state is one reason for this challenge to paradigmatic hierarchies of vision that are frequently seen to be the representational supports for ideological structures of power and hegemony, my intention is to prioritize their aesthetic practice and to do so I employ an enriching selection of theoretical frameworks that dissect this notion of power and vision. To claim that they are unproblematically Spanish is to deny the importance of their sub-national identities, but to claim a space for them as peripheral/minority national cinemas would be to disavow a rich tradition of Spanish cinema and in turn the way in which they fit into a panorama of European cinema marked by the type of experimentation that is so evident in their work.

These films test the limits of their own representational strategies by interrogating the trope of vision, which is the tool of their creativity. To this end I look to theoretical approaches, which examine notions of the gaze anew and in doing so, allow for a greater fluidity of interpretation behind the ideological structures that they have been assumed to support. In each case, through close examination of the films, I investigate theories that explore, expand and reconfigure the trope of vision and the site of perspective. So why have I chosen these directors and these films for this analysis? Of course, their national affiliation sparked an interest in the idea of resistance lying at the edges, but an overriding sense of a play with the limits of the visual is where they find the greatest degree of common ground. These are directors whose works might be considered difficult to fit into a Spanish, Basque or Catalan tradition and who represent an alternative contribution to the border trope, developing a notion of hybrid cinema driven by reciprocity and oscillating subject positions.

Julio Medem articulates a creative riposte to the imposition of the borders and assumptions about the limits of vision. He has, at the time of writing, directed seven feature length films – *Vacas/Cows* (1992), *La ardilla roja/The Red Squirrel* (1993), *Tierra/Earth* (1996), *Los amantes del círculo polar/Lovers of the Arctic Circle* (1998), *Lucía y el sexo/Sex and Lucía* (2001), *La pelota vasca/Basque Ball* (2003), *Caótica Ana/Chaotic Ana* (2007) and *Habitación en Roma/Room in Rome* (2010) – all of which have received a degree of commercial and critical success both in Spain and abroad. He has worked with well-known actors such as Emma Suárez, Fele Martínez, Najwa Nimri and Carmelo Gómez, stars of the Spanish screen. These works have received their fair share of nominations at international festivals, and as Paul Julian Smith asserts, 'Julio Medem has arguably produced the most important body of work in contemporary Spanish cinema' (2007: 30). The excellent work that has been done on Medem draws attention to his preoccupation with the psyche as a defining force on the subjectivity not only of the character of his films but also, and in line with more traditional uses of psychoanalysis in film theory, with the subconscious elements of the films themselves. Medem's inclusion at the outset of this book is an acknowledgement of his deliberate imbrication of vision and subjectivity; the subsequent chapters shift their focus to the affective, material and haptic dimension of cinematic subjectivity.

Medem's works perform tensions between interiority and exteriority of the subjects; their entangled emotional lives are perpetually ensnared within the workings of the gaze and the desire of the other. This network of desire and the gaze, which can present itself as a troubling web of desire through which our limited subjectivities emerge only as they are constructed by powers beyond our control, gives rise to anxiety and decentred subjects that have previously been the focus of Lacanian readings of cinema. Medem reminds us of the imbrication of our subjectivity within the field of the other's gaze but views it as a liberating facet of subject identity, which in Chapter Two I develop in relation to individual freedoms and subjectivities but also relate it to the trap of language as part and parcel of this alternative subject creation.

I am not the first to highlight this facet of his work; Jo Evans's excellent work on the subject locates this struggle with the self through the 'cinematic battle with O/others' and underlines the role of the 'slippery field of the gaze' (2006: 174–175) in this negotiation of subjectivity through a prevalence of Basque symbols and myths of heroic origins. Although the Lacanian lens through which I contemplate Medem's work is a well-trodden path in film studies and has been expertly applied (by Evans and others) to Medem's works, I explore its reciprocal dimension and the implication of our physical selves in this process of reciprocity. To assume, as I do, that perception is always bi-directional and that the perception of the world is an integral element of our creation of cinematic subjectivity enables the anxiety and recognition of lack caused by the outside world, and constructed so often in cinematic gaze theory as a cause for anxiety in the cinematic space to become, for Medem's protagonists, a form of liberation. The premise of a split subjectivity, which we may try to navigate but never master, is not necessarily a position that is overturned; rather I argue that there may be pleasure in the navigation and the journey – a pleasure which is then extended by the theoretical approaches I employ in Chapters Three and Four in relation to a more reciprocal relationship with the world.

The limits of this interpretation of Lacan are precisely that it becomes trapped in vision as our mode of apprehending the world when cinema moves beyond the visual realm and a new ideological and experiential subjectivity is opened up to us. Lacan moved towards it in his reference to Merleau-Ponty in the bi-directional nature of the gaze and its comparison with the intertwining of self and world raised by Merleau-Ponty, relating to what he calls the 'inside-out structure of the gaze' (Lacan and Miller 1979: 82). My theoretical approach is neither unreservedly Lacanian nor does it reside in the seductive approach of phenomenology. My reason for raising this element of the gaze here and reiterating Lacan's own connections among perception, visibility and our relationship with the world around us is to demonstrate a similar theoretical development in the chapters that follow – that is, from the psychological complexities of Medem's characters to the visceral and embodied nature of Bigas Luna's film and then the material emphasis on film and being that Guerín explores. This is a theoretical development that I explore in Chapter One. What should be emphasized at this point and will recur throughout this book is that the stress on contact and the encounter with these films that raises the notion of intersubjectivity and collapses the notion of clearly defined identities is subtended by – if not always explicitly related to the notion of – our being in the world which Merleau-Ponty and Lacan both explore through visibility. Perception is at work in our relation with the world and with others and this threatens but enriches our own subjectivity, and it is in this that phenomenology informs the analysis of Bigas Luna and Guerín: 'As perceiving subjects intertwined with our lived bodies, we are ontologically obligated to reach out towards, and to make contact with the 'horizon' of the visible – the tangible – in order to interrogate our being in the world' (Chamarette 2012: 56).

Of the directors whose work I examine in this study Bigas Luna's output is the most prolific and his career the longest, as he is the oldest of the three directors that are the focus of this analysis. He is also the most adventurous, in terms of his choice of media, as Internet shorts, theatrical productions and installations complement and inform his filmmaking.[2] His works perform the ruptures that break through the borders of time and space in this journey though different media. His feature-length productions number sixteen, at the time of writing, and range in chronology from 1978 to 2010. The ideological resistance that I locate as an element of all of these works is most clearly related to the socio-political context of Spain in my analysis of Bigas Luna. His Iberian Trilogy is the clearest example of this and I do not dwell on these films and their ideological significance in any great detail as they have already been examined in some detail in elsewhere (Weinrichter 1992; D'Lugo 1997; Keown 2008). His pragmatic approach to filmmaking provides something of a bridge between Medem's more conventional art house productions and the experimentation of Guerín, although his early works would fall more clearly into the latter bracket. He is the director who makes his encounter with other media, and by implication the tenuous position of the frame that I explore through Derrida in the introduction, most explicit and in doing so mines rich seams of intertextuality through his reference to other artists that make his works a fruitful example of the enriching potential of new encounters that are the premise of this book.

José Luis Guerín lectures in filmmaking at the Universitat de Pompeu Fabra in Barcelona. He has made six films to date – *Los motivos de Berta* (1985), *Innisfree* (1990), *Tren de sombras/Train of shadows* (1997), *En construcción* (2001), *En la ciudad de Sylvia/In the City of Sylvia* (2007) and *Guest* (2010) – as well as contributing a piece to a collaborative project *City Life* (1988). His work has mainly been distributed on the festival circuit but with the success of *En construcción* – winner of nine awards amongst them the prestigious Goya for Best Documentary and Best Film at the 2001 San Sebastián film festival – has come an increased awareness of this talented cineaste. The increased visibility of the work of this documentary filmmaker has brought his recent title, *In the City of Sylvia* (2007), particular attention at European festivals, where it was accompanied by a photographic exhibition *Las mujeres que no conocemos/ Women We Don't Know* and a cinematic exhibition of still photographs in the short movie *Unas fotos en la ciudad de Sylvia/Some Photos in the City of Sylvia*. The experimentation with media that is the focus of my analysis of *Train of Shadows* would appear to have been extended with his recent forays into video work, including an exhibition of video letters, *All the Letters,* and a digital film, *Memory of a Morning* shot on video, for the Jeanju digital project.[3]

The concept of the periphery indicates an outside in relation to an inside or an edge that must in some way be subordinated to a more dominant centre. The political reality of the Iberian peninsula is one of competing and divergent claims to dominance and calls for devolved power and identities, some of which it will be necessary to engage with through the geographical and linguistic content of the texts under scrutiny.[4] Moreover, these edges invoke selection and binary opposites in a way that constructs alterity through an optical logic of subject and object. This reading of these films attempts to resituate the periphery through an expanded understanding of perspective that constructs it not as a marginalized space at the limits of a binary opposition but rather as the space in which a positive blurring is effected, a position which I expand in Chapter One. It understands the edge as an aesthetic frontier – one that includes taste, acceptability and genre – as well as a discursive construct, a national imaginary and a geopolitical reality. In the cinema it is also a frame, the border of the screen and the (visual) limit of the diegetic space. In what follows I question its obdurate presence and impermeability in the context of subject construction in the works I analyse.

Derrida interrogated this notion of the frame in *The Truth in Painting,* deriving his analysis from Kant's notion of the *parergon* defined, or approached, in the following terms: 'A parergon comes against, beside, and in addition to the *ergon,* the work done [fait], the work, but it does not fall to one side, it touches and cooperates within the operation from a certain outside. Neither simply outside nor simply inside' (1987: 54). Nicole Anderson extends this problem of the frame in Derrida to problematize the notion of alterity and binary oppositions setting up technologically mediated vision as the means by which we can inhabit the border and interrogate the frame as a means of separation: 'If the traditional notion of perspective is constituted in and through binary oppositions, then perspective – in this common 'sense' – also informs not just perspective(s) and points of view on works of art but in conjunction, subjectivity generally' (2006).

According to this reading of Derrida then the interstices are the site of a particular vantage point which does not rely on separation and division but enables a selective re-mixing of the features of two (or more) traditions and paradigms and, as will become apparent, an often pragmatic embracing or refusal of both. The periphery is not constituted by these films as a subordinated or marginalized excentric 'other' to a mainstream. I am aware of the danger of imposing an artificial interpretation of marginalisation and its opposition to Spanish hegemony here, and I acknowledge that networks of distribution, funding, production and an increasingly transnational process of filmmaking would make this a misguided project. To construct Spanish cinema as the dominant other to these directors would be to ignore the status of Spanish cinema as peripheral within a wider, global context. It would also be to conveniently ignore the important position of Medem and Bigas Luna (to varying degrees) within this national cinematographic landscape. Of course in relation to cinema 'the concept of the periphery is not fixed and static but dynamically adjusts to a range of shifting patterns of dominance in spheres such as industry, ideology and taste' (Iordanova, Martin-Jones and Vidal 2010: 8).

In the case of Spain the nation and its borders are both contentious and significant. The autonomous communities within Spain that have the strongest sense of a distinct identity sit close to the borders of the Iberian peninsula. They contain the regional, local and national elements of diverse identities and selectively – according to point-of-view – define their position in relation to the centre and in relation to a European community beyond national borders. This position is inevitably an imaginary one, dependent on numerous historical, cultural, political, ideological, (and in the case of cinema) commercial and artistic factors.[5]

The directors whose works are the focus of this study provoked this reading because of the way in which they exploit these edges and the altered perspective that this entails. They deal with numerous peripheries – locations, nationalities and bodies – by manipulating the focus of their films and engaging with assumptions about identity and subjectivity as they are represented and embodied by their texts. And they do so because their understanding of cinema posits it as a fluid, mutable and affective artistic device. To return to Derrida, 'These questions of matter, of the frame, of the limit between inside and outside, must, somewhere in the margins be constituted together' (1987: 55).

Similarly my critical approach to their work straddles various areas, admitting some contradictions but allowing for the fluidity that these hybrid works demand. This is my attempt to bring the richness and skill of these sometimes underrated cineastes to the fore and in doing so to unfold a reading of a resistance to homogeneity in a complex Iberian cultural context. A re-territorialisation of cultural practice enables a mobile cinematic subject to shift in these liminal spaces and interrogate the positions and the practices that create meaning in this context. The periphery must be understood, first and foremost, as a creative space: 'The cinematic periphery is a constantly shifting constituent in a dynamically evolving relationship. It is elusive and intangible, as the center to which it relates keeps redefining itself' (Iordanova, Martin-Jones and Vidal 2010: 6).

Commercial factors aside, there is of course a place for categorisation of films, and the scholarly attention visited on these categories not only enriches our understanding of minority practice and the cultural products of small nations (Hjort and Petrie 2007) but also has the opposite effect of generating an understanding of creative practice that frequently straddles the globe, speaking to universal tropes and concerns. When we prioritize the national we run the risk, as Andrew Higson reminds us, of 'fetishising the national rather than merely describing it' (2000: 64). He argues that, whilst there are many cases for considering nationality as one factor in the larger picture of cinematic production, there is a great richness to be uncovered if we also take into account 'the degree of cultural diversity, exchange and interpenetration that marks so much cinematic activity.'

It is in a return to the problem of the visual referred to at the outset that these directors contest the power structures embedded within a centralist discourse of the nation (a thorny concept in present-day Spain). Aesthetic practice steps in to interrogate both identity (national and of other varieties) and subjectivity, and to remove the certainty – and assumed power – that resides in both through a revision of the norms of perspective. These films open up identity and culture and subject them to the scrutiny of the camera, paying particular attention to the instances in which the creativity of their cinematic lens crosses the expected boundaries between various types of identities and – perhaps more daringly – across established subject positions.

I seek to demonstrate that when these boundaries dissolve they enable the emergence of new formulations of identity and subjectivity. Possibility and potential are the principal purpose for this exploitation of the periphery in its relation to identity and subjectivity. Of course the periphery is only defined as such when it is viewed from the centre; and despite the various tangents this analysis will follow, the idea of perspective and an obsession with the effect of cinematic looking provides a compelling unifying strand to which all the other features can be usefully linked. The notion of transgression and the breaching of borders which inevitably seeps into peripheral discourse can be more productively configured here as a site of possibility which, whilst it must take into account the violence (actual and cultural) inflicted in Spain's recent past, points to an emerging space of creativity which focuses on the heterogeneous potential of space and the subject in cinema, which does not remain in thrall to the borders established in this recent and fraught past.

At this juncture it is worth clarifying a terminological point which to a degree mirrors the methodological approach and the theoretical 'tool kit' with which I analyse these works. I use the terms text and film interchangeably in this book but not without a degree of calculated imprecision in both cases. The development of digital technology means of course that the term film, derived as it is from the celluloid basis of a moving picture, might justifiably be considered a misnomer. The term text has similarly been criticized as implying an object to be read, onto which we project our culturally embedded, semiotic and symbolic interpretations. Something which, particularly in any phenomenological approach, is problematic to say the least. However, I prefer the understanding of text put forward by Bernard Bentley in 1995, the year that the Forum for Modern Language Studies produced its first edition on the subject of the Seventh Art. He explains that text is employed frequently in 'its etymological sense of *textum*, that which is woven and made up of various components to make a whole. The film should be seen as the end product of many strands and contributions ... all coming together and contributing to the final product: the text or cloth viewed by the spectators' (1995: 1–2). In the context of a reading of these works that exceeds the visual, this description of a text as textural, as admitting its multiple facets and meanings but also drawing attention to its tactile possibility, is productive and fitting as a justification for my use of the term in this book.

In Chapter One I traverse some of the theoretical and methodological terrain that I consider central to the tropes addressed by the directors whom I then subject to scrutiny in Chapters Two, Three and Four. National identity simply provides the point of departure for a fresh reading of the cinematic subject as it is creatively depicted by these directors. Frequently the national, for these filmmakers, acquires significance through oblique reference and indirect or allusive formal and narrative technique. This is a tradition that emanates from what could be termed an Iberian critical tradition, firmly influenced by its nearest European neighbours. I outline the excellent studies that deal with Spanish cinema, and recognize that it is where they have left gaps that this study finds its site of enunciation. I look to the Barcelona School and to Ventura Pons to suggest that a dissident creative practice that was specifically liked to Spain's marginalized places has enacted the same resistance to hegemonic discourse as works examined in the subsequent chapters. The premise of analysis that works through space, place and language as sites of possibility rather than marginalisation is explored in this chapter and I pay particular attention to the place of the city as a site for exploration of subjectivity (as it will later be explored by Bigas Luna and Guerín) and also the fraught relationship that the gendered gaze has had with the practice of cinema in Spain. These thematic interventions set the scene for the three subsequent chapters, which provide a deeper theoretical engagement with each director in turn.

It is in the realm of the subject that this new articulation of cinematic perspective can begin to interrogate the centre/periphery dichotomy. This is initiated through a preoccupation with perspective that I touched upon at the outset, literally examining innovative points-of-view and the doubling of subjects in Medem. Chapter Two focuses on Medem's oeuvre to date and explores his revisitation of Lacanian tropes of subjectivity in his seminar on the gaze (Lacan and Miller 1979).

In psychoanalytic terms the formulation of subjectivity is predicated on the notion of lack. From Freud's explanation of the perceived threat of castration to the Lacanian *coupure* there is a recurring lexicon in the texts that explores these theories of a void or space and that serves as a reminder of our place as split subjects. A cinematic redefinition of these voids – which centres on the potential of the image to both frustrate and indulge our desire for imagined wholeness – seeks to mask them, and ideology (with its indulgence in montage and other innovative editing techniques) papers the cracks that, when left unconcealed, expose an anxiety not permitted in the fantasy zone of cinema. I would redefine these voids as further examples of the edge – a boundary space that represents transformation rather than alienation.

In contrast to both Bigas Luna and Guerín, whose speculation in this area is more conventionally privileged in the topography of the political arena, the ideological project at work is subtler in the case of Medem. His reading of the peripheral experience is justified because of the very literal interpretation he visits on these liminal spaces and, in turn, by an insistence on entirely protean formulations rather than determined and unshifting cinematic subjects.

These are geographical and psychological frontiers in the first instance in my examination of the intricate workings of desire in *Vacas* and *La ardilla roja* and the creative depiction of space and place. I examine the way in which liminal zones and states reveal a space for the production of desire and, in this context, can be understood as on-screen manifestations of trauma, fantasy and desire and the relationship among them, enabling alternative subjectivities to emerge. This chapter works through Lacanian topologies between self and other as language attempts to fill these empty spaces. At all times Medem revels in a creativity which fuses the visual and the psychological in order to question the assumptions that have been made in these areas and that are of such crucial importance in the medium of cinema.

The second part of this chapter engages with the process of cinematic subject creation in the field of language. Here we are the subject of language, particularly in these reciprocal and creative relationships with others. In *Earth* and *Lovers of the Arctic Circle* we witness a doubling at work which problematizes this unified self, and this is extended in an examination of language in *The Red Squirrel* and *Sex and Lucía*. Finally – and continuing this preoccupation with the potential of new technologies – this edge becomes the imagined spaces of a postmodern era in a reading of the creative latency of cyberspace in *Sex and Lucía* and of a sexual voyage of discovery in *Room in Rome*.

If, as established theory has it, desire underpins the labour of the subconscious mind then Medem's obsession with this mechanism leads us to read the desire at work in its numerous guises not only in the protagonists but also in the construction and deconstruction of the cinematic art itself. The peripheries in this instance may be both spatial and temporal, but they lead us back persistently to psychological liminality. These sites are representative of a particular type of freedom in their potential for change – birth, for example, or a moment between sleeping and waking – and invention, standing on the brink.

Chapter Three encounters the peripheral in a slightly different guise in the less well-known works of Bigas Luna. There can be little doubt that the majority of this talented Catalan's eclectic output has received less critical attention that his Iberian trilogy.[6] With their fixation on the condition and nature of Spain and things Spanish these three films encompass a unifying theme on the interrogation of national identity; the triptych also explores the various methods by which the cinema can support or subvert such representations and, by extension, the elements which form the basis of this argument on the intersections between cinema and identity.

Turning attention to the rest of his oeuvre, however, may serve to inform in more detail the trajectory of his concern with identity in general and expose and extend these notions in what may come to be seen, somewhat paradoxically, as a highly polished and adventurous cinematic idiom. Indeed, Bigas Luna's language is so adventurous that redefinitions of cinematic meaning stem from this director's re-evaluation of those familiar signs and symbols which have established cultural meanings, from the Osborne Bull, which dominates the arid landscapes of *Jamón, jamón,* to the familiar and overdeveloped East coast resort of Benidorm in *Huevos de oro/Golden Balls* (1993). It would not be excessive to posit that in the case of this director the weaving together of so many diverse elements makes the works intentionally complex; an abstruseness which is compounded by a deliberately irreverent approach to his subject matter all of which adds a further layer of difficulty. As will be seen, it is precisely these apparent instabilities that demonstrate the indeterminate cinematic elements used in the construction of subjectivity and identity – the elements that Bigas plays with in order to manipulate both.

These notions are particularly apparent in *Bilbao* (1978), an *opera prima* that ostensibly embarks upon a cinematic journey that appears to conform to familiar ideas surrounding the fetishization of the female body with the masculine, and therefore powerful, gaze as the driving force of the narrative. From the very opening of the film it would seem that Leo (Ángel Jové), the protagonist of this piece, conducts the spectator on a tour of his own perverse desire to possess Bilbao, the eponymous female prostitute. Or, in his own words, 'possess everything I like about her.'

However, the recourse to the standard Freudian reading which, in its ubiquity has in itself become as fetishized as the objects of its discussion, limits the scope for recognising the multi-layered significance of these images concentrating as it does on the inscription of male desire onto the body of the female and then onto the film. This is to simplify what is to become a complex interplay of signification and affect, adding a speculative dimension to the discourse that is both innovative and disturbing.

The critical parameters which explore the body as a dissonant site of representational strategies whilst engaging with the potential for an expanded corporeal understanding of cinema's potential is extended by a reading of *Volavérunt* (1997). This dramatized account of the imagined intrigue in the court of the Duquesa de Alba and her relationship with the artist Goya unpicks the relationship between painting and film. This reading of the film tests the borders of both media in their contribution to somatic discourse and (as with *Bilbao*) the unsettling subversion of power that the body – in this case the female body – can engender through its creative representation. In a chapter that observes the tension between the periphery and the physical body, then, it is unsurprising that a coda to this chapter takes the form of a brief and – perhaps somewhat playful – analysis of that which crosses the border between body and world so easily and frequently: food. Linking a Catalan cultural tradition that has exploited the body's baser functions for subversive ends to new readings of the links between sex, food and the subject reiterates the expanded sensorial and interpretative regime which undermines the primacy of the visual.

This chapter enacts a theoretical shift which acknowledges the psychological fascination with Bigas Luna's films but finds a productive line of enquiry provided by the embodied understanding of cinema by Vivian Sobchack, Laura Marks and others. This is not just centred on the centrality of the body in his flamboyant creations but resonates with a deeper understanding of his praxis. These theories acknowledge cinema's interrelationship with our own embodied subjectivity. Here is the other type of edge space that is embraced as Sobchack explains: 'the subjective lived body and the objective world do not oppose each other but, on the contrary, are passionately intertwined' (2004: 286).

Chapter Four locates a similar variety of somatic deliberation, as the edges of the body and the edges of the frame are once more blurred and explored through these moving image texts. This time the objectivity that Sobchack claims can be incorporated within our subjective world becomes, concretely, the objects and images, in their material form, that are the basis for consideration in these film-essays. For Guerín, this self-reflexivity works to interrogate his preferred genre, documentary. He stages the problem of exposition and the political intent of documentary by refusing to clearly state his intentions. The discursive strategies of the documentary mode have a unique relationship with the aesthetics of cinema. There is, for example, an assumed revelatory mechanism at the heart of documentary filmmaking (Grierson and Forsyth 1966; Nichols 1991; Nichols 2010). This strategy of revelation has been assumed to work within certain ethical and political confines. The subjects of documentary are often marginalized – socially and politically – and the works that represent them seek to subvert and expose dominant ideological structures in order to find a voice for these subjects; in other words they take on a clear civic and social function. Guerín deviates from this strategy and locates his work at the intersections between the aesthetic strategies of cinema and the discursive project of documentary.[7] This technique interrogates the falsely erected binaries between genres in an investigation of materiality and its relationship to film history and personal and collective memory.

It is an apt chapter with which to conclude; current debates in film studies preoccupy themselves with the changing nature of moving image representation as the index fades and the digital takes over. At the same time cultural studies in Spain revolve around representations of memory and trauma and an attempt to reconstitute a past through an aesthetic of absence, particularly material absences in the cases where effacement of lives took place in the establishment of a totalitarian regime. In both cases there is a risk of fetishizing the objects of representation, either celluloid or the scant reminders of the past that is lost. Guerín's suggestive approach incorporates the image, its material basis (photography and film) and the objects of memory in order to explore their alternative meanings.

Perhaps not surprisingly, his particular aesthetic shares many features with that of his compatriot Bigas Luna: a preoccupation with the potential of the moving image to be slowed down and stopped; the place of the still – photographic – image within a moving picture that causes a significant rupture and creates a space for a new type of engagement and reflection. This is the type of image that alerts the spectator to its presence, and in doing so restates a self-reflexive relationship with the medium in which the filmmakers work. The effect of this, and a series of other familiar techniques, is to render transparent the status of cinema as a tool of representation, but Guerín extends this examination to explore the moment of encounter with the cinematic image which resists the use of distance in vision and perception and initiates an affective response.

These works are a meditation on and a response to the history of European (quality) cinema. Guerín's focus – in *En construcción* and *In the City of Sylvia* – is the place of the subject in an urban environment, an environment which seeks to contain a material history of place as well as a symbolic, cinematic and representational history. This innovative approach to the construction of the motion picture calls for a new critical paradigm through which it can be explored. The history and critical structure of documentary is explored in relation to *En construcción,* where the nascent aesthetic speaks to theories of the haptic and their approach to cinematic appreciation, in keeping with the work in Chapter Three on *Bilbao.* Finally, the perennial and thorny issue of national identity underlies the geographical transgressions at the heart of these works. Guerín's determination to progress within a European tradition is at the heart of the formal and thematic concerns of both *Train of Shadows* and *En construcción.*

To conclude this investigation of Spain's peripheral cultural practices is to move forward into the international spaces of intellectual and artistic practice. Bigas's films tested the borders and his gallery works have broken out of the confines of the cinema and put into practice the immersive sensorial experience that his films initiated. Guerín's latest works speak to this expanded understanding of what the moving image and its appreciation mean in the twenty-first century. *In Sylvia's City* has a complex relationship with two other productions that, in name at least, would seem to be complementary. The concern with the peripheral spaces of Europe endures as Strasbourg's cobbled streets and eminently French cafes set the scene for this slow and contemplative cinema (another marginal feature as this almost silent picture resists all commercial and narrative imperatives to action).

Spain in Europe

It is not my intention to disregard categories entirely in an attempt to justify the inclusion of what, at first glance, may appear as a disparate and unrelated group of directors. Indeed, the structural logic of this project seems to create some of the categories that the films I analyse attempt to overturn. Much like the members of the Barcelona School (whose work I approach in more detail in Chapter One) they are united by a formal experimentation, to a greater or lesser degree, that coheres around an aesthetic resistance to cultural hegemony.

The pragmatic approach to their national identity taken by these men, pre-eminently Bigas Luna, is well documented. This prefigures a productive approach to analysis of their work. It is situated within certain geographical borders yet its sophistication and attention to its position in a rich history of filmmaking (at least within Europe, perhaps extending to North America, and inevitably, given the linguistic link, also in dialogue with Latin America) demands attention that focuses on this highly developed reflexive approach to the cinematic art and reveals the ways in which identities can be persistently redefined and renegotiated.

Rosalind Galt astutely develops this dimension of flexibility in her reworking of the European Cinematic cartography. Her argument is that these categories are always finally mutable and contingent and (as I will examine during the course of this book) so often depend on a negative: 'European films code internationally as both "not-American" and, in many markets, "not-Asian," "not-Latin American," and "not-Middle Eastern."' Galt emphasizes the 'encrustations of cultural meanings' that compete for dominance according to demands external to the creative process of film production (2006: 5).

I have already hinted at the difficulty of justifying the adducement of these directors as a united group in this study. There was also, of course, an equally problematical decision to be made in the selection of films for scrutiny. Furthermore, the focus of the project necessarily privileges certain theoretical approaches, which move between Spanish cultural studies and film theory and philosophy. What emerges in this interstitial space between national cinema and rejection of it is a persistent refusal to adhere to semiotic and discursive practices which reference a place in the historiographical project of a national cinema, a gendered cinema, a documentary cinema, a fantastical cinema. These directors posit that this space be occupied by a new cinematic subject that can see, feel, speak and perform in it. There is space for this type of analysis to continue, with female directors, the new documentaries that are challenging the political category of this representational art, and other talented directors from the margins of Europe, frequently designated by that equally slippery denominator 'World Cinema', which Lucía Nagib (2006) convincingly argues must also be liberated from its position as other to Hollywood and therefore the peripheral art.

Notwithstanding the amorphous categories of periphery and centre in their geographical manifestation as they are encompassed within the state, there is an unavoidable concentration on the notion of Catalan and Basque identity at work in this study. What merits attention in this respect is the way in which these directors appear to have fallen between two camps. International and universal in outlook, they are also aware of fitting into their regional identity and their state affiliation – unavoidable given their choice of language. Noticeable throughout this analysis is the significance of place and its link to perspective. The pertinence of both in the semiotics of cinema is crucial to an understanding of the way in which cinema is seen to encapsulate meaning. It is still more significant in the case of these filmmakers who with their cameras held at the frontiers are able to turn through three hundred and sixty degrees, offering us new visions of Spain, the periphery and that which lies beyond.

Notes

1. Initially these would have been silent and, as early reports of cinema bear out, concentrated on the magical, dreamlike quality of the image. Excellent work has also been done on sound in film (Chion and Gorbman 1999), and Yale French Studies devoted an issue (no. 60) to this subject in 1980.
2. A number of these short works can be viewed online at http://www.clubcultura .com/clubcine/clubcineastas/bigas/bi-video/home.htm.
3. The other directors selected to create a piece for the 2011 project were Claire Denis and Jean-Marie Straub. For more information see http://eng.jiff.or.kr/b20_ screen/10_section_tap03_01.asp (accessed 25 November 2011).
4. Carr (1982) provides a comprehensive account of Spain's development until the end of Franco's dictatorship. The political situation is succinctly outlined by

Guibernau (2000), and the complex issue of identity is addressed in Balfour and Quiroga (2007).

5. For further elaboration, and problematizing, of these national imaginaries and their relation to cinematic production see Thomas Elsaesser's excellent edition, (2005).

6. Such a prolific and diverse output is difficult to unify under the auspices of a single study, and the divergence in theme and content, as well as the use of several different languages, might be the reason for the neglect.

7. A strategy which has much in common with Keith Beattie's (2008) revision of documentary style and strategy.

References

Anderson, N. 2006. '(De)constructing Technologies of Subjectivity'. *Scan Online Journal*. Retrieved 13 May 2009 from http://scan.net.au/scan/journal/display.php?journal_id=87.

Balfour, S., and A. Quiroga 2007. *The Reinvention of Spain: Nation and Identity since Democracy*. Oxford and New York: Oxford University Press.

Beattie, K. 2008. *Documentary Display: Re-viewing Nonfiction Film and Video*. London: Wallflower.

Bentley, B. P. E. 1995. 'The Film as Text', *Forum for Modern Language Studies* xxxi(1): 1–7.

Carr, R. 1982. *Spain 1808–1975*. Oxford: Clarendon Press.

Chamarette, J. 2012. *Phenomenology and the Future of Film*. Basingstoke: Palgrave MacMillan.

Chion, M., and C. Gorbman 1999. *The Voice in Cinema*. New York and Chichester, Columbia: University Press.

D'Lugo, M. 1997. *Guide to the Cinema of Spain*. Westport, CT: Greenwood Press.

Derrida, J. 1987. *The Truth in Painting*. Chicago and London: University of Chicago Press.

Elsaesser, T. 2005. *European Cinema Face to Face with Hollywood*. Amsterdam: Amsterdam University Press.

Evans, J. 2006. 'La madre muerta (*The Dead Mother*, 1993) and *Tierra* (*Earth*, 1995): Basque Identity, or Just the other?', *New Cinemas: Journal of Contemporary Film* 4(3): 173–183.

Galt, R. 2006. *Redrawing the Map: The New European Cinema*. New York: Columbia University Press.

Grierson, J., and H. Forsyth 1966. *Grierson on Documentary*. London: Faber.

Guibernau, M. 2000. 'Spain: Catalonia and the Basque country', *Parliamentary Affairs* 53(1): 55–68.

Higson, A. 2000. 'The Limiting Imagination of National Cinema'. In *Cinema and Nation,* edited by M. Hjort and S. MacKenzie, 63–74. London and New York: Routledge.

Hjort, M., and D. Petrie, eds. 2007. *The Cinema of Small Nations.* Edinburgh: Edinburgh University Press.

Iordanova, D., D. Martin-Jones and B. Vidal, eds. 2010. *Cinema at the Periphery.* Detroit: Wayne State University.

Keown, D. 2008. 'The Catalan Body Politic as Aired in *La teta i la lluna*'. In *Burning Darkness: A Half Century of Spanish Cinema,* edited by J. R. Resina, 161–172. New York: State University of New York Press.

Lacan, J., and J. A. Miller. 1979. *The Four Fundamental Concepts of Psychoanalysis.* Harmondsworth: Penguin.

Nagib, L. 2006. 'Towards a Positive Redefinition of World Cinema'. In *Remapping World Cinema: Identity, Culture and Politics in Film,* edited by S. Dennison and S. Hwee Lim, 30–37. London: Wallflower Press.

Nichols, B. 1991. *Representing Reality.* Bloomington and Indianapolis: Indiana University Press.

———. 2010. *Introduction to Documentary.* Bloomington and Indianapolis: Indiana University Press.

Smith, P. J. 2007. 'Chaotic Ana'. *Film Quarterly* 61(2): 30–34.

Sobchack, V. C. 2004. *Carnal Thoughts: Embodiment and Moving Image Culture.* Berkeley: University of California Press.

Weinrichter, A. 1992. *La línea del vientre: el cine de Bigas Luna.* Gijón: Fundación Municipal de Gijón.

CHAPTER ONE

(Re-)Defining Spanish Cinema?

This chapter serves as contextualisation for the chapters that follow, both mapping a critical terrain that guides my attempt to offer these new readings and peripheral perspectives, and examining a (sometimes complex) theoretical standpoint that enables these novel approaches to the works that I analyse. Films from Spain are firmly established as a legitimate critical object within both Hispanic Studies and Film Studies, and the critical attention lavished upon them surveys the political, ideological and aesthetic innovation that has been so fruitful on the peninsula (Besas 1985; Hopewell 1986; Higginbotham 1988; Kinder 1993; Smith 1996; D'Lugo 1997; Kinder 1997; Jordan and Morgan-Tamosunas 1998; Evans 1999; Smith 2000; Evans 2004; Smith 2006). I invoke the national briefly here for a number of reasons: these readings develop an alternative approach to the subject of cinema which resides in a dissection of the visual; however, this dismantling of the power of the visual regime begins with a de-territorialisation of the spaces and places that have been inscribed with/by the power of this vision. These are spaces at the periphery of the Spanish state and it is briefly productive to demonstrate the ways in which some (national) certainties are undermined by the films and how a more inclusive and holistic approach to cinematic subjectivity, as it might exceed vision, can also be used to understand national subjects and the subjects of national cinemas. It also serves to remind us of the wider panorama of cinematic creativity into which these works can be placed.

As evidenced by the list above, there has been a welter of recent studies attempting to define exactly this concept of Spanish cinema, commensurate with the increased visibility and popularity of the works and directors who make them. Spanish film critic and scholar Ángel Quintana recognizes that if Spanish cinema does exist then it must be identified precisely by its 'idiosyncrasy' and goes on to examine what he defines as 'orphanhood' in relation to a previous tradition (2005). The infelicity of the insistence on such a futile descriptor (Spanish) is evinced by Quintana's demonstration of the way in which the definition simultaneously problematizes its own argument.

Spanish cinema was once defined within certain parameters. Whether these were the *españoladas* or the later 'official' cinema that emerged during the Francoist regime there was a recognisable and coherent idiom which afforded little difficulty in assigning the label of national cinema to a concrete body of work, perhaps ignoring the works that did not fit easily within a presumed national tradition. These trends are frequently mapped onto a historical/chronological reading of a turbulent and repressive time in Spain's political history. The twentieth century saw cinema emerge as a truly popular art form and coincided with two periods of dictatorship in Spain (Primo de Rivera 1923–1930 and Franco 1939–1975) with the Francoist regime's control of culture proving to be clearly influential in terms of the country's cinematic production. The economic situation, and the burden of production costs – a feature of cinematic production that has so often been cited as a reason for its inability to separate from commercialism, reliant as it is on a degree of investment for its very existence – also meant that state support and intervention was a fiscal necessity that generated a degree of ideological control.[1] Furthermore, aspirations of political acceptance combined with an economy that was increasingly reliant on European tourism as its mainstay complicated the rigidly enforced Catholic morality and the regime's censorship upheld this in the country's cultural output.

The battle with censorship and the lack of funding for anything that did not uphold the state-prescribed ideology made for limited creative diversity in the early years of dictatorship. Nonetheless, there were still ways of avoiding the censor's control and any approach that takes into account peripherality and nationality must surely mention the emerging film movements that registered dissidence and creative innovation even during periods of strict censorship and cultural intervention. The period from 1960 onwards marked a slackening in intervention and control of cultural production, and oblique criticism pervaded the films made in this period. In addition, imitation of the style and techniques of Italian *neo-realism* can be seen in films as early as the 1950s (Evans 2005). Then, as now, competing and divergent styles found a space for expression in spite of a degree of state control and intervention. This aesthetic innovation becomes a mode of resistance, or creativity that pushed against the homogenous view of national identity promoted by a political elite.

The Official Cinema School (EOC, or *Escuela Oficial del Cine*) which was based in Madrid during this period began to distance itself from popular commercial cinema – in fact a distinction between old and new cinema has emerged to distinguish these two historical trends (Faulkner 2006). The 1960s also witnessed another movement which certainly located itself on the periphery – the Barcelona School which was not in fact an academy of filmic production but rather a group of Catalan directors whose avant-garde style and formal innovation was perhaps their sole unifying trait, along with the Catalan reputation for dissidence at a time when once again its culture was severely proscribed. Limited distribution and exhibition meant limited visibility for this latter group (Galt 2007; D'Lugo 1991; Galt 2006).

A picture of the cinema of Spain in this period coheres around a desire to locate dissidence as a national trait, always working within the parameters of an ideological and political resistance to the mainstream, or, to situate an exilic tendency, at the periphery as in the case of the Barcelona School or directors who left Spain in pursuit of artistic freedoms elsewhere in Europe. There seems to be a residual desire to identify paternity for this body of work and, in doing so, to enable a reproducibility of sorts, a putative national continuity. This is unsurprising given the fact that a significant aim of those writing about the cinema of Spain, in the 1980s and 1990s was to bring to the attention of the English-speaking world a rich and varied cinematic industry (Kovacs 1990).

Aesthetic resistance and a new politics of visual representation, one that is acutely aware of the constraints and possibilities of the technologies available, unite the production of Julio Medem, Bigas Luna and José Luis Guerín. Their geographical marginality is significant but, like those directors who were grouped under the banner of the Barcelona School, their narrative strategies and formal innovations are widely divergent. There is, it would seem, a rhizomatic connection, if not a unifying theme, that connects Medem, Bigas Luna and Guerín through this mode of engagement which privileges contact as a form of enrichment and which acknowledges the place of perspective as a factor that might create subjectivity but also undo it. Such a strong aesthetic sensibility would also connect them to their predecessors in a similar way, not necessarily through obvious formal or narrative linkages, but by the strength of an approach which opens out new spaces for interpretation. The Barcelona School became known as such because, as Rosalind Galt and Marvin D'Lugo concur, they differentiated themselves from a centralist Spanish tradition by looking beyond the Spanish frontier for inspiration (D'Lugo 1991; Galt 2007). Their project found inspiration in a strong affiliation with the potential of the cinematic image and a refusal to be limited to what they felt to be an intro-spective Spanish tradition. As D'Lugo observes:

> At its core, these 'positions' voiced by members of the Barcelona School represented a critique of everything dominant Spanish cinema stood for. The essence of that critique was the ideological cleavage between cosmopolitan, universalist culture in Barcelona, strongly identified with the intellectual and artistic currents of the rest of the Europe, and the Francoist Castilianism of Spanish culture and film which was, in their eyes, provincial and anachronistic. (2002: 169)

With this in mind Galt's excellent appraisal of the Barcelona School as breaking out of Catalonia precisely to mobilize a new type of cinema, which is enabled rather than limited by the crossing of spatial and temporal boundaries, anticipates a peripatetic aesthetic to which Medem, Bigas Luna and Guerín all subscribe. Their works, as with the works of the Barcelona School, are not consciously working within a tradition that merits this unifying treatment but it is through this astute awareness of the aesthetics of cinema, combined with a perspicacious comprehension of the critique of hegemony and dominant political structures, that a fruitful connection might be extrapolated. Dissi-dence can sometimes be encountered precisely through a subtle approach which works to counter dominant cultural strategies; as Anna Cox points out with regards to the Barcelona School, 'The School's body of work counters the *ad nausem* displays of uniformity and inclusion representative of a nationalist cinema with its own reiterative expositions that convey an ethics of hybrid-ity and emancipation' (2010: 530). The term hybridity, so productive in Cox's argument, is one that also recurs through analysis of the works in question. While it is a term that must be employed with caution in this context, more of-ten thought of in relation to properly transcultural productions, I engage with it on several occasions throughout the course of the book. Laura Marks argues for the political intent of hybrid cinema in a mode that I believe is discernible from the 1960s films made by the Barcelona School through to the recent ex-perimental installation productions by Guerín; she reminds us of the origins of the term used by Trinh T. Minh-ha, Hamid Naficy, and others but spells out its potential in terms of formal tendencies and their political intent, noting, 'Theories of hybrid cinema argue that a hybrid form, in which autobiography mediates a mixture of documentary, fiction, and experimental genres, characterizes the film production of people in transition and cultures in the process of creating identities' (1994: 245). Furthermore she evidences the resistance to easy interpretation in their necessarily challenging stance: 'They have an archaeological quality that allows it to pose different regimes of truth against each other. They confound official history, private recollection and simple fiction, and point to the lacunae that remain, refusing to be filled by the truth of any of these' (1994: 245).

Pere Portabella provides a more definitive link from the Barcelona School and their output in the 1970s to the works of these directors here. In fact, along with Guerín, he has been actively involved with the highly successful Masters in Creative Documentary at the University of Pompeu Fabra. If, as was certainly the case with the Barcelona School, the films of Medem, Bigas Luna and Guerín are artistically and thematically disparate, then the legacy of those, such as Portabella, working before them must surely be in their acknowledgement of audio-visual media as a potent tool of political critique. Stephen Marsh points to Portabella's deliberately fractured narratives, to the gaps and fissures that he leaves open and unresolved, like the hybrid cinema explored by Marks, in a reading of them that also draws attention to a textural quality rooted perhaps in this potential for dissidence and the tension between the film's materiality and its representational capacity in these early experimental works:

> There is a texture to Portabella's films that is almost tactile, a sensual plasticity. At times, particularly in the earlier, more experimental films, this sensuality takes on an erotic form, similar to that of Portabella's surrealist antecedents, but this is almost never divorced from politics. (Marsh 2010: 557)

It is Marsh's astute reading of Portabella's use of ellipses, empty spaces and his textural (aural and tactile) richness that not only suggests a development of styles and themes from the Barcelona School through to contemporary directors, but also underscores the notion that the hybridity that they raise is indicative of a cinema that points to its alternative national origins (Catalan in the case of Portabella) not in order to narrow the identity politics of this cinema but rather as a reminder of the flexibility inherent in the cinematic image that allows us to think through emergent subjects. As subsequent chapters will illustrate, the location of a unifying theme in the work of these three directors stems from their acknowledgement that they are spatially and temporally at a difficult place with regards to a national cinema, and this is something which inflects their explorations of contact, encounter, hybridity, flexible power structures and ultimately, flexible subjectivity. In other words, the national is present but not limiting and the creativity inherent in their approach, like Portabella, establishes their place within a more inclusive global artistic tradition. This situation, in its spatial and temporal dimension, also calls to mind the complex way in which the nation is constructed through space and time; it is supported by a chronological and political reality and inscribed upon spaces. Medem, Bigas Luna and Guerín seek to reveal the space in which a discontinuity in this temporal progression and its spatial or symbolic rendering might make visible an alternative construction of cinema's many subjects.

Medem does this with overt references to holes, spaces and inexplicable voids. He is, perhaps, the director whose work can most easily be considered 'art house', challenging the norms of commercial cinema but remaining broadly within the category that Bergfelder considers to uphold a white (largely male) version of the form that largely works within the confines of 'the canons and features of Western art and literature' (2005: 317). Nonetheless, his works show him to be uncomfortable in this category, or distrustful of categories in general, and with his documentary feature, *Basque Ball,* and the controversy that surrounded it, he was forced to acknowledge that the aesthetic and the political can inhabit the same space. Indeed, the gaps that are constitutive of his depiction of individual subjects in his feature films surprise him as they become a necessary feature of an attempt to find objectivity in this documentary. As he has claimed in an interview with Rob Stone, 'There's a sense to how the film is edited with the people who are included and even who aren't. To remove something doesn't always mean to erase it. Sometimes silence is more visible, more audible' (Stone 2007: 189).

Bigas Luna, as Chapter Three will demonstrate, persistently escapes classification, and diversity underpins his various artistic projects. His pragmatic understanding of the commercial imperative of cinema is what drives the narrative cinema he has made since the 1990s and has made his name outside of

Spain, as he has said he knows the public wants 'good stories and good images and that's it' (Kogen 2005: 72). This simplicity belies a sophisticated approach to the moving image that will be elaborated in more depth in Chapter Three but his most famous works demonstrate that political critique is to be found in humour, high production values and an irreverent attitude to canonical versions of art and identity that suggests a new poetics of identity, or 'a celebration of the enriching mixture of crosscultural fertilization expressed primarily through the intermingling of body, collective, and location and the possibilities offered by their perennial redefinition' (Keown 2008: 171).

Guerín is the director whose status in relation to the nation is most problematic, but this is not to refute the importance of his work on a national and international stage. He has been labelled 'an idiosyncratic figure in contemporary European cinema because his films are exploratory, experimental essays ... Instead of story, structure and sentiment, his films are intellectual assemblages based more on ideas of collage than montage, on the association of images and sounds rather than their juxtaposition' (Stone 2012: 170). Guerín concludes this book because his reflexive musings on the nature of cinema and its material seem to indicate where its future lies, regardless of geographical strictures; the peripatetic protagonist of *In Sylvia's City* has also wandered free from the confines of the auditorium and into the European gallery, searching out a space for a new European subjectivity in the era of digital, mobile cinema.

What is clear is that despite these differences, their formal considerations do allow for the comparisons that I illuminate in this book. For ease of reference and coherent analysis of the films in question I address each director in discrete studies of their works in the chapters that follow. The notion of the literary author that Barthes examined and Foucault elaborated both attest to the power (capitalist, legal and social) that we assume belongs to the author (Barthes 1977; Foucault 1986). I acknowledge the inevitable tensions created by my organising the following chapters according to director but I attempt to remove the clarity of distinction between author, spectator and film in a reading of intersubjective space that prioritizes none of these elements. This reading goes some way to redefining oppositions and removing them from the power structure in which they have previously been embedded to reveal a 'dynamic subjectivity' (Marks 2002: 3).

Encountering New Spaces and Subjects

As is clear from the brief taxonomy of Spanish cinema presented above, and the place of these directors in it, it is still a significant category, and it seems strange, if not churlish, to set it up as such only to disavow it in order to suggest a peripherality for these directors. In this section I look more closely at the ways in which I see this peripherality as a crucial theoretical tool that intersects, to some degree, with national origin and certainly locates the formal experimentation with a degree of dissidence that presents a challenge to Spanish (cultural and linguistic) hegemony. My approach to these films acknowledges the tensions that this reading raises, as I read them in the context of a certain cultural, historical moment and view them as interventions in this cultural politics. At the same time I hold them up for individual scrutiny, approaching their specific address, as subjects of enunciation and as sites at which pleasure is experienced and subjectivity is challenged. The experimentation with filmic technique represented by these films cannot, I believe, be wrenched from their specific cultural context. Furthermore, it is important to remember (and this is an integral part of my argument and approach) that the encounter with the moving image, the object itself and the extra-textual/ transmedial elements of these works has developed significantly in the space of thirty years that separates the early films I analyse in this book and the more recent productions. This fluidity of the material basis of the cinematic, and indeed the problematic terminology that it gives rise to, are a feature of these complex subjects explored by these directors. From the paint on canvas that is explored in *Volavérunt* to the material focus on a scratched window of the intangible media of digital photography in *Some Photos in Sylvia's City* they all speak to representational uncertainties and freedoms, as I will elaborate in more detail in the relevant sections. My assertion is that the formal experimentation in which they are involved intersects with the tricky notion of the visible, the aural, the corporeal and the material as they are encountered in the moving image (and the photographic and still image at times) and that it is in this encounter, which takes place at the edges, that this book takes shape.

The three directors under scrutiny here integrate the spatial and geographical dimension of the places in which they work not solely as backdrops, but as sites that encapsulate and undermine the many tensions that surround the contested geopolitical areas that make up Spain. In the chapters that follow, the significance of land is acknowledged, but rather than prioritize its exclusive features and role in the various discourses of nationalism that pervade contemporary Europe and – as I have noted – are unavoidable in Spain, I make the land a participant in the play of identity that takes place upon it. To refer to the land here is not to highlight its metaphorical or symbolic associations, although they are undoubtedly present in the films, but rather to prioritize the land as a participant in the evolving visual and narrative circuits of subject creation and renegotiation. The split between urban and rural and a related global and local dichotomy is eschewed when movement through these places and spaces is prioritized, and changing landscapes are not simply subject to the ideological signification that their territorial specificity, as part of the Basque or Catalan autonomous communities implies, but as material and obdurate realities recreated by architectural remodelling (*Work in Progress*), the tourist's gaze (*Sex and Lucía* and *Room in Rome*) and of course the technological apparatus under whose scrutiny they are made visible to us.

Dissident Bodies in Barcelona

As I have already inferred, the representational strategies that have been assumed to function along ideological lines tend to construct binaries and wrestle with hierarchies that must be undone. I do not wish to allege that these are little more than fragile constructs that may be wholly undone by my insistent pursuit of the liminal. As any examination of the place of gender and sexuality within film reveals, the structures of power that work in these representational arenas are nuanced and complex and not easily dismantled. In this section I point out the relationship between city and body and their cinematic representation in order to provide a model for the way in which changing configurations of the urban create new cinematic spaces. This will serve as a theoretical and methodological endeavour to tentatively mark out the ways in which I believe power, vision and bodies are being permitted a space at the edge, which complicates previous ideas. It serves as a prelude to the concentration on the city as a material and sensorial space of filmic immersion, in analysis of *Bilbao* and *En construcción* which takes into account the symbolic function of cityscapes and representations of cities, perhaps more than the lived reality of cities themselves, that precedes this approach.

Colonisation of places through the cinematic gaze, and in other recognisable cultural contexts, means that filming locations are either chosen or avoided as a result of their inherent symbolic value. Cities have provided a unique means of cinematic representation, with the urban experience and its transmission becoming a popular topic for filmmakers. In Europe this has particular resonance in terms of a politics of representation. Stephen Barber explores the phenomenon of city cinemas, pointing to Europe's immersion in this rich history and enlivening the debate on the city's effect on the corporeal:

> Film images of European cities illuminate the past and future of urban forms; the crises and sensations of city inhabitants are projected through European cinema's infinite capacity to juxtapose urban and corporeal identity within a contrary rapport which may be coruscating or cohering, according to each director's particular set of human and technological caprices and convictions. The images that emerge from that raw zone of contact between the human figure and the city provide intricately revealing indicators of Europe's contemporary moment. (2002: 61)

Striking architectural constructions framed by the cinematic camera present an apparently straightforward means of provoking visual recognition and assuming a common understanding of the building in question and the city that it represents. In the case of monumental structures the ideological import and historical specificity make them difficult to redefine in their moving image representations. More than this, they are often used as supports for a master narrative that is reaffirmed and reinforced by its location alongside such edifices, or alternatively as a picture postcard depiction of a city recognisably encoded as exotic and other.[2]

Barcelona, as the most visited city in Spain, is particularly susceptible to this type of depiction and has achieved a status reinforced by its recognisable, picture-postcard vistas of stunning modernista architecture. Woody Allen's 2008 film *Vicky, Cristina, Barcelona* demonstrates this was not solely a trend in Spanish-language films. Furthermore its confusion of Catalan and Spanish symbols combined with fiery characterisation of its two Spanish characters (played by Penélope Cruz and Javier Bardem) would suggest that the stereotype Bigas Luna both imitates and lampoons is still not far from the surface in depictions of this European country and that the subtleties of alternative regional or national characterisation are left unexplored. Bigas Luna's depiction of *Bilbao* is a far cry from Guerín's exploration of the same city almost twenty-five years later. They share a reluctance to subscribe to its mainstream appeal, idealized in its standard visual depictions, and instead admit the competing strands of experience that the cinema has access to through a more sensory mode of appreciation. A darker Barcelona emerges, or at least a city with multiple identities.[3]

What I would like to look at briefly here is the way in which Barcelona both contains and exceeds the identities which have become a part of its symbolic currency. This decentred gaze might engender a unique relationship between city and body that can be elaborated by means of a Deleuzian reading of architectural space that paves the way for a gaze that resists the colonisation of space and underscores a relationship with the city in which the optical works with the tactile in a reciprocal rather than exclusive relationship. Giuliana Bruno attends to this interconnectedness and, similarly to Barber, conceptualizes the contact and reciprocal inscription of the city, cinema and bodies:

> Motion in film is not simply kinetic, nor only kinaesthetic. It implies more than the movements of bodies and objects as imprinted in the change of film frames and shots, the flow of camera movement or any other kind of locomotive shift in viewpoint. Motion pictures move not only through time and space or narrative development: they move also through inner space. Film, like architecture, enables us to journey through the space of the imagination, the sites of memory and the topography of affects. (Bruno 2002: 215)

Here, I turn to another Catalan filmmaker, Ventura Pons, and his depiction of Barcelona's transition through the eyes and senses of one of the city's itinerant inhabitants. If Pedro Almodóvar's concentration on Madrid's Transition created an image of the *movida* as taking place in the centre – the streets of Madrid contained and played host to the experimentation that takes place on so many different levels in his early works – then Barcelona's Transition was subject to alternative cinematic scrutiny. *Ocaña, retrat intermitent/Ocaña,*

Intermittent Portrait (1978) provides a glimpse of a different variety of experimentation that performs its own cinematic moment of transition embodying the experience of Barcelona at this time. It exemplifies the journey that Bruno describes in Deleuzian terms above and moves the cinematic gaze away from the centre and out towards the edges.

Made in the year after *Bilbao* and arguably experimenting with some of the same subject matter, at least in its representation of the marginalized character traversing the city, Pons's documentary enacts and explores the same feelings of displacement and rootlessness and transmits these through a tangible sensation of transition and transience. These metamorphoses predict and acknowledge the specificity of a certain moment in the history of a city, as it reflects the history of a nation and enacts cinema's struggle to capture its fleeting character. This works through the textures of the city as they are ingrained, literally, in the film that depicts them and the way in which the conjunction of still photographic images, a non-diegetic soundtrack and in other scenes an insistence on diegetic sound even when it is distorted by background noises, renders a layered depiction of the city which requires more deciphering than is possible than through a purely detached gaze.

Pons follows an infamous transvestite performer and artist, Ocaña, and captures his movements through the city interspersing them with talking head shots of interviews with him. This is without a doubt a peripheral city housing peripheral subjects. Pons embarks upon an investigation of personal and private, fusing these two aspects of Ocaña's life and in doing so, mirrors a similar merging at work in the migrating and constantly shifting identities of Barcelona which both contains and reveals a new identity in this turbulent and dynamic period of history.

The divided character that he embodies imitates the tension between an engagement with the image at the surface and the depth of the city space that Ocaña navigates. The surface of Ocaña's performance that rests on elaborate clothing and makeup are those scenes in which we see her in the streets – the iconic Ramblas of Barcelona – and are contrasted with the indoor talking-head pieces, in which a face devoid of makeup and more clearly identifiable as masculine talks about a childhood of marginalisation in a village in Andalucia. This doubling troubles the depiction of the other when that other is internalized. Like the traversing of the city that depends on the sedimentation and enfolding of 'imagination, the sites of memory and the topography of affects', this crystallizes the problematic construction of the external gaze and the oppositional forces of identity. In superficial terms Ocaña embodies the fluidity of gendered identity and the national/regional split within Spain that configure Andalucia as a space of regressive tradition and the Catalan capital as the progressive urban centre. This analysis however, works on a narrative level that fails to problematize its assumptions, to see this as a complicated doubling that also contends with the persistent questions of looking as a reductive explanatory practice, a tendency to 'look through rather than at the cross-dresser, to turn away from a close encounter with the transvestite, and to want instead to subsume that figure within one of the two traditional genders. To elide and erase – or to appropriate the transvestite for particular political and critical aims' (Garber 1997: 9). Pons utilizes formal strategies that disorient the viewer and the location of the gaze, as Ocaña's reflection on his performance instigates an internal gaze, which mediates our own and complicates the optical politics of the other sections, those in which we view Ocaña's urban performances.

In this documentary it is also the historicized gaze and the curious and potent temporality that film embodies in its relationship to a gaze that might be both out of space and out of time, which comments on the way in which film creates our relationship with time and history. This is evinced by a sequence in which we view photographs of a demonstration for sexual equality. The demonstration is narrated by Ocaña, who explains the context and the importance of such a demonstration at this time. The footage then changes to black and white (press) photographs of the event. Interestingly the soundtrack is of the chanting at the march, 'llibertat sexual/sexual freedom', divorced from its images and reunited with them here.

It is specifically the cinematic element of this sequence that presents itself as different to the photographic images it utilizes, not simply through the addition of sound but also by its selection of certain areas of the photographs for scrutiny, via a mobile cinematic lens. Both narratively and formally this film epitomizes the complex intersections between developing technology and its roots (specifically in photography), the creative depiction of reality and perhaps most importantly the position of the body in the landscape of a cinematic reality, the body of the screen, the specific bodies of the individuals represented, and our own embodied responses to them. It is only by confronting the gaze and its inherent inconsistencies in the realm of the cinematic that we can approach the space and time of film by means of a gaze that looks for access to the 'other' that is not reductive. As such, the cinematic precedents for this embodied and visual depiction of Barcelona are clearly discernible in Pons's work.

These peripatetic directors remove themselves to 'other' geographical spaces, outside of Spain, where they continue to work with tropes of inclusion and exclusion, redolent of the tense situation in Catalonia and the Basque country, but where the burden of language choice is of less import. From the reading of Medem which looks at alterity as existing in an external gaze through to an analysis of Guerín in which the constructed nature of non-fiction film is always defined against the other from which it is seen to draw its semiotic codes and yet to which it must always be subordinate, the issue of separation, definition and distinction haunts their work.

Subjects of Language

The possibility of self-expression in a language that is imposed upon you is the subject of much consideration. Literary language has understandably taken precedence in these discussions, in its capacity for creation, invention, even corruption; it bears the marks of hybridity and contamination that the mixing of cultures engenders. Cinema works on both a visual and a linguistic level; indeed it works between them too, using semantic codes to structure its visual world. Despite the complex interplay of power at work between the Spanish centre and the peripheral communities in Spain this cannot be conveniently shoehorned into a postcolonial theoretical perspective, and at the same time the visual image escapes these confines to a degree when it casts off the shackles of language. Nonetheless, as has been perceptively outlined by others it is a richly informative structure through which to consider cultural products that position themselves in a liminal space with regards to dominant cultures. Stewart King astutely recognizes in his analysis of Catalan literature that 'in constructing Catalonia as colonized, Catalan critics focus on a single understanding of colonization – that which maintains the nationalist assertion that language equals cultural identity' (2006: 259). Hybridity and reciprocity recur in this examination of an emerging cultural idiom defined not by exclusion but by contact; as King references Homi Bhabha he calls for 'a third space, that is a new hybrid space which is formed by the convergence of two or more cultures' (2006: 260). This may well be a long way from a political reality on the Iberian peninsula but we must credit visual culture and the moving image with an exploration of this type of hybridity, in all its forms. Furthermore, cinema, as I will investigate, revisits this notion of contact and hybridity through its material presence and embodied imaginary (Marks 2002; Sobchack 2004).

Discussions by linguists concentrate on bilingualism and code switching in these areas where Spanish and Catalan and Basque are spoken (Azurmendi, Larrañaga, and Apalategi 2008; Boix-Fuster and Sanz 2008). In these accounts of language terms such as 'interference' and 'contamination' are not uncommon, stressing the effect of contact and interface between the different languages. Territorial border crossings are also a by-product of the languages that move beyond the confines of the nation state as both Basque and Catalan are spoken in French territories.

The negotiation of language and identity and the concomitant politics of inclusion and exclusion in both Catalonia and the Basque country are a neat metaphor for a similar process of intermingling of theoretical and formal conceptions of the structure of subjectivity in these films. But it is more than that, as my forays into the creation of a Spanish cinematic canon identify; there is a tendentious need to simplify a politics of belonging and strategies of contestation of this belonging. Individual subjects in these films perform and embody a complex process of distance, difference, doubling and identification, which complicates their interstitial subjectivities.

The languages that are linked to territories in Spain, as outlined above, create certain expectations surrounding identity. Similarly, the formal analysis of film has led to theories which address the way in which meaning can be created, and subverted, in cinema. Linguistic theory contributed to a structuralist approach and an understanding of cinema's transmission of meaning along these lines: 'Shot relationships are seen as the equivalent of syntactic ones in linguistic discourse, as the agency whereby meaning emerges and a subject-position is constructed for the viewer' (Silverman 1999: 138).

Manipulation of this 'language' along with other filmic marks of identity means that our understanding and experience of film are being revised. The move towards a less comfortable, or at least more complex, cinematic experience as seen in the work of the directors I examine here shuns accepted technique and linear narrative in favour of innovation and multiple splits, which

disavow previous theories of suture and interrogate the potential, or desirability, of the unified subject position, one that might be alluded to through an
apparently discernible point of view. In addition, new geographical configurations and diverse spatial constructions within these films add to the tensions
in significance and interpretation by undermining the notion that there is inherent meaning to be found in certain spaces. As these films situate themselves in anonymous islands, cities without a name, or sites with historical and
ideological import, they make them into new spaces and begin to destabilize
paradigmatic viewing positions.

I would like to suggest navigating a path between identity and the subject,
in keeping with my belief that is at the interstices that a space for new understanding of the import of these moving images might occur. This pays attention to ideology and historical context and, as the first part of this chapter
has set out, cannot avoid the national as a shaping force in all of these films.
However, the acknowledgement of film's ability to alter material spaces and
our experience of embodiment and embodied materiality – which is hinted
at in Medem's use of space and then prioritized in Bigas Luna's and Guerín's
construction of their textural and deep images – entertains the capacity of
our perceptual responses to residue and trace in this context. I think that the
traces of the national and the resulting ideologies cannot be avoided but can
be rethought and challenged by a subject that acknowledges their presence
but, because of the space of film, is liberated – to a degree – from the confines
of being a subject of them.[4]

Thus genre, language, country of origin and nationality of director have
ceased to be sufficient markers for filmic identity. More than this, they have,
in a number of cases, become irrelevant and impossible to define as international collaborative productions mix different sources of funding and directors
look for new and more innovative ways of filming. Numerous geographical locations often resulting in mixing languages in a final production are constantly
enriching a worldwide filmic tradition which looks beyond limiting categories.
One result of this broadening scope of production and its related thematic
widening is that it demands an expanded theoretical appreciation.

Film theory has always been inclusive in its reliance on various theoretical
and critical currents to provide readings of cinematic technique and content.
For the purposes of this study the diversity of the pieces subject to analysis
means that a search for informative theoretical models that inform my reading

encompasses numerous possibilities. These range from the Lacanian structures that speak to Medem's linking of the psychical with the topological to the nascent theories of cinema's sensory appeal which guide my viewing of Bigas Luna and Guerín.

If there is an overriding tendency here it is to look beyond the limiting definitions of alterity, which must always construct an image of the other that reduces that other to the confines of the easily understood and recognisable – a stereotype. Tensions that arise through definitions must be approached and tentatively explored, and the same must be true of a theoretical approach that tests these boundaries. To refer to the semiotic nature of cinema is not to turn to a structuralist reading of cinema, but rather was intended to usher in the notion that language is not universally understood and that at the limits of communication, the sites where we stutter and stumble, an alternative means of communication must be sought. 'In Foucauldian terms, intercultural cinema works at the edge of an unthought, slowly building a language in which to think it . . . The already sayable against which intercultural cinema struggles is not only official history but often also identity politics, with their tendency towards categorisation' (Marks 2000: 29). Artistic innovation is frequently couched in terms of pushing limits and expanding frontiers. In some way each of these cineastes is at those edges and is tentatively or more confidently, both within the confines of mainstream practice and acceptance as well as on the fringes of the commercial production machine that surrounds these endeavours, marking out a space – or various spaces – of innovation and invention.

New Ways of Seeing Cinema

There are three significant moments in three of the films I cover in the discrete chapters on each director which epitomize for me their relationship with the technology at their disposal and their sensitivity to its vicissitudes, ideological pitfalls and more importantly its enormous potential. These are all scenes that prioritize the eye: the cow's eye in *Vacas/Cows,* the detached eyes in *Angustia/ Anguish* and the graffitied cluster of eyes on the crumbling wall in *En construcción.* Unsurprisingly the power of the eye as it has been firmly attached to the bearer of the gaze grounds so much of cinema's formative theoretical descriptions and deliberation, and I attend to them when they are relevant throughout the chapters that follow. This deliberation on the mutable configurations of power that the gaze in cinema has and its seemingly unseverable bond to the formation of subjectivity in visual media have been revised and reconsidered, and I am indebted to the approaches of those who elaborate the philosophical complexities of cinema's approach to the subject, the ontological preconditions of cinema's materiality and the ramifications this has for our embodied experience of cinema and its imbrication of ethics and aesthetics. Where this book articulates to those wider debates on the intersections between philosophy and film and cinema's role as a representational, ideological tool in the construction of individual and collective subjects is in its exploration of three directors from Spain whose work has not been looked at in this way before, and in its intention to interrogate their representational practice in terms of its place within a wider panorama of world cinema but also as a very specific version of cinema from Spain which, implicitly or explicitly, posits a more inclusive version of this subjectivity than has been permitted for a large part of the twentieth century in the country.

In its move from Lacan's seminar on the gaze to the materiality of the gaze and its role in cinematic and cultural memory, this book navigates some difficult theoretical terrain. At its core is a holistic and reciprocal approach to subjectivity that resonates with a phenomenological approach, while not embracing it without reservation. It is the reciprocity that phenomenology sees as integral to our visual and perceptual field which offers a productive model through which this encounter might be staged, an approach that attends to the inseparability not only of subject and object but also of the associated cultural and ideological underpinnings of subjectivity. 'Existential phenomenology and its method thus not only invite us to attend to the material, lived world in order to better understand the lived structures of the emotional, the social and the historical, but also give us a means of embodied analysis that respects the co-constitutive, reciprocal relationship between the perceiver and the perceived' (Barker 2009: 17–18). This is not incompatible with my use of Lacan's gaze in Chapter Two and the analysis of Medem's films. As Todd McGowan reminds us, 'The gaze is not the look of the subject at the object, but the point at which the object looks back. The gaze thus involves the spectator in the image, disrupting her/his ability to remain all-perceiving and unperceived in the cinema' (McGowan 2003: 28–29).

This book seeks to unpack the traces of a moving image and a moving image culture that is latent in the works of Medem, Bigas Luna and Guerín. I do so because in relation to the emergence of a subject at the point where identities can be dissolved these films have challenged the inscription of meaning on bodies, spaces and screens. In this sense they are a productive means by which to identify those edges at which new possibilities, caused by the collisions of possible subjects, are produced. These encounters and collisions at the limits of the visible are then extended in more detail by a new reading in the chapters that follow. Furthermore, the spectrality of the image that is most clearly evident in Guerín's work as he examines the disappearance of film stock in *Tren de sombras/Train of Shadows* or of spaces within Barcelona in *En construcción,* is also the ghostly presence of other images and of previous lives and times which are preserved by cinema and then replayed through repeated projection, technological manipulation of found footage or, and perhaps most powerfully, through our own imaginative and compulsive repetitions. Victor Burgin reminds us that this circulation of images as dreams or daydreams has so much in common with avant-garde films' use of found footage (2004: 24). The repetition of the image in our memory is first raised in Chapter Two, with reference to Medem's film *Lovers of the Arctic Circle,* as the lovers of the title permit us entry into their interior gaze, their remembering of events; dependent on the way in which they saw them are the two sections of the film, which are played out slightly differently according to whose perspective we share.

These imaginative replayings of images that we have witnessed was frequently thought to be the internal mode of vision, the mind's eye. What cinema does for us and what these films are particularly expert at is in troubling the internal and the external. To be visible is not necessarily to see, and that is what makes the gaze so troubling for Lacan: we might be seen and yet not see.

A significant part of this study looks at the nature of the film as document, naturally evidenced by Guerín's output but also approached by Medem in *Basque Ball* (2002). Documentary has a long history and its situation as a problematic representational device was exposed masterfully by Buñuel in *Las hurdes/Land Without Bread* (1933). Criticism of a patronising approach to the documentary subject – which relies on critical distance and examination of a situation from which the camera and its human agent are removed – is exemplified in a scene in this film in which we observe a young girl dying with the voice-over narrating her terrible story and the problem of finding a doctor to treat her. While the camera watches there is no intervention or attempt to come to the child's aid. The sequence necessarily exposes one of the central issues raised by this medium of intrusion and non-intrusion, condescension and interference. The ethical stance of documentary has not ceased to be controversial in this respect but Guerín and Medem follow their predecessor's lead of recognition, exploration and critical self-reflection in their own contribution to this genre.

Revising the Gendered Gaze

My intention is this chapter has been to trace the emergence of criticism surrounding Spain's cinematic production in order to point to the ways in which I will revise and interrogate certain paradigmatic bases for the analysis of this country's filmic production. The aesthetic tropes and formal pursuits that surround the contentious depiction of gender and sexuality become enmeshed within accounts of Spanish cinema. This means that Spanish film remains, to a degree, defined by a view of sexuality that inheres within a paradigm of Spanish identity. In this section I look to the way in which a particular variety of criticism has produced readings of Spanish films that tie national identity – and in particular the perceived moral liberation of the post-Franco period – to gender, in a way that exoticizes and limits meaning, concentrating on received notions of visibility, spectatorial identification and the body which need to be re-evaluated and removed from this limiting gendered dimension if these films are to be appreciated, as I believe they deserve to be, as an interrogation of cinema's capacity to combine narrative and apparatus.

Sexuality and its depiction, as well as the prescription of gender roles that were the product of a rigidly enforced Catholic moral code throughout the majority of the twentieth century, mark the terrain of the body as one of particular critical concern to anyone working on the cultural production of Spain during this period. This is undoubtedly a concern for these filmmakers in the context of their renegotiation of Francoist ideology, which had propounded its own particular brand of gendered behaviour, with its basis in conservative Catholicism, and also specific historic and cultural formulations of the roles of both sexes. Recent explorations of cinematic configurations of this issue are numerous and often couched in terms of a perceived tendency amongst Spanish filmmakers, from the Transition onwards, to opt for excessive depictions of the physical as a backlash to the moral restraint of the previous era:

> Francoism, let us recall, operated on the basis of highly traditional and retrograde concepts of gender and sexuality. This led to the conflation of sexual and political repression in the cultural life of the dictatorship. Along with other forms of cultural opposition to the regime, oppositional cinema was quick to exploit the metaphorical possibilities of the thematics of sexual repression. (Jordan and Morgan-Tamosunas 1998: 112)

Jordan and Morgan-Tamosunas argue that the first signs of this rebellion demonstrated a preference for the presence of more female nudity on stage, thus challenging the restrictive morality of the regime but in actual fact doing very little to challenge the rigidity of gendered positions. Nonetheless, whenever intransigent codes of behaviours are applied there is little doubt that masculinity was also subject to similarly inflexible demands, and the cinematic production was also quick to react to these with subversive representations of the male body. Even in this increased visibility of masculinity the critical examinations of this facet of production 'draw on discourse often built on the acceptance of a national identity or racial determinism or a cultural specificity that allegedly dictates the authenticity of representations' (Fouz-Hernández and Martínez Expósito 2007: 3). Thus carnal pleasure and the excesses of the flesh come to typify national filmic production rather than problematize the assumptions on which the nation is founded, or the surrounding eroticisation of the body (male, female and transgendered).

In the chapters that follow I engage with the notion of gender as it is raised by the films themselves and my readings of them This is often foregrounded because of a concentration on alternative perspectives on the corporeal.[5] Above all, this locates bodies as multifarious signifiers, disruptive presences and – of course – objectified and subjective presences. I seek to demonstrate that these directors here react to the prescriptive morality outlined by Morgan and Tamosunas but their films – narratively and formally – resist the temptation to resort to gender and sexuality as facile signifier of change, progress and alterity. For Stephen Marsh and Parvati Nair 'gender considerations … provide a useful theoretical perspective from which to study the specificities of

Spanish cinema' (2004: 4). For me issues surrounding the representations of gender in these films become most interesting when they present a dual challenge, both to the concept of the nation and to the way in which that concept is often, implicitly, tied to the concept of national cinema.[6]

Whilst there is a recognition that cinematic production from Spain throughout the Transition and beyond frequently attempted to address and challenge this rigid gender dichotomy, the emphasis of analysis in this area has resisted a temptation to combine the readings of sexual difference with a more flexible and fluid approach to positionality and subject matter within the films. If fluidity of identification is embraced then the removal of power from the look – and consequently the look from the gaze – can be read as a way of undermining numerous viewing structures but in particular those which have been assumed to work along the lines of gender.[7] In my readings of these films the premise that visibility does not necessarily render us powerless in the face of the anonymous gaze of the other engages with gender as an element of subjectivity that inheres within the wider and more complex account of the cinematic subject.

Bodies and embodied experience present, in the case of the directors examined here, a problem and a site of creative possibility. The difficulty is persistently one of gender; it is neither true nor helpful to argue that male directors cannot depict female bodies in a way that might offer some liberation from that reductive and ubiquitous rhetoric of objectification. Nonetheless, a brief glance at Bigas Luna's output, and some of Medem's, would seem to at least question, if not undermine, any such liberating tendency.

If bare female flesh on screen were a measure of the degree to which sexual empowerment were being explored then it would be fair to assume that we were a long way from any radical repositioning of gendered subjects. In their approaches to subjectivity, though I believe both men seek a way to negotiate the regressive modes of depiction and the assumed liberation that the Transition brought, they draw attention to a new set of challenges to the creative economy. Bodies and their depiction are part of a complex web of signification and in these films are often used to deliberately draw attention to the spectator's position, ensuring that it is one of discomfort and denial of a purely fetishistic or objectifying gaze.

Medem's 2011 film *Habitación en Roma/Room in Rome,* experiments with the limits of the gaze and its restrictive capacities. Two women, Alba (Elena

Anaya) and Natasha (Natasha Yarovenko) meet in a bar one night in Rome; they are attracted to one another and they return to Alba's hotel for a night of passion. The seduction of Natasha by Alba (Natasha claims to have never experienced a sexual relationship with a woman before, while Alba is in a long-term relationship with a woman in Spain) is the premise of most of the film and it takes place in the hotel room with both women naked for most of the time. I have argued elsewhere in this book that this insistence on sexuality, the camera's refusal to play a game of disavowal or pander to spectatorial voyeurism, implicates us in the relationship with this space. It is the movement between touching and distancing posited by Linda Williams that allows an ambiguity of reference to emerge in this space, one that is underscored by the narrative and the clever use of the camera throughout the film: 'Sex in movies is especially volatile: it can arouse, fascinate, disgust, bore, instruct, and incite. Yet it also distances us from the immediate, proximate experience of touching and feeling with our own bodies, while at the same time bringing us back to feelings in the same bodies' (Williams 2008: 1). Apart from the fact that these two women and the stories of their lives that they recount to one another for the course of the film make this a narrative strongly driven by female desire, the gaze within the film also functions to disavow a reading along purely patriarchal lines.

The rhythm of the narrative is one of continuous deferral. Natasha is a heterosexual woman about to be married, while Alba is in a committed same-sex relationship (at least this is the version of their lives they tell one another at the outset). Their sexual union is delayed by Natasha's doubts; she leaves the room, and Alba, early in the film and then returns because she has left her mobile phone. Initially, the camera is with them in the room, adopting their point-of-view as they frankly appraise one another's bodies – an appraisal in which the spectator is implicated – but as the film progresses the camera seems to try and escape the confines of this space, repeatedly drawing attention to the works of art on the walls of this hotel room.

The desire of these two women drives the narrative and the intrusion of the outside world into this claustrophobic diegetic space comes through their mobile phones and Internet videos – a reminder of life outside of this space and beyond this time – and brief forays onto the balcony from where they view the street below. This technology also draws attention to its ability to distort the self (themes I will extend in Chapter Two), and the juxtaposition of the art that adorns the walls and the old maps of Rome remind us of a changing perspective, a developing scepticism about the function of the eye and vision as the tools of understanding. It extends the premise of embodied vision and the subject/object dichotomy that subtends my readings of these films.

There is a tension between the technological eye which Medem integrates into his narratives and the bodies that look. The fixed, specific bodies of certain doubly marginalized subjects – female and homosexual – adopt the technological gaze as that which allows them to manipulate their existence as sexual and gendered subjects beyond our expectations of them as (naked) female subjects on screen. Gender and sexuality are shown to be enmeshed within a technologically mediated politics of vision which in Medem's universe, as I will show, is always entirely contingent. Gender and sexual relations become imbricated within the field of a wider reading of subjectivity and can be seen more as an exchange in which power is implicated on neither side but rather externally located in the field of the gaze as Lacan understands it.[8] It is not to deny that in the history of cinema from Spain the various depictions of feminine sexuality and the female body have been inevitably caught up in an ideological and political structure which has a particular relationship to nationality as already outlined, and which has been explored by other scholars (Martin Márquez 1999; Davies 2004). Nonetheless, as various hierarchical structures are revised with an altered politics of vision, it is inevitable that alternative constructions of gendered subjects and the relationships between these subjects are also redefined.

There is no doubt that films from the peninsula have for some time now offered strong female subjects whose psychology and actions propel that narrative in a space in which empowered female subjects are granted a great degree of freedom. It is also true that the social and cultural context of the images of female flesh must take into account a time when the visibility of the female body was, in itself, a provocative political act. The nuances of such representation and their place in the history of art is explored in Chapter Three on *Volavérunt*, in which I argue for a complex interaction between the ideological implications of the objectifying gaze and its deconstruction here in the context of a fraught political environment.

Redrawing a symbolic analysis of the relationship of the nation to gender is not the concern here, but there must be some investigation of the way in which the visible and the marginal work together in order to attempt to define a new, participatory and fluid means by which the intertwining of the visible and the material, and the twofold appreciation of the physical that they entail, can cut through some of the previous restrictive ideas of gender and sexuality. In these peripheral spaces these representations suggest and seek out alternative, more inclusive depictions, or at least challenge previous ones. Queer theory has, of course, already addressed tropes of gender and its cultural deconstruction. In acknowledging the Foucauldian regulation of bodies that works, in part, through a regime of the visual perhaps the queer bodies of Spanish cinema have become important sites of resistance (Feenstra 2011). But if queer is, as Halperin claims, 'whatever is at odds with the normal, the legitimate, the dominant' (1995), then we must also look at the bodies on the margins of this new space in Spanish cinema and the representations of gender that trouble the previous hegemonies as well as the new, assumed, liberation.

Underlying this endeavour to look to the edges to find a space in which overlaps are found and contours are less clearly defined, then, the reliance on vision and visibility as markers of imbalance and power that relates to gendered subjects can also be approached from a variety of different, marginal perspectives, including a suggestion of learning to look and to experience in ways that are not dependent on vision. Removing the object/subject split that seems to be the structuring logic of this economy of the gaze finds alternative ways of looking defined by Irigaray (although not referring to the cinema in this analysis) as 'contemplative, passive as well as active, capable of discovering an other or a world always unknown. What it is to see is not already defined, and our eyes can thus remain open upon and infinity of views, of sights' (2002: 150).

Sexual relationships and alternative readings of the representation of gender within film are often viewed as peripheral, either inherently or as a result of the spaces in which they occur. In this respect it is unsurprising that they are relevant in the context of this wider reading of the marginal and peripheral. It is evident that previous conceptions of gender and sexuality and their filmic representation are subject to continuing renegotiation as established formulations are pushed aside to make room for new and constantly shifting perspectives – perspectives which move beyond and between established theoretical positions in 'a space to maintain previous and new theories together in which past, present and future co-exist as in a Deleuzian rhizome' (Block 2008: xviii).

The subject/object binary – which can no longer be facilely assigned to either gender – is expanded by an approach to objects, and by extension objectification, which sees them given the potential for subjectivity in a cinematic space that deliberately seeks to untether vision and power. 'If we regard the eye as an interface between spectator and film, we can distinguish among several configurations that shape the look and the activity of seeing in different ways', according to Elsaesser and Hagener (2009: 84). As we will see from the cow's eyes in *Cows* to the graffitied, disembodied eyes at the beginning of *En construcción* these directors are involved in a project of interface. They posit a cinema which interrogates the look and the gaze and which always places it as the point of contact, imagined or actual, between two regimes of knowledge, two spatial territories or two bodies. In this way it is opened out at these edges to readings that resist and question the hegemonic configurations of nation and gender.

Traversing Boundaries

It is their astute recognition of position and the importance of a new type of cinematic gaze that is considered by the following chapters on each director. Their manners of exploration of this are diverse but at their cores the emphasis of their work on perspective speaks to an obsession in the history of film with the representational strategies that appeal to a certain way of looking and that construct an imagined spectator within the confines of certain ideological, and frequently patriarchal, positions. An attempt on behalf of a filmmaker to escape such restrictions is not new but the way in which national origin influences this trio is interesting both in the context of a study of film from Spain and also in terms of its wider ramifications for the study of cinema. Here we return to the reduction of the other into simply the site of our gaze. This book works through the wrenching of the gaze from the human subject and the ensuing liberation of entrenched structures of vision that this permits through a re-appraisal of vision and ideology in the films examined.

Re-positioning individual subjects and focussing on vision and its potential as both expansive and limiting re-evaluates power, not in order to shift its focus, but in order that we might see it as a constantly shifting element in the networks of other relations within which cinema is caught. Returning to

Bhabha this repositioning might be thought through in terms of the specific-ity to images and their meanings; his political project depends on a separa-tion of the two through a questioning of the very discourses that have created these positions. Oppositional stances comply with the desire to separate and classify and have become accepted as legitimate terms of definition. In the cinematic arena these oppositions may be likened to the distance required between spectator and screen which aids the illusive sense that by being able to visually focus we also necessarily occupy a position of comprehension. This is what Bhabha defines as an illusory mastery: 'The fetish or stereotype gives access to an "identity" which is predicated as much on mastery and pleasure as it is on anxiety and defence, for it is a form of multiple and contradictory belief in its recognition of difference and disavowal of it' (1994: 75).

What all of these directors do is to recognize that difference may exist, but they show that it is outside of our control to properly represent it, and thus it surprises us – in the external gaze and performative power of language in Me-dem's films, in the material world in Bigas Luna's and in the power of the image to disrupt our expectations of time, history and the representation of lived experience in Guerín's. This cinematic flexibility then rests on the disempow-ering of our gaze by the gaze that looks back, and the disruptive and mutable presence of the material world which includes our bodies, in these works.

The inscription of the body and its materiality as a sensory presence in the presence of the film is initially suggested by Lacan's external gaze and elabo-rated by Sobchack as she seeks an expanded gaze in cinematic space: 'Look-ing *back* at us, the significant object also looks *beyond* us to an *expanded* – if deferred – *field* of visuality and meaning that subsumes and absorbs the re-ductive, if invested and consequential, questions asked of it by our contingent, local and personal gaze' (Sobchack 2004: 93).

The combination of Medem and Lacan in Chapter One dovetails neatly with the work of Bigas Luna and Guerín in its oscillation between the imag-ined gaze and the material insurrection of meaning, or non-meaning in the form of coincidence and chance in the field of the visual. All of this provides a theoretical basis for the processes and practices with which these filmmakers engage. They suggest that the visual is not the only means by which we can organize the world and ensure our power within it; there is a more positive facet to being looked at by the other that does not simply reverse a structure of power but as Sobchack suggests expands on it: 'our gaze and the gaze that looks back and beyond is not structured according to the "harsh dialectics" of an opposition between self and other or subject and object. Rather, embodied and enworlded in the manner – and matter– of that at which it looks, our gaze serves as a synthesizing "transfer point" of the commerce between and commingling of matter and meaning.' (2004: 100). So when Medem's soaring bird (*La pelota vasca/Basque Ball*), jukebox (*La ardilla roja/The Red Squirrel*), futuristic underground telescope that surveys the woodlice (*Tierra/Earth*), and a cow's eye (*Vacas/Cows*) look back, it can be considered, as I argue in Chapter One, a way to represent the mobile gaze as a site of freedom, which precisely due to its location in a cinematic space is wholly liberating for the subject and may also represent the world as flesh which furthers my argument for a democracy of vision that might suggest alternative structures of understanding the other, which are not ultimately dependent on division and mastery:

> The cinema mechanically projected and made visible for the very first time, not just the objective world but the very structure and process of subjective, embodied vision – hitherto only directly available to human beings as an invisible and private structure that each of us experience as 'our own'. That is, the novel materiality and techno-logic of the cinema gives us concrete and empirical insight and makes objectively visible the reversible, dialectical, and social nature of our own subjective vision. (Sobchack 2004: 149)

The dichotomies that are subsumed within this more holistic visibility are not just those that rest on ideological divisions in the present but also extend to the temporal divisions and their contested meanings within this space.

Contact as interference and as interface is the outcome of any exploration of the edges. This is an attempt to remove the Foucauldian regulatory gaze from its position in the panoptican and enable its embodied disjunction so that the subject of the look and the object of the gaze can be interchangeable and interrelated. This is where Spain's edges – geographical, somatic and creative – speak to the perceptual field that defies categorisation and preferences experience as a means of democratic participation in the space of cinema and, by implication, in the space of the world. In this moving back and forth of preceptor to perceived subject to object, then, difference is not effaced but acknowledged and approached. 'At the limit, film and spectator are like parasite and host, each occupying the other and being in turn occupied, to the point where there is only one reality that *un*folds as it *en*folds, and vice versa' (Elsaesser and Hagener 2009: 11).

It is in the realm of the visual and through a creative manipulation of this look that film is uniquely placed to question accepted positions. This involves a new conception of the gaze as active, external and involved as opposed to static, powerful, internal and always functioning at a distance. In its ability to interact and its position as external to our material body it functions as a mediator – a third term – shedding new light on both the ideological and aesthetic dimension of these films. Its unique use of space and motion coupled with an ability to constantly switch perspective gives it the potential to highlight this 'recognition of difference', acknowledged by Bhabha, at the same time as it disavows it. Dialectical relationships functioning through a network of time, space, place, time, touch and vision combine in these readings through the innovative cinematic creations of Medem, Bigas Luna and Guerín.

Notes

1. For a thorough and perceptive survey of these periods, see Bentley (2008).
2. A pertinent example might be the depiction of Tokyo in *Lost in Translation* (Dir., Sofia Coppola 2003): the city is as we expect it, lived through its images, but it resists this easy inhabitation and colonisation and the tourists in the film are lost because of this gap between the city they think they recognize and the one they fail to understand.
3. This is an underside to the city that has also been explored in the film *Biutiful* (Dir., Alejandor Gónzalex Iñárittu 2010).
4. I recognize that identity is often contested, overdetermined and the result of a desire to categorize and therefore subjugate certain groups; however, I believe that certain identities are played with and undermined in the films I look at and that the term is a productive one in these contexts. Subjectivity is a much slipperier term, and it is one that alters in significance throughout my readings of these films because as Elspeth Probyn recognizes, it is always 'a relational matter' thought through in terms of the surrounding context (Probyn 2001: 290). In this book individual subjects (films, people and sometimes objects and spaces) seek to unsettle the assumptions made about certain types of identity.

5.   This is particularly the case in the chapter on Bigas Luna whose overt and prob-
     lematic depictions of sex and naked flesh make it hard to avoid this particular ele-
     ment of his filmmaking.
6.   Paul Julian Smith's work in this area is insightful and richly suggestive of alternative
     approaches to the categories of gender and sexuality.
7.   I am thinking particularly of criticism of the type initiated by Mulvey (1989), and
     then revised and developed by numerous critics such as Studlar (1992) and Doane
     (1991), which located a spectatorial identificatory gaze based in a psychoanalytic
     reading of gender following and critiquing Freud.
8.   This is the premise of the argument that I elaborate in Chapter Two.

References

Azurmendi, Maria-Jose, Nekane Larrañaga, and Jokin Apalategi. 2008. 'Bilingualism,
     Identity and Citizenship in the Basque Country'. In *Bilingualism and Identity: Span-
     ish at the Crossroads with other Languages,* edited by M. Niño-Murcia and J. Roth-
     man, 37–62. Amsterdam: John Benjamins Publishing.

Barber, S. 2002. *Projected Cities: Cinema and Urban Space.* London: Reaktion Books.

Barker, J. M. 2009. *The Tactile Eye. Touch and the Cinematic Experience.* Berkeley and Los
     Angeles: University of California Press.

Barthes, R. 1977. 'The Death of the Author' In *Image Music Text,* 143–148. London:
     Fontana/Collins.

Bentley, B. P. E. 2008. *A Companion to Spanish Cinema.* Woodbridge: Tamesis.

Bergfelder, T. 2005. 'National, Transnational or Supranational Cinema? Rethinking Eu-
     ropean Film Studies'. *Media, Culture & Society* 27(3): 315–331.

Besas, P. 1985. *Behind the Spanish Lens Spanish Cinema under Fascism and Democracy.*
     Denver: Arden Press.

Bhabha, H. K. 1994. *The Location of Culture.* London: Routledge.

Block, M. 2008. 'Dissidents of Patriarchy'. In *Situating the Feminist Gaze and Spectator-
     ship in Postwar Cinema,* edited by M. Block, x–xiv. Newcastle upon Tyne: Cam-
     bridge Scholars Publishing.

Boix-Fuster, E. and C. Sanz 2008. 'Language and Identitiy in Catalonia'. In *Bilingualism
     and Identity: Spanish at the Crossroads with Other Languages,* 87–106. Amsterdam
     and Philadelphia: John Benjamins Publishing.

Bruno, G. 2002. *Atlas of Emotion Journeys in Art, Architecture, and Film.* New York and
     London: Verso.

Burgin, V. 2004. *The Remembered Film.* London: Reaktion.

Cox, A. 2010. 'A New "Cinema of Attractions"?: The Barcelona School's Exhibitionist
     Loops'. *Hispanic Review* 78(4): 529–549.

D'Lugo, M. 1991. 'Catalan Cinema: Historical Experience and Cinematic Practice'. *Quarterly Review of Film and Video* 13(1–3): 131–146.

———. 1997. *Guide to the Cinema of Spain*. Westport, CT: Greenwood Press.

———. 2002. 'Catalan Cinema'. In *The European Cinema Reader,* edited by C. Fowler, 163–173. London and New York: Routledge.

Davies, A. 2004. 'The Spanish Femme Fatale and the Cinematic Negotiation of Spanishness'. *Studies in Hispanic Cinema* 1(1): 5–16.

Doane, M. A. 1991. *Femmes Fatales: Feminism, Film Theory, Psychoanalysis*. London: Routledge.

Elsaesser, T., and M. Hagener. 2009. *Film Theory: An Introduction through the Senses*. New York and Oxford: Routledge.

Evans, P. 2004. 'Contemporary Spanish Cinema'. In *European Cinema,* edited by E. Ezra, 250–264. Oxford: Oxford University Press.

———. 2005. 'Cinema, Memory, and the Unconscious'. In *Spanish Cultural Studies: An Introduction,* edited by H. Graham and J. Labanyi, 304–310. Oxford: Oxford University Press.

Evans, P. W. 1999. *Spanish Cinema: The Auteurist Tradition*. Oxford: Oxford University Press.

Faulkner, S. 2006. *A Cinema of Contradictions: Spanish Cinema in the 1960s*. Edinburgh: Edinburgh University Press.

Feenstra, P. 2011. *New Mythological Figures in Spanish Cinema: Dissident Bodies under Franco*. Amsterdam: Amsterdam University Press.

Foucault, M. 1986. 'What is an author?'. *The Foucault Reader,* edited by P. Rabinow, 101–120 London: Harmondsworth Penguin.

Fouz-Hernández, S., and A. Martínez Expósito. 2007. *Live Flesh: The Male Body in Contemporary Spanish Cinema*. London: I. B. Tauris.

Galt, R. 2006. 'Mapping Catalonia in 1967: The Barcelona School in Global Context'. *Senses of Cinema Online Film Journal* 41(November). Retrieved 19 August 2009 from http://sensesofcinema.com/2006/feature-articles/barcelona-school/

———. 2007. 'Missed Encounters: Reading *Catalanitat,* the Barcelona School'. *Screen* 48(2): 193–210.

Garber, M. 1997. *Vested Interests: Cross-Dressing and Cultural Anxiety*. New York: Routledge.

Halperin, D. M. 1995. *Saint Foucault: Towards a Gay Hagiography*. New York and Oxford: Oxford University Press.

Higginbotham, V. 1988. *Spanish Film Under Franco*. Austin: University of Texas Press.

Hopewell, J. 1986. *Out of the Past: Spanish Cinema after Franco*. London: British Film Institute.

Irigaray, L. 2002. 'Being Two How Many Eyes Have We?'. *Paragraph* 25(3): 143–151.

Jordan, B., and R. Morgan-Tamosunas. 1998. *Contemporary Spanish Cinema*. Manchester: Manchester University Press.

Keown, D. 2008. 'The Catalan Body Politic as Aired in *La teta i la lluna*'. *Burning Darkness: A Half Century of Spanish Cinema,* edited by J. R. Resina, 161–172. New York: State University of New York Press.

Kinder, M. 1993. *Blood Cinema: The Reconstruction of National Identity in Spain.* Berkeley and Los Angeles: University of California Press.

———. 1997. *Refiguring Spain: Cinema/Media/Representation.* Durham and London: Duke University Press.

King, S. 2006. 'Catalan Literature(s) in Postcolonial Context'. *Romance Studies* 24(3): 253–264.

Kogen, L. 2005. 'The Spanish Film Industry: New Technologies, New Opportunities'. *Convergence: The International Journal of Research into New Media Technologies* 11(1): 68–86.

Kovacs, K. 1990. 'Demarginalizing Spanish Film'. *Quarterly Review of Film and Video* 11:73–82.

Marks, L. 1994. 'A Deleuzian Politics of Hybrid Cinema'. *Screen* 35(3): 244–264

Marks, L. U. 2000. *The Skin of the Film: Intercultural Cinema, Embodiment and the Senses.* Durham and London: Duke University Press.

———. 2002. *Touch: Sensuous Theory and Multisensory Media.* Minneapolis and London: University of Minnesota Press.

Marsh, S. 2010. 'The Legacies of Pere Portabella: Between Heritage and Inheritance'. *Hispanic Review* 78(4): 551–567.

Marsh, S., and P. Nair, Eds. 2004. *Gender and Spanish Cinema.* Oxford: Berg.

Martin Márquez, S. 1999. *Feminist Discourse and Spanish Cinema: Sight Unseen.* Oxford: Oxford University Press.

McGowan, T. 2003. 'Looking for the Gaze: Lacanian Film Theory and Its Vicissitudes'. *Cinema Journal* 42(3): 27–47.

Mulvey, L. 1989. *Visual and Other Pleasures.* Basingstoke: Macmillan.

Probyn, E. 2001. 'The Spatial Imperative of Subjectivity'. In *Handbook of Cultural Geography,* edited by K. Anderson, M. Domosh, and S. Pile, 290–299. London: Sage.

Quintana, A. 2005. 'Modelos realistas en un tiempo de emergencias de lo político'. *Archivos de la Filmoteca* 49:11–31.

Silverman, K. 1999. 'The Subject of Semiotics [on Suture]'. In *Film Theory and Criticism: Introductory Readings,* edited by L. Braudy and M. Cohen, 137–147. New York and Oxford: Oxford University Press.

Smith, P. J. 1996. *Vision Machines: Cinema, Literature and Sexuality in Spain and Cuba, 1983–93.* London: Verso.

———. 2000. *The Moderns: Time, Space and Subjectivity in Contemporary Spanish Culture.* Oxford: Oxford University Press.

———. 2006. *Spanish Visual Culture: Cinema, Television, Internet.* Manchester and New York: Manchester University Press.

Sobchack, V. C. 2004. *Carnal Thoughts: Embodiment and Moving Image Culture.* Berkeley: University of California Press.

Stone, R. 2007. *Julio Medem.* Manchester: Manchester University Press.

———. 2012. '*En la cuidad de Sylvia/In the City of Sylvia* (José Luis Guerín, 2007) and the *durée* of a *dérive*'. In *Spanish Cinema 1973–2010: Auteurism, Politics, Landscape and Memory,* edited by M. M. Delgado and R. Fiddian, 169–182. Manchester: Manchester University Press.

Studlar, G. 1992. *In the Realm of Pleasure: Von Sternberg, Dietrich, and the Masochistic Aesthetic.* New York: Columbia University Press.

Williams, L. 2008. *Screening Sex.* Durham and London: Duke University Press.

CHAPTER TWO

Julio Medem
At the Margins of the Self

Underpinning the narrative of all of Medem's visually sumptuous experiments in the fundamentals of cinematography is the enigma of the self in the process of creation. This process of subject creation in its performative dimension is expanded and interrogated through his cinematic investigation of individuality and cinematic identity that is looked at here through the lens of Lacan's formulation of the gaze and language. I outline the ways in which this reading of his works exposes and engages with their creative approach to the construction of the subject before I move to a closer analysis of specific films.

In all of these works, liminal spaces function as mirrors for the psychological processes at work in Medem's cinematic subjects. The transformative power of the image renders them as positive, desiring, dialogic spaces rather than being solely the negative spaces of missed encounters, or the Lacanian voids that necessarily define the subject. Medem's deliberately ambiguous style supports this reading in his preference for narratives that are altered as they progress and whose filmic protagonists accept and adapt to their changing realities. A structural approach has seen psychoanalysis adopted – and adapted – to inform the relationship between spectator and screen, locating the desire of the former as a fundamental component in the projection of the latter (Metz 1982; Mulvey 1989). Symptomatic readings of films as representing the repressed, mirroring our unconscious and imitating the structures of the mind as Freud and later Lacan established them, have led scholars to seek within the moving image a means to assuage this anxiety. In doing so they have invested the image with a power to involve and placate this spectator who must be invested in the fantasy world on screen. Jean Pierre Oudart famously accounted for this concession to spectatorial desire in his writing on suture, drawing on the work of Lacan's disciple Jacques-Alain Miller, and the invocation of cinema as a discourse in which we must be able to identify ourselves as something other than the lack as which it initially configures us. The concept arose from the spectator's realization that the world on screen was demarcated – and thus profoundly separate from her – by a frame. Dayan elaborated

Oudart's theory in these terms: 'The viewer discovers that the camera is hiding things, and therefore distrusts it and the frame itself, which he now understands to be arbitrary' (1974: 126).

Since these initial examinations into the system of representation that has now become ubiquitous, there has remained a fascination with the cinema as a discourse of subject – and subjective – creation. The limits of the frame are being constantly redefined and yet that founding science of the self seems to offer itself anew to these reinvigorated debates on the relationship between self and cinema. This would seem particularly pertinent when the cinema engages with new technologies, which offer themselves as extensions of the self at the same time as they create multiple possibilities for its alternate understandings. The 'Vision Machine' that Paul Julian Smith borrowed from Paulo Virilio to examine his contention that 'visibility is constantly inflected by sexuality and nationality' is now ubiquitous but, as Smith argued and as I believe these films prove, this is not to the detriment of our experience of reality (Smith 1996: 2). In fact, to acknowledge that the self is constituted by externalized technologies is to embrace the capacity for them to add to our potential for alternative subjectivities, rather than detract from or alienate the subject from reality. In other words, we must accept that they have become so ubiquitous that they are our reality.

Medem acknowledges the power of the image in a system of visual representation, furthermore, and it is in this that he offers himself and his works up for Lacanian analysis, noting the impossibility of existence outside of desire, language and the scrutiny of the Other. However, he has discovered in cinema an outlet for subject creation that can play with the structures that were previously depicted as limiting, or limited by the frame. It is here that we return to the edge, the split subjects (perhaps mirroring the split national/regional identities at work), and engage with this division, because the mediation of the cinema enables them to find themselves outside of themselves and be there, where the other is, in order to see themselves. Medem finds, in the technological apparatus of the cinema, the perfect outlet for these Lacanian narratives. It points to the absence that is constitutive of our desire and which Lacan formulates as the gaze, but it then employs suggestive – and fantastical – means by which the subject can confront this gap without surrendering his or her sense of self. Fantasy in this regard does not equate to a cinematic genre, although it has something in common with it; it is rather the psychoanalytic definition glossed by Todd McGowan as 'an imaginary scenario that fills in the gaps within ideology. In other words, it serves as a way for the individual subject to imagine a path out of the dissatisfaction produced by the demands of social existence' (2007: 23).

(Re)imagining the Gaze

Vision and desire make us aware of what we cannot see, of the futility of an attempted encounter with the Real: 'We can apprehend this privilege of the gaze in the function of desire, by pouring ourselves, as it were, along the veins through which the domain of vision has been integrated into the field of desire' (Lacan and Miller 1979).

This reading moves away from the Lacanian theory of the cinema that depended on the Imaginary identification of the mirror stage and owes much to Todd McGowan's critical repositioning of Lacan in this arena. Limiting the gaze to the position of the eye would not suffice in Medem's cinematic universe where we are allowed to soar through the air, or disappear into holes under an island or behind the eye of a cow. If the dichotomy between self and other – that is mirrored by the fraught politicization of identity in the Basque context – can be removed through a fantasy construction of expanded visual possibility, then Medem is content to expose the cracks in ideology (or at least in the damaging effects of externally enforced and false configurations of subjectivity and identity) through this gaze which can be exposed through the strange and yet enhanced visuality of cinema. Lacan surmises that this 'is not a seen gaze, but a gaze imagined by me in the field of the Other' (1979: 84).

The world of images engages initially with the spaces of freedom – actual and symbolic – in *Vacas/Cows*, and it moves more explicitly to the doublings of self that speak to Lacan's theory of repetition and the drive in a reading of *Los amantes del círculo polar/Lovers of the Arctic Circle* and *Tierra/Earth,* and in *Lucía y el sexo/Sex and Lucía* and *Habitación en Roma/Room in Rome* the invention of the self is imagined anew as Medem finds in new technology an ideal structure for unending revision and creation of the subject. All in all, the concerted revision of previous technique and conventions resists the facile imposition of a power structure. The lines between fantasy and reality are deliberately blurred; an indistinction that obliquely refers to greater issues of representation, language and freedom of the subject.

During the opening sequence of *Earth* the camera transports us through space to earth, staging the locational grounding which is constitutive of the film's narrative structure. Paul Julian Smith reads it as 'the shift from darkness into light recreating a pagan cosmogony, the creation *ex nihilo* of the earth (and, perhaps of cinema)' (2000: 153). This return to the origin, to the nothing that precedes us, sets the stage for a new formulation of the self, of the mediated subject in a cinematic universe which resists the negative pull of the absent signifier and prefers to open out the spaces at the edges, the spaces between self and other and the spaces in between politically defined territories, to alternative linguistic and spatial conjugations. Ángel, the film's divided protagonist, embodies the themes that I will examine below. He is able to traverse that edge and inhabit the external gaze, and he has privileged accessed to the other's desire as he embodies it. Nonetheless, this is still a thwarted attempt to fully inhabit the space of the other as he encounters the desire of the two female characters as an obstacle to his dual selfhood.[1]

The director's obsession with cinematic modes of looking, which he revises and recycles throughout these works, demands a revision of the location and meaning of the gaze, a revision that Lacan undertakes in his seminar on 'The Eye and the Gaze'. In simple terms, power has been taken out of the hands of its usual owner, the subject who looks and says, 'I see only from one point, but in my existence I am looked at from all sides' (Lacan and Miller 1979). What is more it now inhabits the realm of an external object. As a result, this control is now converted into anxiety, as our look is no longer equated with the powerful gaze of conventional wisdom but reminds us of our status as split subjects.[2]

Studies of Medem's cinematic output have frequently concentrated on this innovative employment of the gaze as it is depicted by an endlessly mobile – frequently dizzying – camera. Nonetheless, there remains a persistent project to assign this gaze some ideological significance. It has been read as a site of conflict, a spectral presence of a Basque identity, which recurs at each moment of its apparent disavowal (Gabilondo 2002). Paul Julian Smith reads this transitory mode of vision as an inevitable symptom of a postmodern condition, of which film is the artistic movement *par excellence*. This reading of *La ardilla roja/The Red Squirrel* is informed by Gianni Vattimo's 'identification of the false transparency of contemporary society with the visual apparatus of cinema' (1996: 142).

Theories of cinema, which depend on various configurations of the gaze, have, at their base, a preoccupation with positionality, which at times has appeared to eschew its fundamental ability to adopt multiple subject positions throughout the duration of a film. This occurs both through the process of spectatorial identification but also as cinema works, as a quasi-subjective entity, to produce subject positions in and of itself. There has, of course, always been an acknowledgement of the eminent and inherent mobility of the cinematic camera intensified by the process of editing which manipulates this moving sequence of images. Fascination with this element of the motion picture drives much of the early speculation on this unique aesthetic vehicle (Benjamin 1992). These musings centred on the ability to look at the world anew; Stan Brakhage is rapturous in his imaginings of the perceptual possibilities of this mechanism, stating, 'Imagine an eye unruled by man-made laws of perspective, an eye unprejudiced by compositional logic, an eye which does not respond to the name of everything but which must know every object encountered in life through an adventure of perception' (1963: 228).

What both varieties of deliberation have in common – those marvelling at the potential of the new technology and those seeking to limit its political project through its function on the psyche – is their preoccupation with the subject and its imbrication, even entrapment, in the workings of desire, configured as a desire to see. Godard, in *Histoires du cinema,* claimed that the cinema was that which allowed Odysseus to look at Eurydice without killing her. This is what these doublings and improbable positions do: the imagination is that which – etymologically – inheres in images, and this image world suggests alternative modes of being. Elsaesser's double occupancy provides the perfect philosophical space for cinema to do this. After Derrida it is, 'the capacity of textual space to let us see both itself and something else' and it is also the 'sign of the co-extensiveness of two perceptions in a single representational space' (Elsaesser 2005: 110).

The notion of separation within what we think of as a coherent whole is more than a convenient metaphor for the positioning of the Basque country; it acknowledges an ability to inhabit two spaces precisely because we feel we are part of them both. This is Elsaesser's utopian definition of double occupancy, a site at which we can be self and other: 'utopian, insofar as under certain conditions ... it opens up ways of sharing the same space while not infringing on the other's claims' (2005: 111).

Place and Space: Constructing the Self at the Edges

Cinema's ability to traverse the boundaries of time, place and space grants it a certain privileged position at the interstices. It is not usually an entirely abstract and virtual space in the way of the programmed graphics of computer games (although the advent of increasingly sophisticated CGI means that virtual spaces are becoming indistinguishable from the topographical realities on which they are modelled), but it is frequently a space of extended freedom, possibility and becoming. On the one hand we are always distanced, temporally and spatially, from the world on-screen. On the other, we have the potential to inhabit a place in the future, or to recognize a place that we may already have inhabited at some time in the past. This complex synthesis of time and space as it is made manifest through technologies of the visual is perhaps most succinctly demonstrated through the motif of chat rooms and the use of cyberspace in *Sex and Lucía* and the exploration of virtual topographies as a new space of invention and encounter in *Room in Rome* to which I will return later. For the moment the concrete locations of filming and their relation to the narrative – as well as their slippery relation to the recognisable cartography of Spain – will be the subject of interest in terms of their topological relation to the workings of desire. In keeping with my reading of a shifting site of identification in these films, then my analysis oscillates between the concrete location of political identities and a subsequent evasion of them. I do not claim that Medem's project in relation to space is always tied to that of place and therefore ultimately political, but I do believe that his narratives and their visual innovation with regards to the location of their unfolding are inevitably inflected by the residual meanings (historical, social and political) that underpin these sites and their depiction.

Place and space are fraught notions, not only in their filmic context, but also in their formulation as territory, implying ownership as well as the right to residency. Such a spatial delineation, of course, encompasses an exclusivity surrounding national spaces. To include or exclude members of a nationality from a particular space assumes that boundaries can be drawn. Medem does not preclude himself from any involvement in the debate on spatial practice but he does try and proffer a new way of viewing and performing subjectivity (and other ways of non-visual filmic appreciation which I will examine later) which in its mobility challenges the assumption that it is indeed possible to create these sections which rely on inside and outside and, as a corollary, the subsequent establishment of groups according to inclusion or exclusion. This intersection of cinematic and spatial practice as it functions in Spain has already been aired: 'The dominant feature of Medem's meditation on the nature of Spain's imagined communities, is the effort to erase confining borders and to break out of the old ideological traps that had positioned Spain, even in the minds of Spaniards, as exotic and different' (Harper and Rayner 2010: 126). In this resistance to stereotype this Basque director posits a more productive relationship between these spaces and their inhabitants which sees the borders as useful sites for creation and interaction. This is an extensive, actual and metaphorical conceptualisation of spaces and their edges which works from a position where the subject (that is, both diegetic subject and the subjective capacity of the moving image texts) transgresses these limits in its expression of a desire to radically alter its subject position in various ways, through perspective, language and the mediation of both through technology.

(Re)viewing Reality in *La pelota vasca/Basque Ball* (2003)

To demonstrate this resistance to fixed identities and their ideological facet a comment on the aesthetic depiction of the political at work in his contentious and only non-fiction production is insightful. *Basque Ball* was Medem's attempt to address the conflict of his homeland creatively, constructing a political dialogue through cinema, a conversation which in reality could never have taken place and therefore relies on technological mediation and intervention. The voices that Medem prioritizes in this troubled piece are enmeshed with his ideas on place and space although in this context this attitude to space takes on an explicitly evasive reference.

The documentary subjects (a variety of politicians, cultural commentators, academics and artists with a connection to the Basque country and its ongoing political struggle) are depicted in several different locations, mainly outdoors, explaining their understanding of the issues at stake. The locations of the interviews have a deliberately ambiguous function. On the one hand, they resonate as both a site of conflict and a representation of the reason for the struggle. It is the land that unites the Basque people and the land that is fought over, a struggle for self-rule and, implicitly, of ownership of this very terrain. On the other, the extrication of social actors – especially political leaders – from the physical immediacy of their ethos also works as a representational strategy of neutralisation. In this way, forcing the participants into an external space implicitly adds a further layer of interest and potential meaning to these images as sites of both conflict and neutrality.[3] The cinematic journey that began with *Cows* returns here to the lush verdant landscapes of the Basque country and similarly it is the spaces of freedom that become the catalyst for dialogue. As Nathan Richardson claims, 'While getting his interviewees into the mythic space of nature – a general topic of all nationalisms – he, at least, moves them from place to space. In so doing, he gets them out of those sites most heavily charged with personal and political meaning. Medem, then is fully aware of the charged nature and charging potential of geography' (2011: 116).

The pre-titles of the film, lamenting the absence of those who refused to take part in its filming, establish a sensation of loss and bereavement which pervades the whole of this cinematic investigation. The purpose of referring to this film in this context is to introduce two features that will later be expanded upon in relation to the variety of marginality explored by this Basque director: the relationship of cinema to place and space and the way in which this relates to actual events, and the ways in which cultural memory is excavated.

Given the concentration on point-of-view exemplified by structures of vision, then, locality is imbricated in these structures because of its bearing on positionality – the place from which we look. The vertiginous style of shooting which is a feature of all of Medem's films is still in evidence in this work, particularly in the rapid interspersion of interview footage with other filmic material, often unattributed, which ranges from Orson Welles waxing lyrical about the Basque people to excerpts from Medem's own work with various clips from *Cows*. The dialogue which Medem posits as the only solution to this age-old conflict can be made possible only by these shifting perspectives and in these neutral liminal spaces as the camera attempts to occupy the place of the other.

There are occasions when the interviews appear to have been almost scripted to fit with the aesthetic project of their director, as a musician at the beginning of the film reminds us that 'Now it seems that things are black or white, you're either with me or you're against me. We forget about the whole range of colours that is found in between, which are perhaps the most beautiful and the most enriching.'

If this broad spectrum of colours is incorporated into this filmic project, then the difficulty of defining identity with any certainty is not only made more difficult but is also made into an irrelevant project. The redefinition of identity, which film as a liminal space within the domain of the other allows for, interrogates the validity of national and gendered identities and nurtures a holistic and inclusive consciousness which promotes human identity as multiple and fluid. As one of his interviewees says, 'Basque society has a basically plural identity' – an identity as fluid as will be seen in the repeated swish of the balls through the air from the game of *pelota* which becomes an aural motif for the desired harmony, speed, excitement and (physical) control in the face of the prosaic chaos and cacophony of the political discourse.

Border Crossings and the Other Within

The Lacanian gaze is that which troubles the unproblematic visual consumption of the image; it obstructs our access to it and threatens to look back, to implicate us in this experience by crossing the border of the frame. Lacan claims that the gaze is an inversion of perspective and as such it designates the shifting I/eye.

Initially this reading is dependent on location as a function of the gaze, the function that, as I will return to repeatedly, is a defining feature of Medem's output. As Medem engages with location (both in terms of the geographical settings of these films and on a smaller scale the actual position of the camera) he does so by deftly undermining positionality to establish an intersubjective space in each work. A space in which the gaze is revealed is a space in which problematic subjectivities are exposed rather than concealed by ideology (Žižek 1989).

The edge is frequently for Medem the space separating self and other. Lacan's formulation of being engages with these edge spaces as his configuration of the subject engages with spatiality. The subject for Lacan exists in a position of doubt – that is, the doubt that forms the desire to see ourselves from where others see us. Desire is therefore dependent on a spatial formulation.

An examination of this use of space through the films is extended to a tentative exploration of a link to place on some occasions. What is suggested in this investigation is that the shifting gaze that constitutes the subject's redefinition is aligned with places that, for variously assigned political and ideological motives, are containers for a certain reading of the subject and the terms of his or her desire.

This is illustrated here by means of the filmic trajectory mentioned above (from the Basque country in *Cows* to another European capital in *Room in Rome* which will be more fully explored in the course of this chapter). It has already been examined in terms of its ideological implications as a self-conscious removal from a troubled site of inhabitation into spaces where there is more scope for creativity and freedom, analogous to the spaces in the subject that are created at the moment of the founding split, yet which cinema is able to fill. Medem, optimistically, seeks a freedom in places that represent these spaces yet to be defined:

> In some way, in nature I feel closer to instincts and, above all, to my own feelings, perhaps because of this fear of the real that I spoke about earlier. I feel as though these spaces give me more freedom to invent, to situate or create stories that, as they develop in nature are able to escape the ties of realism that inhere in the urban, because it is unable to impose its rules there. I live in a certain reality, that of a city like Madrid, I know what it's like and how it affects me, and sometimes I think that if I leave this urban environment and get away to another place a calmer untouched place, perhaps I can express more of what is within me. Perhaps there my feelings are more comfortable in an environment that is less familiar and has a more primitive dimension. (Heredero 1997: 560) (translation mine)

Like the director, critics have analysed this as a pragmatic removal, a distance which permits a greater level of creativity and freedom: 'Young directors seem to be searching for new "spaces" and formal strategies, expanding territorial and representational limits in order to incorporate "other" settings and stories, allowing themselves to use fabulation and metaphorical discourse, freed now from the *burden* of political or nationalistic representation' (Santaolalla 1998: 332). The spectre of Medem's nationality haunts this variety of interpretation as he is unable to escape from the 'Basqueness' of his works.

Although a facile interpretation of a complex political problem, it is true that the cultural construction of 'Basqueness' is seen as other to 'Spanishness'. The co-existence of the two, as strong and legitimate national identities, would apparently be incompatible. Whichever (one) of these two cultural identities we configure as other, Lacan's spatial formulation of desire and the subject means that we, through cinema, can incorporate the desire of the other and the desire to be other within our own conceptualisation of the cinematic subject. The dynamism of Medem's ludic gaze enables this idealized, inclusive permutation of a Spanish-Basque subject, an inclusive cultural subjectivity.

As he moves away from the Basque country (in the gap between *Cows* and his problematic return with *Basque Ball*) the spatial representation of desire becomes more problematic as the other is internalized for the protagonists of *Earth* and *Lovers of the Arctic Circle*. Once again Medem preferences the ambiguity of temporal and spatial limits as perceived through the cinematic lens. He is fascinated by the way in which our inhabitation of space is transformed and facilitated by a mobile camera that becomes our surrogate eye and moves us into places that may otherwise be forbidden to us.

In the main these places are located outside a naturalized view of time and space. This is not wholly novel in the context of the cinema; formal devices have frequently relied on the creative use of the camera in order to reinforce and enhance spectatorial knowledge of diegetic events. Nonetheless, these devices have tended to remain within the confines of the mimetic on-screen world, utilising flashback for tricksy temporal leaps or explicitly resorting to generic categories that allow for such invention (science fiction or fantasy).

Medem departs from such convention on two levels, as the temporal and spatial jumps are not always explained. Of course, the point-of-view of animals is an innovative means of representing these discrepancies in time and space, but Medem takes it further. The camera temporarily loses its subjective association with a human eye, permissible and exciting in this fantasmatic space, enabling an imaginative projection through the eyes of another.

At the Edge of the Forest: *Vacas*

Medem's first feature film, as I have already mentioned, roots us firmly within the space of his origins. The rural environment functions, it must be assumed, as the blank canvas to which he referred in his earlier quotation. The plot centres on the rivalry between two families, the Mendiluze and the Irigibel, which is channelled through the competitive act of wood chopping with an axe as both men are *aizcolari* (the Basque name for the participants in this custom). The links between the two families are complex and involve an adulterous relationship between Ignacio Irigibel and Catalina Mendiluze, the result of which, the illegitimate Peru, produces the possibility of an incestuous relationship later in the film when the youngest generation of the two families, Cristina and Peru (now adults) leave their troubled homes and escape to America. The three temporal divisions in the film enable Medem to use the same actors to play three generations of family members. Conflict marks all three sections, with the Carlist War opening the film and the Civil War raging at its end. The family conflict that the narrative focuses on is the source of discontent in the middle section.

If the narrative is marked by these national and familial divisions, then the formal properties of this innovative piece are almost compulsively located in the potential of the camera to exceed the limits of vision. It is a compulsion that is supported by the narrative. Anne M. White comments pertinently on the unifying motif of vision in *Cows* as a means by which we begin to acknowledge, if not comprehend, the eccentricity of the grandfather and his link with the cows and his two grandchildren. She observes 'an obsessive concern with the act of looking, and more particularly, a focus on the pleasures of seeing the world from different, occasionally baffling, viewpoints' (1999: 1). Once more the alternative and bizarre point-of-view shot is seen as the defining feature of his auteurist style. What this 'obsessive concern' does illuminate is the relationship between space, the gaze and subject formation (which has as its corollary the definition of national identity in these Basque spaces).

It is this film which presents the most complex depiction of space in terms of its relationship to nationality. It is set in the valleys of the Basque country with character names that are indubitably Basque. This is not an urban milieu with its connotations of a central and recognisable politicized agenda of nationhood; these people are living in a place where the rivalry between two families is of much greater significance to them than the issue of a disputed governance of their land. It is the first in a series of borderline spaces – spaces that present the view from the edge. As is typical of Medem, it places the individual and the issue of personal identity at the forefront of his aesthetic, making any political or ideological point secondary to the characters' depiction.

Furthermore, the space of much of the action within the film, and certainly the place where the more bizarre and illicit elements of the film take place, the wood, is another exoteric site. This wood propels the action forward and is the locus of several key moments in the narrative: the illicit coupling of Ignacio and Catalina; the film's final scenes of civil war; and the second generation of the two families clandestine union, repeating the behaviour of the previous generation at the same time as they choose their own happy ending with their flight from this conflict ridden land.

This escape at the end privileges individual freedoms above collective identities, a trait established by our first visit to the wood at the beginning of the piece. In this scene Manuel, the first generation, escapes in a truck of dead bodies, having faked his own death during a battle in the Carlist War. Falling to the ground in the forest that becomes a central and significant space in the narrative, and unable to walk, after the cart has run over his leg, he looks up to find himself staring into the eyes of a cow. The camera then moves to occupy Manuel's point-of-view and in doing so stares into the eyes of the stationary and curious beast. This is the first iteration of the black hole that becomes a motif of spatial and temporal mobility and that is representative of a liminal space of freedom throughout. In this instance the camera moves towards the eye until the screen fades to black. The soundtrack to this sequence is the incessant buzzing of the flies that surround the cow's eye (an evident citation of Dalí whose work is of latent significance to Medem and Bigas Luna) and a harsh repetitive electronic soundtrack, evocative, in its rhythms and tonalities, of the usual aural accompaniment to the tense and suspenseful moments in the horror genre. After a short interval of black a small circle of light appears slightly off-centre and grows to reveal a country house with an old man in the foreground seated at an easel. Medem's inter-titles tell us it is the same Manuel, travelled forward in time some thirty years (now played by Txema Blasco).

The subject of the painting that Manuel is working on at this easel is another cow; the next shot is again a close-up of a cow's eye surrounded by flies. The eye, as it stands for vision, is unsettling in this scenario, revealing the unexpected instability of vision within a visual medium. It is perhaps the most

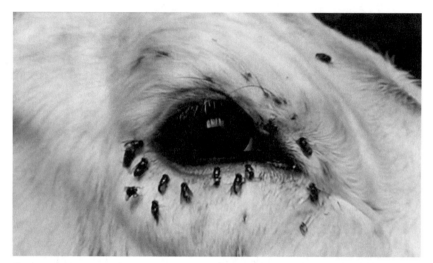

Figure 2.1. Cow's eye surrounded by flies, from *Vacas* (1991), by Julio Medem

apt rendering of Lacan's gaze as *objet a*, initially because it seems to be that absolute other space which transforms into a black hole. Our first encounter with it draws us in and threatens our obliteration in the space of that black void. If it were a space of this desire it would, of course, remain as a threatening void; to remove the threat is to remove the possibility of desire. Slavoj Žižek, perhaps the best known 'translator' of Lacan into popular culture, and film in particular, explains that 'anxiety occurs not when the object-cause of desire is lacking; it is not the lack of the object that gives rise to anxiety but, on the contrary, the danger of our getting too close to the object and thus losing the lack itself' (1991: 8).

It is Manuel and his granddaughter Cristina (Ane Sánchez) who understand the function of this blackness and seem, in their eccentricity, to remain calm when presented with their apparent lack. Three young girls flank the cow, the subject of the painting in this scene. As they stand patiently and their grandfather paints, the eldest speculates as to which part of her is being rendered according to where she assumes the grandfather's gaze falls. She asks if they are in the picture, and he assures them that they have to be as a cow will not stand still unless held, and much less so in a picture. The girl with the blond plaits, a young Cristina, already established as complicit with Manuel by virtue of their shared knowing glances, disagrees; she knows that they will not be in the picture, a belief corroborated by our privileged view of the painting under construction which is, indeed, lacking in human subjects. Cristina and Manuel are united precisely because of their understanding that the gaze does not equate to what we can see, but is defined by the unsettling knowledge that we can always be seen; the sister that wants to see herself in the painting is limited by her understanding of the field of vision. At the end of this sequence the cow starts and escapes into the forest, followed by Cristina, who is allowed access to this liminal creative space because she understands the fluidity of desire that enables the fantasy of the black space in the forest not as a destructive force but as a space of fantasy and potential, the space of cinema that functions beyond the field of vision.

Joseba Gabilondo argues that Medem's alternative perspective and innovative use of the cinematic lens is used deliberately to 'construct a point of view that defies historical positionality', a point of view which means that the viewer occupies the gaze of the other (2002: 269). But this reading rests on an idea of negative identity in its designation of Basque identity as other, as present in its disavowal. Manuel's response to his granddaughter locates cinema's potential to display and conceal without the associated disavowal, as the black hole designates. Lacan's complex formulation of desire can usefully be related to this black hole:

> If it is merely at the level of the desire of the Other that man can recognise his desire, as desire of the Other, is there not something here that must appear to him to be an obstacle to his fading, which is a point at which his desire can never be recognised? This obstacle is never lifted, nor ever to be lifted, for analytic experience shows us that it is in seeing a whole chain come into play at the level of the desire of the Other that the subject's desire is constituted. (Lacan and Miller 1979: 235)

The gaze as present in this film is an instance of this phenomenon as not necessarily traumatic because of its occurrence within this space – of cinema – which can alter its appearance with such fluidity and frequency. Basque identity becomes a possible presence, amongst numerous alternative identities. Desire is located in the founding split of subjectivity; and pleasure is afforded through our repeated efforts to return to the origin of the split.[4] Exploiting the potential for play within this space, rather than concentrating on the limit at which our desire no longer functions, is the function of the transparency of the gaze in Medem's adaptation of Lacan.

The spatial link between the black hole and the forest exemplifies this excess as a site of ideological liberation. From its first appearance this black void constitutes the space in which we are allowed a greater freedom than would usually be permitted; it does not offer access to a greater understanding of reality but reveals the excess that may designate the real in this fantasy space – the possibility that the other's desire is present here, co-existing with our own. Todd McGowan (2007) argues that this excess comes to signify precisely in terms of its position in the narrative; in other words it is not there to be enjoyed simply as a moment of excess but precisely because it points to the gap that cannot be reconciled by ideology. The symbolic dimension of these spaces is not foreclosed by the reference to their psychoanalytic redolence but adds to our understanding of the peripherality of the visual domain in this film. The black hole – represented by the cow's eyes and the *ajugero encendido* (*the lighted hole*) – are located in a deliberately, and symbolically, indeterminate space of meaning.

The *ajugero encendido* is a hollow tree stump in the forest. The three protagonists, Manuel, Cristina and Peru, are the only ones who access this privileged space. This hole is designated as magic; they throw live mice into it and wait to hear the fire catch them, a fire that we see no evidence of. Here I contend that it functions as a site of desire. In this early film it hints at those elements of Medem's oeuvre which critics have found confusing or challenging and as such typifies McGowan's (2007: 69–74) premise that a cinema of desire is difficult precisely because of its refusal to pacify the spectator and hide the troubling reality of unfulfilled desire.

Symbolic readings of the forest and the black hole attend to the gendered and national signification of this enigmatic space which is configured as an autochthonous political symbol by some (de Ros 1997; Evans 2007) or allied with a female space outside of the Symbolic order (Sánchez 1997: 150). The feminine here is figured as the space for any subject marginalized by the mainstream and patriarchy. The relationships of the characters to the places that they inhabit unite critiques of these films through their investigation of the way in which these spaces mirror the functioning of the psyche or – to take this further – are a part of the film's unconscious, which has also proved a fruitful area of investigation. Isabel Santaolalla refers to the peripatetic dimen-

sion of his first three works as 'the best possible expression of what psycho-
analysts call *transitional space*' (1998: 33).

Cinematic spaces are inscribed with ambiguous and complex meanings
which do not always bear a direct relationship to geographical place, as their
occupation of space transforms them, offering the spectator a way of inhabiting them anew. The screen is established as a desiring site that simultaneously sets up and breaks down the oppositions which create this desire and
at these cinematic junctures anguish and possibility combine. It is difficult, on
numerous levels, to define and delimit these works either spatially or temporally; Medem's sophisticated technique ensures a perpetual state of becoming which defies neat interpretation. The challenge to the spectator that the
confrontation with the black hole represents is entwined with a more positive
but no less ambiguous reading of subjectivity. McGowan insists that 'film does
have the ability to insist on the gaze as an absence rather than attempt to
obscure it through the illusion of presence' (2007: 74). The black hole exists to
remind us of the limitations of our field of vision, and the gaze is outside the
field of vision. Manuel, Cristina and Peru are untroubled by this limit because
despite its threatening presence they recognize its concomitant possibilities:
in this topological dimension it literally opens out this space to the potential of
that which is extrinsic to the visual field.

If these spaces are always sites of transition, in psychoanalytic terms, then
we have moved into the ultimate halfway position, caught between life and
death, this world and another. Once more the significance of this entirely
commutative state of being is that construction is privileged above the completed product, not only ensuring endless interpretative possibilities but also
significantly engaging with the transmutable potential of the cinematic.[5]

Doublings and Splittings in *Earth* and *Lovers of the Arctic Circle*

In *Cows* the complexities of the generational conflict played out against the
backdrop of the Basque countryside are underlined at the same time as they
are obfuscated by Medem's choice of actors and their representation of various members of one family. Carmelo Gómez is the young Manuel prior to taking on the role of his son Ignacio then finally playing the youngest of the male
line, the grandson/son Péru. This can be read in light of Medem's concern,

elaborated in the next two films that I examine, surrounding the impossibility – or desirability – of a separate and powerful notion of self. The earlier reference to the opening of *Earth* engaged with the specificity of location, the definite grounding that is staged by this cosmic descent at the outset. The voice-over that we hear during this improbable cosmonautical journey addresses itself to an as yet unknown Ángel:

> Death is nothing but if you were completely dead you wouldn't hear me. So here you are Ángel, in the middle of the greatest unknowable ocean that you can imagine. Existence is always accompanied by a background noise, called anguish.

If the defining colour of *Cows* was green, then here we move into the burnt red of the arid Spanish landscape in Zaragoza and Navarra. After this opening sequence – in which the camera moves through blackness, increasing in velocity as stars rush past at speed – the first inhabitant of the earth that we encounter is the woodlouse, a subterranean insect that causes the wine in the area to taste like the earth of the title. The camera has moved us from the cosmos to underground – improbable points of view in both cases. The sound that accompanies these sequences is redolent of the amplified heartbeat that moved us into the black spaces of *Cows*. This time it is Ángel who has privileged access to this void. As with the grandfather in *Cows,* he is on the outskirts of society, a misfit. The previously held negative connotations of this type of 'madness' are re-defined in both films as a variety of personality that embodies yet another type of freedom.

Ángel has been contracted to get rid of the woodlouse, and we meet him for the first time as he drives into the arid terrain of the title, amongst those vines whose fruit are contaminated. His eccentricity is established from the outset as he converses with a shepherd who has been killed by the lightning strike that we witness during the opening storm. His character develops, as is Medem's preference, through a series of enigmatic stories and his complicated pursuit of the two female protagonists of the film, Angela and Mari. From the very beginning of this film the notion of self – in terms of any separate and clearly defined entity – is problematized. The merging of fantasy and reality, inside and outside, that conveys this blurring is crystallized by the opening sequence and extended through the trope of the split personality.

I have already examined the means by which psychoanalytic narratives locate desire as the intrusive element into all intersubjective relationships. As well as revisiting the relationship between power and desire in these films, Medem's cinematic technique locates a place for this desire and a reading of it within the films at these liminal sites. In *Earth* this internal desire traverses the boundary that confines it to the mind (and body) of the desiring subject and allows it a physical presence, in the cinematic space, as Ángel's alter ego.

Returning to the conception of suture that I touched upon earlier in the chapter, this time the gaze, or that which should remain hidden, is manifested in the location of the split subject on-screen, undermining the comfortable and powerful presence of the ideal spectator. A split subject opens a rupture in which a new conception of this cinematic space emerges. Medem's use of this on-screen doubling is initially adumbrated by means of the auditory, as a voice-over intimates a dialogue with an alter ego – although at this point the presence of an interior monologue is possible given the absence of visual explication. Later on in the narrative, however, we are faced with the dual presence on screen as the alter ego argues with the character over the provenance of the dead sheep that he offers to Angela and her family.

The by-product of this maintenance of ambiguity is the second instance of the removal of spectatorial power, pleasure and certainty. Accumulation of knowledge throughout a film creates similar feelings of indulgent certainty and control that function as support for the identification with the image. In this case, however, there are various moments of deliberate dual meanings and confusion which disavow any such possibility with regard to Ángel's 'true' identity. We are fully aware of his time in the psychiatric hospital. Yet his explanation for his internment – on the grounds of an overactive imagination – appears to satisfy his recent acquaintances. Despite the connotation of schizophrenia raised by his split personality, we are not allowed a comfortable solution: the dénouement resists closure and explanations, creating a new and ambiguous liminal space for the spectator, which mirrors the apparent limbo of the protagonist.

The split between subject and object – self and other, signifier and signified – acquires a visual dimension in Lacan's consideration of the scopic drive. The concept of the drive is taken from Freud's work on the instincts, which Lacan highlights as a mistranslation of *Trieb* (drive), differing from an instinct in that it is a specifically human trait. In this work these drives, as well as being closely associated with the idea of the split that is all pervasive, remain fundamentally linked to the idea of repetition: 'What is fundamental at the level of each drive is the movement outwards and back in which it is structured' (Lacan and Miller 1979: 177).

Ángel's movement between the two psyches (his repeated arguments with himself, particularly concerning the two women in the film) are a cinematic acknowledgement of the removal of limitation and the manifestation of the technical manipulation that offers the potential for many alternative points of view. As Paul Julian Smith sums up, 'In his use of enigma, Medem is advocating a practice of looking and listening as if for the first time' (1997: 12). Once the black space of freedom – that here represents that split in which we obsessively engage in a repetitious movement – is established, the subject vacillates in this space literally split by a desire for two women in the film's narrative and simultaneously exploring the potential to inhabit a desiring space, impossible outside of this fantasy scenario, which posits the imbrication of the other and their desire within the subject. Cinema's unique point of view enables the internalisation and externalisation of the self simultaneously, reinforcing the porous boundaries of the subject – bodily and psychologically – already hinted at by the use of the same actors mentioned above.

The indistinct separation marked by the doubling in *Earth* is extended by his subsequent film *Lovers of the Arctic Circle* which also privileges subjective freedoms but this time links them more explicitly to the desire of the other. The ethereal title sequence gradually reveals the actors' names and production details as they peep through clouds. Its bleached whiteness hints at a heavenly location, otherworldly and certainly peripheral. The sounds are those of a deserted space with prominent gusting wind giving way to the haunting melody of *Sinitaivas* performed by Olavi Virta and the Harmony Sisters. As the title of the film emerges from the mist in this snowy sequence it suggests that we find ourselves in the northerly location which that same title announces.

This richly evocative movement creates a space which seems uniquely open to inscription of cinematic meaning. It is literally a blank, clean and white site, haunting in its emptiness. At this point there is only the title of the film to ascertain any geographical specificity but this also marks the location out as liminal and restricted, by the boundary of the circle. As the mist both obscures and reveals the names that appear on-screen, the fragility of the cinematic subject is rendered visibly apparent. The shapes that appear through the mist and partially covered by the snow on the ground underline this vulnerability. The close-up and fragmented camera work at this point means that these are little more than unidentifiable shapes lying half buried in snow and ice. The image here privileges surface texture and foregrounds the intrinsic visual interest of shapes and colours and this surface, prior to the inscription of narrative on this space. Little by little the wreck of an aeroplane fuselage is discernible (interestingly only in two shots, one that reveals the name of the director and the other the name of the film).

The wreckage hints clearly at a traumatic event, or at the very least a significant rupture.[6] This as-yet unknown narrative becomes foundational to the fiction created by Medem, a fiction which continues to pivot around unknown elements or at least frustratingly unexplained stories and missed encounters. The nature of the binary narrative and its deliberate inconsistencies establishes this inconclusive structure, as the differing accounts incite suspicions of inaccuracy and the possibility of deliberate deception. In these twisting and overlapping accounts of two such initially intertwined and then wholly separate lives, Marian Via Rivera discerns the structure of a labyrinth. If this maze-like structure is viewed as a game with its own particular rules in which resolution always depends on deferment, the aim must not only be to find the centre but then also to locate the exit. Pleasure, similar to the pleasure to be gained in the pursuit of desire, is the result of precisely this lack of resolution, and like the Freudian desiring drive, revisited by Lacan, it is the enigmatic object, often absent, which becomes the space around which we relentlessly circle in a game which depends on its futility – our never finding the centre of the maze. As Via Rivera explains, 'the place that has so meticulously been kept secret is usually an empty space – the blind spot. Thus the effort of finding it seems pointless and the subsequent satisfaction of the conquest is immediately transformed into a strong sense of disappointment' (2004: 207).

The narrative pivots on the overlapping stories of Otto and Ana, who meet by chance in their infancy, as they leave school one day, and whose parents later marry. Forced to become step-siblings, they enter into an intense intimacy (becoming lovers) and then an enforced separation, after Otto discovers his mother dead in her flat and flees. Otto and Ana tell their own stories; Medem marks the alternating sections of the film with their names alerting us to the point of view of each section. Palindromic names chime with the circle of the title, and the repetition and its relationship with desire and its interminable circuit, as well as the connotations of fate that this construction entails, are all constitutive of this intricate and complex fable.

There is an element of overlap with Rivera's observations on the blind spot and the Lacanian formulation of vision as a constraint rather than a revelatory device. Postulating further on the essential disempowerment that our acknowledgment of the gaze entails, Lacan says, 'In this matter of the visible, everything is a trap, . . . There is not a single one of the divisions, a single one of the double sides that the function of vision presents, that is not manifested to us as a labyrinth' (1979: 93).

Missed encounters, unanswered questions and overlapping paths are certainly features of a maze that are imitated by the narrative of this film. In one scene, after Otto and Ana have lost touch, they both find themselves in Madrid; they pass within metres of each other in the Plaza Mayor. Indeed our frustration as we watch Otto and Anna miss one another, despite their physical proximity, comes from an inability to control this cinematic gaze or identify with either one of these protagonists in an attempt to understand how it is that they fail to see one another. Relating this missed encounter to the mapping of the film locates Madrid as the centre of the maze and the site of potential encounter, yet these two fail to meet and return once more to the geographical periphery in order to continue in the pleasure of the pursuit and the repeatedly missed encounter.

This instability of vision calls into question the reliance on the visual that the cinema promotes. Medem's obsession with the modes of cinematic looking and the relationship with self and other suggested by these scopic conventions is related to subjectivity and the imbrication of our relationship to the other in this creative version of subject formation.

Otto and Ana create ego ideals in one another, in the sense that Lacan explains: 'You will then see that it is in the Other that the subject is constituted as ideal, that he has to regulate the completion of what comes as ego, or ideal ego – which is not the ego – that is to say, to constitute himself as an imaginary reality' (1979: 144). They merge themselves narcissistically, becoming one in their narrative and their idea of their subjectivity. In this way they have traversed the space that was supposed to separate them, and, in doing so, they propose a new type of spectatorship which draws us closer to the film in our appreciation of it. Furthermore, they trouble the established boundaries suggested by the spatial, geographical and human territories in this film.

The temporal disjunction and character doublings, with one actor playing several parts in the same film, have led to criticism of Medem's films for inspiring certain disaffection. Jonathan Romney in his review for *Sight and Sound* defined the narrative structure of the film as a 'jigsaw principle' that he considers 'alienating'. He sees the complications and repetitions as a test to the spectator:

> Medem tests us further by spinning us what purports to be a narrative of grand destiny, while repeatedly exposing its twists as cavalier string-pulling. ... The notion of plausibility is swallowed up in an intricate game, in which every element is there simply to reflect another, and in which every part has to be accounted for before the game can reach a satisfying conclusion. (2000: 48)

If these repeated reflections are indeed the key to an intricate game then it is a game which unfolds within the visual realm and plays with the artifice of these images as they present a simulacrum of ourselves which is an illusion of a coherent whole self. Referring again to Lacan, the moment of self-definition in the mirror stage is unquestionably a spatial identification, and it is this, in part, which has led so many theorists to apply it to cinema.

However, this mirror is always presenting an inverted and artificial form of our material body. Not only this, it also opens up the space that lies between this body and the mirror itself, a space reflected by Medem's symbolic circles. The ability of the circle to create new space is exploited by Lacan as he uses circles to sketch his topologies of the self in relation to the Other. Circles allow the greatest flexibility in this project because of their ability to join and link and still retain their own individual spaces. The endless deferment, the cinema as the mechanism of construction rather than resolution, is precisely the aesthetic means by which the contours of difference can be navigated. There may indeed be some metaphorical redolence with the inhabitation of self within other and the doublings at work which refer to the problematic space of Basque identity within the Spanish state, but I think this reduces the complex and layered signification at work here. It accords with McGowan's understanding of the manifestation of desire in the visual realm as that which can be there but hidden or which the mechanism of cinema can precisely render transparent and yet still unsettling.

The flexibility of vision and its role in subject formation deviates here from the oft-cited version of identification that proceeds from a (mis)reading of Lacan's mirror stage. Otto and Anna's reflections enact projections of their imaginary and idealized versions of one another. Unlike the mirror the cinema allows them, via an objective and selective embodied gaze, to break down their images of one another and represent them in their own spatial and temporal terms. Here, the construction of the screen image is significant both in its aesthetic precision and stylized composition as well as in the symbolic depth of connotative meaning of the various components of this image. In this way the symbol not only creates a liminal space – the Arctic Circle – it also pervades the narrative with palindromes and circular narratives and enables the reflective recurrences of the dual narrative, remoulded each time according to the perspective of these protagonists, lending weight to Lacan's assertion that 'repetition is not reproduction' (1979: 50).

Ana and Otto epitomize the circularity of Lacan's repetition in both their palindromic names and their obsession with the Arctic Circle within the film. The pair are split subjects defining themselves in relation to the other within their simultaneous narration. The maze-like structure suggested by Rivera concurs with these circles, as the centre of the maze eludes us and the same paths are trodden time and again in a quest for this elusive ending. The ambiguity of the narrative lies in the doubt of the spectator as to whether they are continuing around the void in the middle of the circle, the *objet a* which pins their Imaginary, Symbolic and Real together, or whether their confused ideal egos of one another are causing a malfunction in the workings of their desire.

Narratively the opening of the film suggests that the latter may be the case as Otto admits that life is circular but the problem in his life is that it 'has only gone round once'. He is caught in a specular image with Ana. At the beginning of the film Otto looks down at Ana and as the spectator we are allowed to briefly assume his point of view, we see his eyes reflected in hers. Suddenly there is an apparent confluence of those two things that should remain separate; this same image closes the film as we too are confined within this circularity repeating the same circuit over and over.

Ambiguity and enigma are inevitable consequences of this inconclusive mode of cinematic representation. The film's beginning announces its ending, with the debris from the plane crash pre-empting the possibility of the death that may, or may not, befall both protagonists. Alternate endings – Ana run-

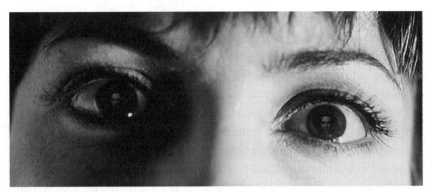

Figure 2.2. Otto reflected in Anna's eyes (Najwa Nimri) in *Los amantes del círculo polar* (1998), by Julio Medem

ning up the stairs to her other Otto and the young Otto crashing his plane and never being reunited with Ana – are presented, and we are given no clue as to which we are to believe. That there may be inherent truth in either situation is of less concern than the notion of perspective and the reality that inheres in the gaze of the viewing subject.

The possibility of truth in representation returns us to the grandfather's painting in *Cows* and moves the discussion forward towards the nature of performance and reciprocity in Medem's other films. This awareness of being under the gaze of another that being the subject of a painting highlights brings to the fore another key dimension of Medem's work, that of cinematic performance, or subjectivity as coming into being but also as necessarily related to a performance of being which is extended and enabled by the screen and yet still regulated by our interaction with the other and an awareness of being under their gaze and subject to their interpretation of us, this time through language. Language for Lacan is always limiting; it is an imperfect means of communication which cannot help but allow meaning to slide through the cracks at the limits of its failures.

Language, Performance and the Creative Subject

If the subject is conceptualized and depicted by Medem as always in the process of construction, as fluid and labile and not reduced by the vision of the other, then in language his cinematic subjects discover a further outlet for this version of creativity. Just as the gaze was shown to be manipulated by a skilful and motile camera, so the performance of self can engage with language, in this mediated world, as a further means for creation. Language is traditionally assumed to be a source of authority. It is through language that we are thought to create subjectivity, as we use it to describe who we are. However, it is a structure that predates us and that we are forced to adapt to our needs and desires. Lacan's contribution to the Freudian understanding of the unconscious stems from his premise that he sets out in Seminar XI: 'The unconscious is constituted by the effects of speech on the subject, it is the dimension in which the subject is determined in the development of the effects of speech, consequently the unconscious is structured like a language' (Lacan 1989: 149).

The other is always implicated within language if we view it as a structure of lack. It can never truly represent us to the other. Reciprocity is imbricated within this structure, in the same way that it was an inevitable, if threatening, component of the gaze. Medem demonstrates a view of language as constitutive in the creation of experience rather than fulfilling a descriptive function: 'It's an interesting, strange relationship between the teller of fables, or the suggestor, and the person who is receiving the suggestion' (Mottram 2002). Language, for Medem, is ambiguous. It has, on the one hand, the potential for creativity and through this creativity can also exercise powers of deception. It is at once more powerful than the protagonists and insufficient for their needs.

The Red Squirrel establishes this potential for deception and creativity in its opening scenes. This film creates an alternate reality which is, apparently, driven by the tenacious assertions of its main characters and the narrative pursuit of these frequently outlandish constructions. The premise of the film is the amnesia suffered by the female protagonist Elisa/Sofía (Emma Suárez) as a result of a motorcycle accident at the beginning of the film. The quest to uncover her true identity is at odds with Jota's (Nancho Novo) desire to create in her an ideal/fantasy lover, perhaps based on a previous relationship, which is obliquely referenced in several scenes during the film. The violent pursuit of Elisa/Sofía by a man claiming to be her husband Felix (Carmelo Gómez) forms a menacing subplot as he approaches the eponymous campsite where the new lovers are on holiday together. As with *Lovers of the Arctic Circle* the expected explication of plot, the recognition of a contained cinematic reality that will play out to a conclusion, is resisted. When Felix finds Sofía she escapes both men and they are involved in a car chase, which ends in Felix's death. A further set of improbable connections involving Sofía's brother and a radio talk-show allow Jota to find Elisa/Sofía, and he claims that he never believed her to be suffering from amnesia, ending the film as it began with the mendacious capacity of language and its capacity to deliberately mislead.

Sex and Lucía in similar fashion combines two narrative strands, temporally disjointed but overlapping, and in common with *The Red Squirrel* structures a plot on the basis of a misunderstanding. This has more in common with *Lovers of the Arctic Circle* as it presents the binary plot structure as clearly labelled separate strands, appropriately named 'Sex' and 'Lucía'. The film opens with Lucía and the unexplained end of a relationship followed by a traumatic misunderstanding, and Lucía's escape to an unnamed island. What follows moves us back in time to the island and the coupling of two strangers on holiday before 'Sex' establishes the primary relationship of the film as Lucía and Lorenzo meet and establish their life together. Lucía recalls her life with Lorenzo from the island, to which she fled because she believed Lorenzo had been killed in a car accident. Language is both the limiting and creative factor in these relationships as it becomes a means for the characters to create alternative versions of reality.

Both of these films employ confusing plots in order to highlight the elusive version of identity that cinema enables. In *The Red Squirrel,* for example, we see how Jota and Elisa use it in the first place to create the artifice of a relationship and when they realize its limiting power they move on to actions which, however exaggerated they might seem, give credence to the words they have spoken. In both works under scrutiny the creative power of language in film is developed from the suggestive conversations between Elisa and Jota to the more sophisticated idiom of cyberlanguage as Medem tackles technological innovation as an ideal means by which to establish his implausible subjective points of view. As might be expected from a director who has proved so capable in his manipulation of filmic technologies, the Internet provides him with a further avenue by which he can open up the dialectic space through which his protagonists negotiate and unravel their identities.

Language facilitates creation and deception and in psychoanalysis it both legitimates and undermines the subject who speaks. It highlights our separation from the other and our dependence on them to confirm our existence.

The openings of *The Red Squirrel* and *Sex and Lucía* are similar in their uterine emergence from underwater depths. Thus the films visually perform a birth as the camera is born from these waters – an earthly amniotic sack. For Elisa the baptismal qualities of the water in her re-naming take on a significance that then inflects the entire narrative. From the watery credits that open *Sex and Lucía* the enforced splits and gaps become the spaces in which the story is allowed to unfold. In *The Red Squirrel* when Elisa crashes through the barriers on her motorbike before falling to the beach below, a shockwave shudders its way along these barriers that then cracks in between Jota's hands, enacting another physical split. He had been gazing at the sea below and trying to summon up the courage to jump, to return to the water that represents both oblivion as well as the positive space of rebirth.

As is ever the case for Medem it is a coincidence, Elisa's accident, that prevents Jota from leaping to his death, and it is the first verbal exchange between this pair that restates Medem's preoccupation with the organ of sight and the truth of deception which is fundamental to the remainder of this film. As Jota stares down at the face of Sophia encased in her helmet (a shot echoed at the end of *Lovers of the Arctic Circle*) he lies to her about the colour of her eyes. The first question posed by Jota to Elisa, 'Who are you?', is logical in this scenario. More than an inquisitive aside, it is constitutive of the structuring logic of this film, in which the creation of narrative and its dependence on language are not only transparent but in their unexpected dimension create tension and underline the provisional delicate nature of the self. This would appear to be borne out to a degree by this scene on the beach, in which Jota encourages the female protagonist to invent a self, instructing Sofía/Elisa, 'Say a name, the first that comes into your head'.

This emphasis on the lack of authority in language is programmatic: it destabilizes the notion that it may express fundamental truths, but in a style typical of Medem this is not interpreted as a negative. Amnesia is positive because, real or feigned, it provides this woman with the ideal opportunity to reinvent herself. It goes further than this though, by locating the legitimate subject on the side of performance at least in this fictional space. Escape, invention and their relationship to language and visibility are once more the primary concerns.

In this final section I will bring together this performative and creative power of language and demonstrate how Medem adapts it to his needs, enabling a variety of cinematic performativity that relies on language, the gaze and the inherent creativity of technology to reassign meaning to both. J. L. Austin's work on the performative power of language initiated an interest in its potentially transformative power. For Austin the performative capacity of language concurs with Medem's explanation of storytelling. To this effect the theorist is concerned with utterances which he proceeds to label 'performative': statements which purport to offer a declaration of fact but which, in their creation, actually alter reality, literally performing an action through their words. 'The name is derived, of course, from 'perform', the usual verb with the noun 'action': it indicates that the issuing of the utterance is the performing of an action-it is not normally thought of as just saying something' (Austin 1962: 5–6).

To return to Medem in relation to this performative aspect: in their acceptance of the amnesia (which appears to be fabrication that neither of them now wishes to question) Elisa and Jota enter into a considered negotiation as they (re)construct her life linguistically, specifically through speech. They enter into a contract which apparently involves them speaking their wishes, desires and memories in order to legitimize them.

An early scene at the hospital anticipates and frames this function of language in its dual performative and revelatory capacity. Elisa is visited by a psychiatrist specialising in cases of amnesia, the first treatment consists in her naming a series of people in photographs based on a view of the backs of their heads. In a film which centres on the elusive nature of identity – and a concept of it as alterable and influenced as much by external suggestion as by any degree of autonomy or internal volition – the naming of anonymous, faceless humans is pertinent. In a cinematographic style typical of Medem, the presence of the photographs at this point of the narrative and their relation to the structure of film and its indexical link to reality make this scene at once useful and highly provocative in its wider relationship with film.

As Elisa leafs through these snapshots rapidly assigning names to each one, they reveal the way in which a false sense of movement is created in the cinema via the projector. The uncanny aspect of this scene makes its presence felt as the name Felix recurs and the photographic image begins to move, becomes in fact a mini-film within the film. We will learn later that this is the back of her husband Félix's (Carmelo Gómez) head. This can be read as a cinematic rendition of the performative dimension of language, the power of the utterance to bring into being, which mirrors Jota's earlier naming of Elisa.

Elisa and Jota must voice truths before they can act on them, but once spoken they seem, uncannily, to become real. Much of this linguistic invention and intervention takes place in the presence of other people, adding a further layer of legitimation to the words as they are spoken. The first example of this takes place when Jota and Elisa are invited to dine with the family at the campsite. Jota is anxious that Elisa should not let slip the fact that she is amnesiac, and the conversation at dinner focuses on the interplay between the couple as they are forced to concur on the minutiae of their lives, neither knowing what it is the other is about to claim as fact. They invent stories about their past together in response to the older couple's questions about them.

Given our privileged knowledge of their situation, dramatic tension is created as we listen to stories that are apparently detached from reality, because if they met for the first time at the site of the accident then there is no way that they could know these things about each other. Jota claims that Elisa is a champion swimmer and that is how they met; she in turn at a later meal boasts of his skill with a motorbike, despite the fact he has already told her that he cannot ride one. These need be little more than interesting fantasies of these two characters but Medem extends this preoccupation with the creative power of language in the construction of the subject as Elisa proves her swimming prowess and Jota performs an implausible stunt with the motorbike. Rob Stone relates this invention to the wider issue of identity and memory:

> A sense of identity is based on memories of ourselves but memories change with time, becoming, in effect, an edited version of events that show us in a better light – a 'director's cut' that lets us all be auteurs in the new, improved version of our lives. Lies have this useful habit of turning into truths, with the result that fabricated memories do not necessarily result in a false sense of identity. (2007: 169)

The extent of personal volition and the necessary involvement of another party are interrogated by the episodes in which they create this new identity. This 'useful habit' of lies based in the power of language to create an 'other' and to assign him or her with certain characteristics is assumed in this interpretation of language in psychoanalytic terms:

If speaking is acting, instead of an utterance being the voicing of a statement about the world which then becomes implanted or transferred into the mind of the other, then only one party can commit the act – whatever part the other has to play, he or she is not the agent. Indeed certain speech acts will undercut the supposed freedom of the listener in the very act of their utterance. (Forrester 1990: 152)

In establishing the psychoanalytic framework as a legitimate one through which to examine these as speech acts, we are working with the suggestive power of language, with the words uttered and with the interpretation drawn from them. We must also accept that we are creating speculation as to the nature of the relationships within the film. Thus far, I have elided the problematic relationship that psychoanalytic interpretations have with the concept of gender, and in furthering an argument about performativity I have also not engaged with, arguably, its most significant critical manifestation, that of gender.

Performing a Feminine Self?

As is the case with Bigas Luna, Medem's films have a tricky relationship with their depiction of female characters. This is confounded by their national position, or their exteriority to the Spanish national identity that has traditionally had a troubled relationship, politically and culturally, with stereotypical national versions of gendered identity, which I examined in Chapter One. In films which rest on the playful and ultimately indefinable nature of the subject, where do we locate the problematic facet of the gendered body, particularly the sexualized body? If the camera attempts to elide constructions of power based on binaries of repression and dominance in this new visual regime, then the gaze is detached from the body and liberated from (some?) of its original/ limiting definitions. Jacqueline Rose's riposte to the psychoanalytic criticism of cinema in the late 1970s – and what has come to be known as 'gaze theory' – lamented the 'elision of sexual difference' and mused that 'the concept of sexual difference functions as the 'vanishing point' of the theory' (1986: 200).

The elusive identity of the female protagonist combined with the sensual appeal of the actor Emma Suárez, in *The Red Squirrel,* invite readings of macho overtones, which is unsurprising given the premise of the narrative which is ostensibly the creation of (a) woman in the image of (a) man. Medem re-doubles the notion of sexual difference in order to challenge the location of the gaze and the stability of sexuality and gender as signifiers in a cinematic world. We have seen how the quest for fulfilment in the films thus far has been consistently derailed by the acknowledgement of the lack that is the thing we think we seek. This time it is the elusive sexual relationship that slips out of our grasp. In doing so the sexual subjects fail to comply with the codes that would be expected in such a relationship.

Elisa's ostentatious sexuality is a significant attraction, an attraction that is aided by the personality and physical presence of Emma Suárez, one of Medem's preferred female leads. Sexuality and erotic codes are utilized as another means of communication when language is seen to be insufficient for the needs of these characters; but this sexuality is not confined within the normative heterosexual practices within which previous cinematic objectification of the female was assumed to function.

The character of Elisa never demonstrates the fear or mistrust that might be expected of an amnesiac patient who is removed from a hospital by a man she claims she can't remember. When they arrive at the campsite she signs her name S. Fuentes and challenges Jota to correct her with a pointed stare. As the couple are shown to their plot the camera contemplates her rear in tight-fitting white trousers. A cut to the suggestive look of a shorthaired woman, an employee at the campsite, exposes her as the bearer of the look in this instance. In a film that pivots on unsettling expectations, this is unsurprising: it is not simply an example of the adoption of lesbian desire which adopts the active gaze for a homosexual relationship that still depends on objectification; it is a recognition of the pitfalls of that same objectification and its concomitant assumptions in cinema. It must also take into account the national tradition from which it stems and which, I argue, it seeks to interrogate, playing with a feminine stereotype that is inseparable from a national stereotype at certain periods in Spain's cinematic history.

Desire is initially established as Jota's desire to create Elisa/Sofia in his image, and it is hinted that this is the image of his previous partner. We expect the films to work through the process of this project; tension is created through our knowledge of Sofia's amnesia and the possible recovery of her memory and revelation of her true identity. As this is dismantled and we are confronted with an autonomous sexually confident female who appears to collude in the creation of this alternative reality, the anticipated structure is overturned. There is to be no resolution of desire within this sexual relationship, or at least not in the terms that we might expect. Lacan affirms that although we may seek what we desire in an other they will never fulfil that need because the desire is a desire for nothing. Lacan's gaze represents that nothing. This time the site of the gaze is both concealed and revealed by the performance of subjectivity in which Jota and Elisa engage. Their performance each time points to the empty signifier and to the site of the external gaze. Medem shows himself to be fully aware of the medium within which he works and the paradigmatic structures of gender-driven spectatorship prevalent in film and its theory, and the above scene is an ironic nod towards these many and varied theories of the gaze.

This in no way constitutes, I would argue, an attempt to elide the serious ethical issues of sexual representation but rather signals the initiation of an inclusive approach that permits an exploration of feminine sexuality wholly independent from a rigid and controlling male gaze. As such, the slippage, which I will contend is the effective and characteristic cinematographic technique through which he can open up the dialectic spaces in his work, takes precedence and is effected by means of a ludic mobile gaze that defies ideological assignation. This is because I read the gaze as separate from the assumption of mastery that was involved in its original reading. Of course, gaze theory as it has been applied to film was not only the result of Lacanian structures of viewing; it has been caught up in gendered accounts of pleasure and spectatorship which have been debated and revised since Mulvey's seminal essay on the subject in *Screen* in 1977.

The manifestation of feminine sexuality in *The Red Squirrel* depends on a linguistic performance which is not bound by its corporeal representation as it is defined by the cinematic apparatus. It's a return to Lacan in its reliance on the impossibility of definition of the self, and an identity that literally in the case of this film depends upon the desire of the Other. This is explained by Jacqueline Rose: 'Sexuality belongs in this area of instability played out in the register of demand and desire, each sex coming to stand, mythically and exclusively, for that which could satisfy and complete the other' (1986: 56).

To accept the notion of these roles as a performance – not simply in the space of the film but an extended deliberation on the nature of authenticity which tests the linguistic and geopolitical hegemony of the Spanish state

– encompasses gendered concerns but refuses to prioritize them. Frequent speculation on the nature of representation of identity in the cinema has postulated the presence of various oppositions: authenticity/inauthenticity, reality/performance, frivolity/seriousness. Paul Julian Smith, in his excellent reading of the film, argues that its particular attraction lies in an ability to retain a certain amount of ambiguity in those things which pertain to these divisions – that can be broadly summarized as reality versus performance – demanded by postmodernity of its artistic creations. Reading Medem through Gianni Vattimo's version of postmodernity and its effect on artistic production relating to 'the identification of the false transparency of contemporary society with the visual apparatus of cinema' (Smith 1996: 130) reveals the play at work and the role of speech within this play, shaping and reflecting its own superficiality and transience in relation to the identity of the characters.

Once more this is not out of place within Medem's rich aesthetic but rather constitutive of it. Working within a media with such capacity for negative deception or positive fluidity means that he has little choice but to embrace the technology which makes this possible and the society which recognizes his filmic idiom:

> As the film develops, we see that such an intensification of the aesthetic experience is characteristic of the society of generalized communication, whose supposed transparency is dangerously and fruitfully muddied by the possibilities of performance and play afforded by the mass media. (Smith 1996: 152)

'Generalized communication' and the 'mass media' are synonymous with this infinite capacity for deception that relies on a combination of language and technology as a tool for this reinvention and redefinition. In Medem's subsequent films, and the final objects of my analysis here, this preoccupation is continued and extended.

Epilogue: New Technologies and New Subjects?

This final brief section is my attempt to draw together the Lacanian reading of Medem that drives this chapter and to suggest that it is in developing technology, both exemplified by and embedded within, film that the performance of self, through language and by other means, finds a further outlet and enables creative new subjects to emerge. *Sex and Lucía* was a tricky response to the unexpected success of *Lovers of the Arctic Circle,* and one that Medem intended to invert the pessimism of the earlier film's ending by moving us from 'death to life' (Medem 2001). Life in these films, and for the women in the three films I end with here, is the life that they are able to create and represent with the tools at their disposal. New technologies creep into the equation in these three films, and while they are not the focus of any of the films I would argue that their role here is to question the fundamentals of performance and the way in which we understand subjects in spaces that are so easily manipulable, and perpetually in flux. In so doing they speak to tropes of slippery subjectivity, human and spatial, that have been the focus of this chapter.

As we have seen, language for Lacan is tricky in that it traps us as our only means to represent ourselves to the Other. Literary language is ostensibly the language of creation and in *Sex and Lucía* the purpose of Lorenzo's profession as an author is to create with this type of language. Furthermore, as the meeting between Lucía and Lorenzo demonstrates, it is so powerful that she has created a love affair from the words on the page which she now seems to believe she can bring to life. She initially pursues him because she says his novel has taken hold of her and won't let her go. Even here there is an idea of power and control embedded into the type of language that can create and shape reality. The intertwining of author and his work that Rob Stone uses in his analysis of this film sheds light on this element of the creative process, but it also limits it. To ally Medem with Lorenzo is to foreclose the notion of filmic language as different, and to enclose the film's narrative within Lorenzo's. Clearly the novel is pivotal and shapes or inflects the progression of the film. However, I believe that the visual at times clashes with the literary and what we view in the process of the film is the resistance of the gaze which sits outside of language.

In answer to Stone's question, 'Is Lucía a free-thinking individual or is she just following the path that Lorenzo, a stand-in for Medem, has described for her?' (2007: 155), I would argue that in the gap between the words that Lorenzo writes and the space into which they are received, the image proposes a site of resistance and a space beyond the page and the mind of the author.

Multiple selves (read by Stone as the means by which Lucía embodies multiple varieties of femininity designed for the fulfilment of Lorenzo's/Medem's needs) and autonomy of self-definition are precisely the positive facets of technologically mediated, performed existence. The potential for self-invention in this fantasy space is mirrored by Lorenzo's story which he has been writing and sending to Elena and which Lucía had read secretly before her and Lorenzo's (accidental) separation. It is a narrative that can be altered according to the reader's desire, thanks to a hole in the middle, which enables release and re-entry into the novel at any given point.

In Rob Stone's excellent analysis of Medem's latter films he builds an argument, a convincing one, around the notion of the figure of Lorenzo, as author of Lucía's life, as being elided with the ultimate authority here, Julio Medem. If this were the case then the liberation that I believe is a facet of all of these works would seem to rest within the problematic codes of the male as author of the female's fate. He draws attention to a moment in the film when, after secretly reading Lorenzo's new novel, still a work in progress on his computer Lucía switches it off and we see her naked reflection on the screen which he describes in the following terms: 'Lorenzo's theft of Lucía's identity culminates in the shot of her naked reflection in his unplugged computer monitor suggesting she is trapped on the inside and helplessly looking out' (Stone 2007: 171).

I would offer an alternative reading of a similar scene in the parallel version of this story, Lucía's time on the island. In Elena's guesthouse she is introduced to the world of chat rooms. The first conversation that Lucia takes part in centres on the importance of names and self-invention. Elena's moniker is

Figure 2.3. Lucía (Paz Vega) and Elena (Najwa Nimri) in a chatroom on the Island in *Lucía y el sexo* (2001), by Julio Medem

'alsi' which she explains to Lucía is *isla*/island backwards. Turkle claims, 'When we step through the screen into virtual communities we recognize our identities on the other side of the looking glass. This reconstruction is our cultural work in progress' (1997: 177). It is not the mirror, although it can invert as is evidenced in the choice of name; instead it is quite clearly a site of freedom. This time Lucía's inhabitation of the narrative within the space of the screen underscores her own volition in terms of her subject creation which, as she converses with a virtual community, liberates her from Lorenzo's imagination and attests to the subjective capacity of the film itself, free from the authorial binds of both Lorenzo and by implication, Medem.

This space beyond is developed as a technological site of possibility – the use of the Internet in *Room in Rome,* as I suggested in Chapter One. It is in the external mediation of the subject that these new technologies suggest both a lack of control and a pleasurable and creative potential of the self:

> In the work of Jacques Lacan, for example, the complex chains of associations that constitute meaning for each individual lead to no final endpoint or core self. . . . In this he joins psychoanalysis to the postmodern attempt to portray the self as a realm of discourse rather than a real thing or a permanent structure of the mind. (Turkle 1997: 15)

Room in Rome is the story of two women who meet in a bar in the eponymous city, and they go to Alba's (Elena Anaya) hotel room where she persuades the Russian Natasha (Natasha Yarovenko) to spend the night with her. The premise of the lesbian (Alba) seducing the feminine, heterosexual Natasha is problematic in its attempt to suggest new interpretations of developing subjectivity. However, if in 2001 Medem discovered with chat rooms and emails the perfect interactive space for the creation of the self, then 2010 opens up a word of possibilities to him and the his two female protagonists. This time the four walls of the darkly lit hotel room where the action takes place are relieved by the laptop, camera and mobile phone screens that intermittently become part of the dialogue between these two women and in the words of one critic work 'to open up the piece both spatially and temporally' (Buckeridge 2011).

They function as technological extensions of the self in this game of invention, as the two women recount their life stories to one another changing them as they go. It is a similar trope to the invention that took place in *The Red Squirrel* but in this instance the performance of the self takes place through the stored moments on the screen in the form of family videos and the photos from Google Earth. The representational cartography that has moved from the hand-drawn maps of Rome from another time that they peruse, almost unrecognisable today, has become a digitally photographed and enhanced copy of reality. Medem undermines the authenticity of these digital images by allowing the women to reinvent themselves in relation to what they see on the screen. These images don't necessarily corroborate their stories; they seem to be a trigger for further invention. Multiple spaces allow for multiple versions of the self: 'The internet is another element of computer culture that has contributed to thinking about identity as multiplicity. On it, people are able to build a self by cycling through many selves' (Turkle 1997: 178).

Finally these have become literally many selves in Medem's film Caótica Ana/*Chaotic Ana*. This is more complex film, given that Medem made it as a tribute to his sister, who was killed in a car accident while he was making *Sex and Lucía,* and it features her paintings as well as a protagonist with the same name. At first glance of course, this reinforces the claim that we should not be too quick to separate fiction from our lives, that there are always and inevitably blurrings between the two, and it restates the complex imbrication of the male author with a female character that Stone elaborated. This time it is a male psychoanalyst whose hypnosis of Ana suggests a problematic relationship of power and suggestion once more enmeshed within the use of language.

Ana (Manuela Vellés) is a young artist living with her father on the island of Ibiza and selling her paintings to visiting tourists. One such tourist, Justine (Charlotte Rampling), offers her the chance to develop her artistic talent in a residence for young artists in Madrid. While she is there Ana meets and falls in love with a troubled young man named Said (Nicolas Cazalé) and allows herself to be hypnotized by Anglo (Asier Newman). These sessions of hypnosis see Ana inhabiting the bodies of women in history who have met violent ends at the hands of men.

The opening of the film is a visual incarnation of the essay that accompanied Medem's documentary, *Basque Ball,* a reflective and discursive piece by the author titled *A Bird Flies Through a Gorge. Caótica Ana/Chaotic Ana* revisits this avian theme as in its opening, a sequence that appears disconnected from the rest of the narrative, a dove flies through the air and as the camera is in such close proximity to it, the sound of the wind and the flapping wings are amplified. These are the sounds that open the film, accompanied by the credits and prior to any visual orientation. We cut to a falconer holding a hawk, a small leather helmet covering the bird's eyes. A man dressed in hunting garb and holding a gun explains to a group of men, also dressed as if to go hunting, the hunting method of the hawk. He concentrates on the power of the bird's eyes, saying that it fixes its prey with a powerful gaze and then goes on for the kill. This is then demonstrated as the dove we saw in the opening shits on the larger bird's head and the falconer releases it to kill the dove. It's a symbol that recurs in the film's later intense depictions of violence experienced through Ana's subconscious and Said's dreams in which the bird tears the flesh of the murdered family members.

Ana's liberation comes with a move from the significantly dark and literal cave on the isolation of an island to the centre and the capital city. As the falcon's eyes are cleaned at the beginning, her eyes are opened in this commune where she mixes with other young bohemian artists all searching for their own way to see the world, at the same time as they scrutinize one another repeatedly. It is Linda, Ana's friend (played by the singer Bebe), who finds the technological eye through which she is able to create her own technologically and artistically manipulated version of reality. It is thanks to her handheld digital camcorder (a nod to the democratization of the filmmaking process perhaps?) that Ana's sessions of hypnosis are filmed and then later played back in numerous scenarios, one of them an apparently public cinema-like screening to the other young members of this bohemian *madrileño* residence. (The similarity of one of the scenes from this film to Charcot's earliest sketched depictions of his hysterical female patients is impossible to ignore and calls into question the naivety of the gender politics evidenced at other significant moments in the narrative).

The artistic experimentation that takes place in Justine's residence is a metaphor for Medem's own forays into this more experiential style of filmmaking. Despite the reliance on vision that would seem to be suggested by the bird of prey at the beginning, there are also several hints that Medem is losing faith in its power as an infallible method of understanding the world. The similarities with his other films are numerous: this time the will to escape sees him travel from Ibiza to Madrid and then New York. Ana's liberation comes when she frees herself from the women who inhabit her subconscious mind. Here we return to Medem's interrogation of a fixed subject. Indeed the final section of this film in which Ana moves to New York sees her final reinvention, and as she takes her revenge on an American politician it would seem that Medem has finally found the feminist tale that was never quite successful in his previous works. Paul Julian Smith believes that despite the critical failure of this film, within Spain at least, its success lies in its 'visual recreation of a poetics of everyday life' (2007: 33).

Notes

1. For an excellent survey of Medem's work and detailed synoptic accounts of his films, see Evans (2007).
2. As Lacan establishes earlier in this Seminar Series, 'Thus the unconscious is always manifested as that which vacillates in a split in the subject' (Lacan and Miller 1979: 28).
3. This is not a uniform strategy. Some of the participants have been allowed the comfort of a familiar internal environment (Felipe González).
4. Repetition, as the return of difference, is constitutive of the narratives of *Lovers of the Arctic Circle* and *Sex and Lucía,* a trope that illustrates the pleasure to be found in returning to the limit on each recounting of the story, a story that alters with each telling.
5. In this sense I am referring to those qualities traditionally thought to be 'of cinema' yet which have a wider epistemological significance with regards to the construction of the image and the field of the visual.
6. For an excellent theoretical extrapolation of the significance of these ruptures in Medem's narrative, see Davidson (2008).

References

Austin, J. L. 1962. *How to Do Things with Words.* Oxford: Clarendon Press.

Benjamin, W. 1992. 'The Work of Art in the Age of Mechanical Reproduction'. *Film Theory and Criticism: Introductory Readings.* New York and Oxford: Oxford University Press.

Brakhage, S. 1963. 'From Metaphors on Vision'. In *Film Theory and Criticism: Introductory Readings,* edited by L. Braudy and M. Cohen, 228–234. New York and Oxford: Oxford University Press.

Buckeridge, J. 2011. 'MQFF Film Review: Room in Rome'. http://australianfilmreview .wordpress.com/2011/03/29/film-review-room-in-rome/ 2011.

Davidson, R. A. 2008. 'Conceptualizing "the Impact" in *Los amantes del círculo polar*'. In *Burning Darkness: a Half Century of Spanish Cinema*, edited by J. Ramon Resina and A. Lema-Hincapié, 195–209. New York: State University of New York Press.

Dayan, D. 1974. 'The Tutor-Code of Classical Cinema'. In *Film Theory and Criticism: Introductory Readings*, edited by L. Braudy and M. Cohen, 118–129. New York and Oxford: Oxford University Press.

Elsaesser, T. 2005. *European Cinema Face to Face with Hollywood*. Amsterdam: Amsterdam University Press.

Evans, J. 2007. *Julio Medem*. London: Grant and Cutler.

Forrester, J. 1990. *The Seductions of Psychoanalysis: Freud, Lacan, Derrida*. Cambridge: Cambridge University Press.

Gabilondo, J. 2002. 'Uncanny Identity: Violence, Gaze and Desire in Contemporary Basque Cinema'. In *Constructing Identity in Contemporary Spain: Theoretical Debates and Cultural Practice*, edited by J. Labanyi, 262–279. Oxford: Oxford University Press.

Harper, G., and J. Rayner. 2010. *Cinema and Landscape*. Bristol: Intellect.

Heredero, C. F. 1997. *Espejo de miradas: entrevistas con nuevos directores del cine español de los años noventa*. Alcalá de Henares: Festival.

Lacan, J. 1989. *Ecrits*. London: Routledge.

Lacan, J., and J. A. Miller. 1979. *The Four Fundamental Concepts of Psychoanalysis*. Harmondsworth: Penguin.

McGowan, T. 2007. *The Real Gaze: Film Theory after Lacan*. New York: State University of New York Press.

Medem, J. 2001.'Lucía y el sexo: memoria de la película'. http://www.juliomedem.org/ filmografia/lucia_memoria.html.

Metz, C. 1982. *Psychoanalysis and Cinema: The Imaginary Signifier*. London: Macmillan.

Mottram, J. 2002. 'Julio Medem Interviewed by James Mottram.' Retrieved 18 September 2007 from http://www.bbc.co.uk/films/2002/04/26/julio_medem_sex_and_ lucia_interview.shtml.

Mulvey, L. 1989. *Visual and Other Pleasures*. Basingstoke: Macmillan.

Richardson, N. 2011. 'From Herria to Hirria: Locating Dialogue in Julio Medem's *La Pelota vasca*'. *Arizona Journal of Hispanic Cultural Studies* 11(1): 113–119.

Romney, J. 2000, Review of *The Lovers of the Arctic Circle*. *Sight and Sound* 10 (2): 48.

Ros, X. de 1997. '*Vacas* and Basque Cinema: The Making of a Tradition'. *Journal of the Institute of Romance Studies* 5:225–234.

Rose, J. 1986. *Sexuality in the Field of Vision*. London and New York: Verso.

Sánchez, A. 1997. 'Women Immune to a Nervous Breakdown: The Representation of Women in Julio Medem's Films'. *Journal of Iberian and Latin American Studies* 3(2): 147–161.

Santaolalla, I. 1998. 'Far from Home, Close to Desire: Julio Medem's Landscapes'. *Bulletin of Hispanic Studies* LXXV(3): 331–337.

Smith, P. J. 1996. *Vision Machines: Cinema, Literature and Sexuality in Spain and Cuba, 1983–93.* London: Verso.

———. 1997. 'Angels to Earth'. *Sight and Sound* 7(8): 12–14.

———. 2000. *The Moderns: Time, Space and Subjectivity in Contemporary Spanish Culture.* Oxford: Oxford University Press.

———. 2007. 'Chaotic Ana'. *Film Quarterly* 61(2): 30–34.

Stone, R. 2007. *Julio Medem.* Manchester: Manchester University Press.

Turkle, S. 1997. *Life on the Screen: Identity in the Age of the Internet.* London: Phoenix.

Via Rivera, M. 2004. 'A Journey into the Labyrinth: Intertextual Readings of Borges and Cortázar in Julio Medem's *Los amantes del círculo polar* (1998)'. *Journal of Iberian and Latin American Studies* 10(2): 205–212.

White, A. M. 1999. 'Manchas negras, manchas blancas: Looking again at Julio Medem's *Vacas*'. In *Spanish Cinema: Calling the Shots,* edited by R. Rix and R. Rodriguez Saona, 1–11. Leeds: Trinity and All Saints.

Žižek, S. 1989. *The Sublime Object of Ideology.* London: Verso.

———. 1991. *Looking Awry: An Introduction to Jacques Lacan through Popular Culture.* Cambridge, MA: MIT Press.

CHAPTER THREE

Bigas Luna
Physical Frontiers

If Medem's challenge to perception lay in the psychological interrogation of separation that implicated us and his characters in the desire of the Other, then Bigas Luna's testing of the border has a much more physical slant. It is my intention in this chapter to concentrate on some of his lesser-known works, bringing together and analysing the concentration on the somatic and corporal dimension of this flamboyant Catalan auteur. The emphasis on the body – depicted in frequently provocative ways – highlights its place within a wider tradition of artistic production. This ranges from the explicit citations of painters and filmmakers such as Goya and Dalí to the perhaps less considered intersections with both previous and contemporary artists, the textural invocation of Antoni Tapiès perhaps. The director's installations and Internet shorts engage with and extend his musings in this area, and the influence of the alternative representational strategies of these varied media is patent in his feature-length works for the big screen.[1]

Any evocation of the body exposes a number of contradictions in terms of its place as a locus of meaning and signification. A desire to separate mind and body in philosophical thought alerted us to a need to think through apparently naturalized divisions and question the body's place in representational systems. From Foucault's foregrounding of the body as a primary element in the inscription and wielding of power, numerous thinkers have revisited the body as a site of critical tension (Foucault 1979, 1981).

Problematic cultural inscriptions of the body have added a further dimension to the debates that surround its materiality and how we are able to 'think' this body with regards to its representation in works of art. The body's relationship to gender and the way in which gender is represented in cultural production is one way in which these added layers of corporal meaning have been thought through. The turn to affect and an embodied understanding of perception, which inform my reading of *Bilbao*, challenge us again to rethink these somatic (un)certainties. Vivian Sobchack and Laura Marks pursue the positive potential of the open body as it interacts with the screen, basing their investigations on a phenomenological understanding of the body's experience of the world in line with Merleau-Ponty, in the case of Sobchack, while Marks also includes Merleau-Ponty in a philosophical and analytical framework that draws heavily on the work of Deleuze and Bergson.

Bigas Luna's output is prolific and diverse and it would require several volumes to engage fully with his fascinating and varied oeuvre. These productions have, on the whole, been well-received on the international stage, and interestingly it is the three works that deal specifically with the Iberian national character that have brought him this international recognition (it seems likely that the emerging and attractive stars in the shape of Penelope Cruz and Javier Bardem contributed to this popularity). This chapter provides a survey of the unifying themes concentrating on the corporal as a signifying and significant trope and then examines in more detail two of his films which I believe mark this concern and yet develop it in quite different ways, demonstrating a progression that moves his work from the darker concerns of the earlier works to a pragmatic consideration of commercial priorities. These works demonstrate an aesthetic interweaving of sumptuous visuals and popular historical plotlines that maintain this concern for the peripheral concerns of representational practices and, as will become apparent the persistent interrogation of the edges, of the body and its place at the nexus of consumption, representation and a variety of sensory experience.

Despite my contention in Chapter One that there is a case for presenting these directors as peripheral to a certain reading of Spanish cultural and filmic history that selectively includes them under the auspices of regional or Spanish cinema, I have not, as yet, considered this within the wider historical context in any great detail. My reading of *Bilbao* provides a degree of political and historical contextualisation. This film demands this type of analysis in order to assess a new critical framework that arose in a very specific moment in the history of this country.

Bilbao engages with the signification of the city as a cinematic site of meaning with precise reference, surprisingly not to the Basque capital as the title suggests, but to the topography of Barcelona as a site of changing meanings and a new urban lifestyle. This may be informed and influenced, to a degree, by the 'new Spain'[2] in which a focus on the city became a liberation of sorts for a generation that needed a symbolic site for the creation of this new identity: the urban represented a crucial rupture with the idealized rural way of life that had typified the Francoist rhetoric on the make-up of the nation.

Bigas Luna's cinematic city however is distinct from the *movida madrileña* which exists as a hermetic cinematic universe thanks to the films of Almodóvar.[3] Barcelona's streets are loaded with a much deeper and more problematic political resonance and the Barcelona of *Bilbao* still struggles with these tensions. The strobe lighting of the club where the eponymous stripper Bilbao performs and the edgy contemporary soundtrack that accompanies most of the city scenes are symbols of the youth culture that flourished after the end of the regime.[4] A refusal to grant the viewer the cityscape shot of the type preferred by Almodóvar in *The Flower of My Secret* (1995) and *Live Flesh* (1997) or to revel in the cinematic tourism of films such as *All About My Mother* (1999) deliberately avoids the temptation to replace a centre of dissidence with a constructed image of a famous city. Thus, the contradictions of Barcelona and the wider implications of the filmed city are explored by other means.[5] As such, this alternative form of urban enquiry becomes one method of mapping a new identity by means of the mapping of a new space.

In this chapter the possibility of multiple effects and their concomitant experimental means of representation take shape within the context of speculation on the haptic dimension of visuality in *Bilbao* and are extended in an examination of a later work, *Volavérunt,* through an innovative employment of Goya's famous paintings to provoke debate once more on the means of representing the female body. As we shall see, in the case of the later film a holistic incorporation of a variety of sensual invocations resists a simplistic reading dependent on objectification via optical structures, as sensation becomes paramount to engagement with the space of the film. In this respect, however, Bigas's ironic sense of fun and exaggerated cinematic style cannot be ignored, and his concentration on the gastronomic as it relates to the sexual is a further element of this, which also has a more serious side. In a reading of the relationship between food and sex as capable of opening out new relationships and ways of thinking through representation, this chapter will end with a return to his less mainstream works with an examination of these issues in *Bámbola* and *Lola* with reference to the Iberian trilogy and his installation *Ingestum*.

Establishing a Transgressive Cinematic Style

There is, as critics have noted, a reasonably clear division between Bigas's early works (from *Tatuaje/Tattoo* (1976) to *Las edades de Lulú/The Ages of Lulú* (1990)) and his perhaps more commercial work which begins with the Iberian trilogy in 1992. This early work nonetheless set the scene for his explorations of the darker side of the human psyche, or what Carolina Sanabria terms his '*etapa negra*', or black period. Here I trace some of those themes and the aesthetic style, which is then clearly located and developed in my readings of *Bilbao* and *Volavérunt*.

Bigas took the nature of the fetish to excess in *Caniche* (1979), a title which translates as 'poodle' but which also, as Sanabria points out, resembles a contraction of the words *can – dog* and *fetiche – fetish* (2010: 32). A brother and sister, Bernardo (Àngel Jové) and Eloisa (Consol Tura) – Bigas returns to the trope of dysfunctional male-female relationships – are bored in their inherited mansion and become involved in butchering and eating dogs. Eloisa owns a poodle that she treats as though it were human, sharing medication with it and smothering her labia in honey so that the dog might lick it off. Her brother, Bernardo, prowls the streets in the search for stray dogs that he uses for his own sexual gratification (penetrating them) in the basement.

After a mixed reception to this deeply inventive yet, according to the director himself deeply flawed, work Bigas turned his attentions to the English-speaking market with *Renacer/Reborn* (1981) and *Lola* (1985). Pragmatism plays a very large part in this director's commercial decisions and this linguistic, cultural, and geographical shift represents his quest to explore the economic (and artistic) potential of an alternative market. Thematically and formally, *Reborn* has much in common with *Bilbao*. Male appropriation of the female body and the body's resistance to that appropriation is focussed this time on the body of Maria (Antonella Murgia), a Sicilian woman whose body is the site of stigmata and who is 'bought' by an American TV evangelist Tom Hartley (played by Dennis Hopper) for him to use in his tour of America; Maria will be the living proof of the (faked) miracles that earn his living and fund his opulent lifestyle. The overt critique of this commercialized religious practice, usually associated with the United States, is inflected by the mysticism and belief in symbolism that typifies the Catholic faith of the Mediterranean and for which, aesthetically at least, this director shows a certain fondness.[6]

The contextualisation of my reading of *Bilbao* within a very specific and liminal moment in the history of Spain raises issues of representational tensions precisely due to this transformative moment. *Reborn* engages with the trope of vision once more, this time at a remove from the ideological struggles taking place in his native country. The emphasis on the visual manifestation of miracles that the evangelist's TV show encourages through its format, and by extension in the tour of the United States that he undertakes, reiterates the fragile relationship between vision and veracity, and our optical apprehension of the world. Television as an increasingly popular medium is subject to interrogation as Bigas moves his scrutiny to the commercialized visual culture of the United States, home of the cinema.[7] If seeing is not believing, then by what means can we relate to and understand the world on the screen? Once more the techniques that Bigas employs deliberately resist the faith in vision that was overturned in *Bilbao*.

Sensational Cinema?

In her reading of contemporary French cinema Martine Beugnet argues for a cinema of sensation that pushes the spectator to occupy this position of sensory and experiential subject rather than powerful voyeur. She explains: 'Denied the distancing effect of explanatory introductions and establishing shots, the viewer is left to experience the powerful perplexing affect of the imaginary' (2007: 7). Bigas's biting critique of blind faith in *Reborn* is initiated by precisely the cinematic technique outlined by Beugnet which places the viewer in the position of incomprehension faced with a powerful, yet partial, view of the diegetic world. As the film opens, a mobile camera (an aerial shot which may well be taken from the helicopter which reappears throughout the rest of the piece) shoots an unnamed town/city at night. The only discernible feature of the landscape in this night sky is the flickering neon cross. The repetitive electronic soundtrack, which varies in intensity and volume, and which furnishes the soundtrack to many of the scenes in the film, utilizes vibrations and frequencies that seem to connect to our body and, prior to a cognitive and analytical viewing, immerse us in an emerging space of embodied perception. We inhabit the space of the film before we attempt to step back and analyse the various elements of an image, and we are dislocated in a non-specified space.

This pre-discursive, pre-ideological engagement with the image in a film about faith plays with the notion of belief and experience and our need to witness a miracle in order to believe it. Moreover, in terms of its place in the oeuvre of this director it begins to develop the darker, psychologically driven aesthetic of his two earlier films into a more narrative-driven style that still utilizes these haptic and sensational techniques.

To view his work as a developing aesthetic and in particular to relate this to the intermedial productions with which he has been involved is to locate a curious nexus of styles which bring together an acuity and precision around the image and our relationship with it, a relationship based on psychological engagement and affective responses but which always privileges the material of its creation. It may well be this element of his work that seems to have made him a difficult director to address critically, and why films such as *Reborn* are often elided in analysis of his work. Sensation in film is often assumed to diverge from narrative, as to experience film sensually is to derive pleasure from a pre-linguistic regression which foments the idea that the two are incompatible. Furthermore, Bigas cannot escape from accusations of sensationalism which centre on the excessive scenes of a sexual nature, frequent displays of bare flesh and as I mentioned above, bestiality and sexual violence. If we tease out a reading of his output which privileges sensation and embodied responses then I believe there is a counterpoint to this analysis that liberates them from accusations of sensationalism and revels in the ambiguity that is constitutive of the works themselves.

It is difficult to reconcile the various facets of this work around a consistent theoretical reading, and I do not attempt to do so. The apparent disparity of form and theme throughout his work means that selection for critical scrutiny has often been with discrete films that demonstrate some thematic and formal unity. An attempt to trace a certain aesthetic development provides fertile ground for discussion in relation to the undermining of power that lies in the interstices. This reading converges on the two possible renderings of the sensational that are suggested by Beugnet in relation to a body of contemporary French films. This is expressed as a productive tension through the analyses that Beugnet undertakes, and I hope to locate a similar tension here. The textural and tactile image which privileges sensation is allied with narrative rather than distanced from it in Bigas Luna's films, and the moments at which these forms of encounter are evoked invite a pause in which an alternative regime of knowledge directs us to alternative responses and modes of understanding. I identify the movement between haptic and visual, posited by Marks in my reading of *Bilbao*. This sliding from one regime to another unsettles the critical thinking that allows us to rely on vision as a way to create a secure sense of the subject, or as Beugnet puts it, 'The effect is an unsettling of the conventional vision-knowledge-mastery paradigm, in favour of a relation where the spectator may surrender, at least partly, a sense of visual control for the possibility of a sensuous encounter with the film – where the subject affectively yields into its object' (2007: 68).

It is clear that alternative forms of spectatorship must be theorized for the appreciation and understanding of Internet video work and the plastic arts with which Bigas Luna is involved, but I would argue that creative sensibility in his films is informed by the other types of work that he has done. As with the plastic arts Bigas has a developed sense of the manipulation of the material of his craft, and the same can be said for the bodies with which he works – the bodies of the films and the bodies of the actors and the characters that they represent. This is not to say that they are objectified, but that in the problematisation of subject and object, of the matter of the art form and its material basis, these bodies become the contested sites of representation. In the manner of their depiction, which persistently works to undermine vision, we are forced to understand our own bodies as sentient and lived, like the filmic bodies, demanding an ethical interaction that moves away from the criticism of this objectification of women. Fouz-Hernández has gone some way to unpick the complex layering of meaning that inheres in the more challenging films, those that deal with sexual violence. He seeks to implicate an ethical spectator who seeks a redemptive slant to these images, which are violent and terrifying, but which are also so extreme as to deliberately alienate a spectator and undermine the notion that we are somehow enjoying the power that these images offer to us. Looking at *Bámbola* through the work of Patricia MacCormack on *cinesexuality* he goes some way to at least problematize, although not entirely discard, 'the politics and value of desiring positions of power' (MacCormack 2008: 37; Fouz-Hernández 2011).

The commodification of the woman's body in *Reborn* is expressed through its visibility: Maria must appear on stage with Reverend Hartley, the evangelist, in order that her miraculous appeal be witnessed by the crowd. She is prepared physically for this appearance. As her appearance is modified, her armpits are shaved and her face made up so that her body conforms to the semiotic codes that this market will understand and can willingly consume, even down to the costume in which she is robed, a hybrid version of a liturgical gown and a choral vestment. Her body resists this codification; the stigmata cannot be controlled and neither can her excessive bleeding. Even her act of resistance with Mark, who is initially her captor who works for the evangelist's team and with whom she has a sexual relationship and as a result becomes pregnant, makes her body into a tool of resistance as it bears her child.[8] The lived capacity of the body exceeds its representational purposes here. Vivian Sobchack reminds us of the ethical dimension of our lived and sentient bodies and their capacity to push at the limits of the visual to which contemporary culture seems to try to reduce them: 'In a culture like ours, so preoccupied with images of bodies and bodies of images, we tend to forget that both our bodies and our vision have lived dimensions that are not reducible to the merely visible' (2004: 179).[9]

Touching the City: Barcelona in *Bilbao* (1978)

What is there beyond this 'merely' visible to which Sobchack refers and how can it contribute to an alternative understanding of the edges and a removal from the dominant cultural hegemony in Spain that frequently foregrounds a tendentious account of nation, strongly linked to stereotypical accounts of gender? Bigas couches this in tactile terms: 'When I worked as a painter and designer I could touch what I was making. When I started to direct cinema I couldn't touch my films and my fetishistic instinct, my love for objects, felt lost' (Bigas Luna and Canals 1994: 5).

The liminality implied by the interstitial period of the Transition anticipated a new type of cinema which not only placed itself at the borders but which exploited the numerous thresholds associated with the cinematic art, refusing to remain confined by them. As such, frontiers – physical, cinematic and metaphorical – became crucial sites for renegotiation. And precisely one of the central features of Bigas's deliberation in *Bilbao* is a critical reconsideration of the timeworn relation between power and vision. The film's exploration of one man's tenuous grasp of his own position as spectator comes to attest to a lack of faith in the reputed primacy of the visual and elicits a similar critical revision of the power structures which this represents. It is my contention that, in its tentative marrying of two forms of creation – where haptic joins with visual – *Bilbao* offers new possibilities for experience on collective and individual levels.

Bilbao constitutes a dissident filmic essay as pre-existing configurations of power, reinforced by paradigmatic experiences of viewing, are questioned and a dysfunctional pursuit of one man's desire proves ultimately fatal. In this way, *Bilbao* is the beginning of a journey which leads this flamboyant auteur to repeatedly thwart spectatorial expectations and experiment with the seemingly endless potential of cinema to subvert, question and create. It is easy to see where the critique of organized religion in *Reborn* was initiated and how the ultimate rejection of visual power in *Angustia/Anguish* (1987) emerges (Friedman 1999).

This cinematic world is dark and perverse, and interpersonal relationships are immediately exposed as dysfunctional and unfulfilling. Leo lives with an older woman, María (María Martín), who besides being his sexual partner acts as his protector and receives money for doing so. Leo spends his days pursuing Bilbao (Isabel Pisano), a prostitute, through the streets of Barcelona. He pays her to perform oral sex but refuses to speak to her and expresses frustration when she tries to engage him in conversation. He repeatedly communicates the desire to posses her and, in true collector fashion, obsessively accumulates material reminders of her which he then arranges in bizarre *mises en scène* to photograph (the director's tactile manipulation of objects which can then be visually captured, as alluded to in the previous quotation). His strange fantasies eventually lead him to kidnap Bilbao, drugging her and suspending her from the ceiling in a variety of bizarre poses before killing her accidentally by letting her head knock against a chair as he is moving her drugged body. He confesses his crime to María who helps him dispose of the body in a pig butchering plant.

Bigas initially pays lip service to the expectations of this orthodox mode of spectatorship as evinced by a series of subtle visual asides early in the film. A close up of Bilbao's high heels, for example, seen from the point of view of Leo as she has sex with a client in a parked car parodies the function of the psychoanalytic fetish.

This type of viewing, however, fails Leo on two counts: the fetish does not placate his castration anxiety, and he receives little satisfaction in his voyeuristic activities. It is in this way that Bigas begins the deconstruction of the power structures that Leo is set up to represent. The sensorially holistic method of filmmaking explored in this, at times primitive, movie is indicative of the adventurous efforts to push back the boundaries which had confined cinema within the edges of a flat screen. This approach is both suggestive and inclusive and challenges the separateness of screen and spectator, hinting at the potential for spectators to enjoy and share a space of pleasurable (or otherwise) sensual experience. This manifest attack on vision and the limits of the cinematic frame cannot be referred to without making reference to *Anguish*, an English-language horror movie in which the trope of the movie theatre as a site of the action dissolves the safe distance between viewer and viewed. Furthermore, in the film within the film, *The Mommy,* we and the diegetic movie audience watch as the protagonist, John Pressman (Michael Lerner) is involved in the removal of the organ of vision when he gouges out his victims' eyes on the instructions of his mother. The eyes do not help him see, and although this is a heavy-handed metacinematic representation of the over-reliance of vision as a tool of comprehension and enlightenment, it certainly has echoes of the more attenuated approach to alternative modes of perception in *Bilbao*.

Haptic discourse – in apposition to the purely visual – comes to the fore through the ways in which Leo relates to the city and to the object of his obsession. The most important elements of this reading are that of failed vision which gives way to the potential of tactile perception. In Leo's case his inability to relate visually or haptically to his surroundings results in frustration, which the director relates more widely to the feelings of displacement and inner exile at work in the psyche of his protagonist. Coalescence of haptic and visual representation proffers alternative means of experience, a potential that resonates sharply with the wider socio-political context.

Movement is an important function of Leo's apprehension of the city space and is informed here by Giuliana Bruno's explanation of haptic space within film as it is predicated on this notion of dynamism. Bruno explains her derivation of this term and its relation to motion pictures in the following words:

> As the Greek etymology tells us, haptic means 'able to come into contact with'. As a function of the skin, then, the haptic – the sense of touch – constitutes the reciprocal contact between us and the environment, both housing and extending communicative interface. But the haptic is also related to kinesthesis, the ability of our bodies to sense their own

movement in space. . . . Here, the haptic realm is shown to play a tan-gible, tactical role in our communicative 'sense' of spatiality and motil-ity, thus shaping the texture of habitable space and, ultimately mapping our ways of being in touch with the environment. (2002: 6)

Leo's inhabitation of the city, portrayed as a marginal activity, highlights this motility and its associated sensory merging in its emphasis on the combi-nation of touch and vision. Close-ups of eyes and bodies within this film mean that previous theories of visual enjoyment are subject to cinematic revision as other senses are drawn into the arena of film. One of the film's opening sequences sees Leo travelling around Barcelona on the metro and then the bus. These crowded forms of transport are metonymic of the way in which we travel around the city, and their use in this context highlights a stylistic endea-vour to immerse the filmic subject in his immediate environment.

The movement of this transport and the contours of buildings and peo-ple in this urban milieu highlight the depth of the cinematic image extending the possibilities of representation beyond the visual plane. The proximity of the people packed into these uniquely urban forms of transportation is re-corded by a camera that mingles with them in its observance of Leo's trajec-tory around the metropolis. Separation is not possible because of the nature of these crowded vehicles. Distance as constitutive of perspective and in its relation to comprehension in the aesthetic tradition of cinema is disavowed by these passages. Thus from the very first sequences a mistrust of vision is registered and the spectator, like the photophobic Leo, is obliged to consider alternative modes of comprehension.

Cohabitation with the city in this respect, encouraging a recognition of its encroachment on all the senses, emphasizes touch and fragmentation. The city alters the field of vision and the individual walking the streets is engulfed by crowded cityscapes. The camera's proximity to its subject renders it un-able to fulfil its expected function and allies it with Leo's photographic camera. Promoting mistrust of technological mediations of vision in this way is a delib-erately self-reflexive musing on the limitations of this chosen medium. In de-pictions of Leo's sexual encounters with both of 'his' women, the director opts for close-ups of faces rather than focussing on the act itself, not only removing these episodes from accusations of gratuitous voyeurism but once more dis-avowing the supremacy of vision implicated in conventional representation.[10]

The dynamism that Bruno sets out as integral to a haptic relationship with space is clear in these outdoor city sequences. The close-ups that persist in the claustrophobic domestic surroundings which Leo shares with Maria are recorded by a relatively static camera but are – like the city scenes – experienced via the protagonist's corporeal relationship to these his environs, and their depiction centres on touch and contact. Washing, teeth cleaning, affixing plasters and eating are examples of the physical relationship at work in this domestic space. These activities are accompanied by harsh diegetic tonalities, which emphasize the roughness of touch in opposition to the more conventional choice of melodic pieces, the conventional intensifier of amorous sequences.

A perspective that oscillates between voyeuristic shots from a distance and discomfiting close-ups is complicit in the representation of these two types of vision. Laura Marks sets out a functional relationship between these two modes of perception as operating in a dialectical relationship: 'The difference between haptic and optic visuality is a matter of degree, however. In most processes of seeing both are involved in a dialectical movement from far to near, from solely optical to multisensory' (2002: 3). This is posited as a way of entering into a relationship with the film that exceeds vision and breaks with previous tropes of viewing.

What is at work is a rejection of the traditional when it is no longer sufficient to represent new experience. Alternatives are not established solely as a reversal of a previous convention, a simple turning on its head of an existing set of power relations; rather this is a more fluid and labile approach to the construction of subjectivity within the space of cinema, an approach which allows for a relocation of the subject that is not solely guided by the look but in its inclusion of a wider sensory perceptual field and becomes a more inclusive and flexible experience.

It is frequently assumed that a haptic mode of perception more closely involves spectatorial interaction with the screen, an acknowledgement that film viewing is not solely a detached cognitive process based on images experienced visually and aurally but also makes possible embodied perception. Rather than reading this as the limit of vision, it might be better welcomed as a latent imagining of unending possibilities for both representation and appreciation, as Vivian Sobchack explains:

Even at the movies our vision and hearing are informed and given meaning by our other modes of sensory access to the world: our capacity not only to see and hear but also to touch, to smell, to taste, and always to proprioceptively feel our weight, dimension, gravity, and movement in the world. (2004: 60)

At the very least the techniques which challenge visual means of appreciation or provide alternative routes towards comprehension of filmic space are often formulated and shot with scant regard for the presumed comfort of the spectator. Whilst we do not actually touch the screen the element of contagion and implication is encompassed by these modalities that linger too long on the uncomfortable detail and compromise personal space with excessive proximity, getting so close that our ability to focus on separate objects is removed.

It is through Leo that we are made aware of the alternative possibilities that the senses promote. Yet this same figure is a malfunctioning spectator and subject: he himself proves unable to decode these alternatives. Haptic appreciation of space presumes an immersion in that space and a concomitant loosening of the ties by which we are rooted to a secure understanding of our subjectivity. Marks writes:

Like the Renaissance perspective that is their progenitor, cinema's optical images address a viewer who is distant, distinct, and disembodied. Haptic images invite the viewer to dissolve his or her subjectivity in the close and bodily contact with the image. . . . The viewer is called on to fill in the gaps in the image, engage with the traces the image leaves. (2002: 13)

Just as in this type of spectatorship we are called into a different relationship with the world, so Leo is forced to accept a certain permeable relationship between himself and his environment. However, his demeanour suggests a total resistance to any kind of interpersonal relations: a tightly fastened coat and sunglasses protect him from the contamination of his environment. His obscured eyes hint at the naivety of the child who covers his face and believes that he is hidden from view, protected from the penetrative gaze of the outside world that exceeds his control.

Thus it becomes apparent that neither touch nor vision will resolve the lack of control for Leo. The two modes of perception are interlaced and presented as an enticing possibility for interaction with a cinematic screen that need not represent the distant space of fantasy but hints at a physical immersion, which assumes an experiential, almost phenomenological, appreciation.

The representation is problematized because Leo appears not to have learnt how to appreciate or read – somewhat ironic given his name which translates as 'I read' – either sense. His clumsy handling of Bilbao that causes her death would indicate a similar 'tactile blindness' on his part. This results in a lack of reciprocity in his relations with the two women of the film. Leo feels that the inevitable acceptance of recognising other subjects outside of our control and with whom we must interact is a threat to his subjectivity. His refusal to answer María's questions and repeated desire that Bilbao should not talk to him are proof of his attempts to remain separate, giving nothing of himself. He assumes that the objects, which succumb to his handling and manipulation, are merely material extensions of himself and once he appropriates them they stand for examples of the power he is able to wield over them. As Bigas reveals these beliefs to be delusional, he places the subject's position in a material world in doubt, whilst revelling in the possibility of an enriched and enriching sensory relationship with and in the world.

The desire to look whilst simultaneously remaining invisible has long been postulated as the impetus for a primarily voyeuristic practice of film viewing. Revisitation of the psychoanalytic paradigm of desire as it functions through the scopophilic model extends the possibilities for interpretation of desire and identification. Whilst haptic visuality exposes this looking as limited, it also promotes a new type of viewing pleasure which is dependent on our experiences of our own bodily inhabitation of the world. During long sections of this film we are denied a coherent image as shadows and patches of darkness obscure detail on the screen. This type of vision is less dependent on mastery and more on an acknowledgement of new and more fluid types of subjectivity.

In this respect the tactile approaches made by Leo are based on a misunderstanding. Filmically they refute the idea that mastery inheres in vision; but his desire for mastery and control cannot be accommodated through recourse to touch. Touch for Leo is the means by which he experiences the city when he realizes he is unable to capture it visually, and contact becomes the only means by which he can 'make sense' of it. It is when spying on the object of his affection is exposed as insufficient that he takes refuge in material reminders of her. Following her through Barcelona is not solely a means of optical control but has a distinctly physical and corporeal function. This is an acknowledgement of the traces that reside in material objects as the result of a kinaesthetic inhabitation of the city's streets.

Bilbao, for Leo at least, is representative of the city of Barcelona: she is a streetwalker, part of the metropolis's seedy underworld. Leo is left following her trace, replacing the encounter with her by numerous encounters with replacement objects and with the map of her route through the Catalan capital. As Leo traverses the city and experiences repeatedly frustrating encounters with the prostitute, the director's method of filming represents Leo's psychological condition at the same time as it exposes the instability of vision. When he fails to hold Bilbao in his gaze he looks for replacement objects in order to hold her in his hand. Long sequences that follow him through Barcelona describe his attempts to find fetishes through which to appropriate a substitute for the body of the object of his obsession. Action in these sequences unfolds slowly and is driven by the sparsest of dialogue, usually Leo's voice-over.

There are several instances in which we see Leo's actions before he describes them to us, adding interest to the aural domain and its slippery relation to the visual. This use of voice-over, a standard omniscient form of discourse in cinema, is compromised in this instance in its accompaniment by diegetically tactile noises, unmediated in the soundtrack. Another example of this director's subversion of cinematic convention presents Leo – this time by means of this voice-over – as no longer dominant but enfeebled and requiring the complicity of others who collude to save him. Furthermore, the voice-over in the Castilian original is not that of Ángel Jové, who does provide the voice in the Catalan version, a blatant challenge to the standard supremacy afforded to the aural domain. Leo's commentary is unreliable, and his actions are exposed as futile.

The Fetish

In *Anguish,* vision and its physical corollary, the eye, are both fetishized and then revealed as unable to fulfil that fetishistic intent. The eyes are displayed in jars; detached from the body they are little more than an object for scrutiny, deprived of their ability to see. In relation to the function of the fetish as able to represent in Marks's words 'the material conditions of displacement' (2000: 79), the objects themselves become the closest Leo can get to the physical presence of the object of his desire, like John Pressman and his eyes. The importance of these objects is in the power he can wield over them through touch. As Marks elaborates, 'All fetishes are translations into a material object of some sort of affect . . . theories of fetishism describe how value comes to inhere in objects that is not reducible to commodification' (2000: 80). Leo's relationship with this woman is exposed as dysfunctional when he fails to grasp the meaning of these objects and returns to the visual, taking photographs of them that he then obsessively handles, arranges and re-arranges, perhaps in a further futile attempt to impose meaning.

Lingering close-ups of hands evoke their function as an important interface between self and world; hands are certainly important as representative of contact for Leo but they are portrayed as unreliable in the same way as his eyes. Not only is he optically challenged; he appears also to be touch-blind. Through an emphasis on texture, these objects become integral to this cineaste's multi-sensory aesthetic project and acknowledge once more the tactile potential of the cinematic image. Leo's hands are the vehicles by which the spectator appreciates this textural variety: from the nylon fabric of tights which he stuffs with crackling, crumpled paper to the smooth shiny surfaces of his photographs and the scaly fish in whose mouth he places a sausage (in a thinly disguised imitation of the sex act he has recently engaged in with Bilbao). This spectrum of textures generates images of depth even as they play with surface and superficial structure. Engaging with vision at the surface in this way is a feature of haptic visuality that allows for a widened appreciation of the spectatorial experience. In this instance, it is a technique that acknowledges the material qualities of the objects and derives pleasure from these qualities when meaning cannot be grasped.

Bigas sets out at first to expose this power structure as unstable. He sets up his male protagonist as exaggerated voyeur, trailing his object of desire in trench coat and sunglasses. Here there are hints of the parodic excess for which this boisterous Catalan has since become renowned. Many of the visual contradictions in the film stem from the cross-cuts which alternate with extreme close-up shots from Leo's point of view, apparently as though we were to be afforded a privileged perspective which we may share with him in his sta-

Figure 3.1. Leo's (Angel Jové's) hands arrange objects in *Bilbao* (1978), by Bigas Luna

tus as the epitome of the filmic voyeur. Nonetheless, these close-ups have no revelatory function, being too close for optical focus. They plunge us deeper into a confusing, multisensory urban environment.

The challenge to optical supremacy is also, of course, a challenge to rigid representation of the many different identities encompassed by film. Leo's displacement enacts the situation of the piece and the director's refusal to grant him optical or tactical understanding opens the way for a more fluid concept of the negotiation of space and the senses within the cinematic world. In the movement from visual to haptic, previous power structures are interrogated and destabilized, opening the way for a new appreciation of the work.

A resistance to an anchoring of the signifier to signified by this daring reformulation of the semiotic codes related to cinematographic technique is evidenced not solely in the adventurous experiments with tactile vision. The nomenclature is carefully selected for its connotative value and relation to two significant sites of political conflict and proves that this slippage is integral to this film. The identity of Barcelona and Bilbao as centres of dissidence under the Franco regime ensures their linking in this way – via the film's title and location – which enables them to flaunt their newly won freedom. Franco's destruction of these two cities was the result of a combination of appropriation and neglect made possible through the collusion of those implicated in the support of the dictator's authority. Leo's unhealthy pursuit of Bilbao that leads to her murder is facilitated by the same collusion and is the result of a similar combination of (mis)appropriation and inadequacy.

Further evidence of the significance of nomenclature comes in the form of the inevitable evocation of Da Vinci – or Leonardo as he is known to Spaniards. In contrast to his namesake, the Renaissance artist knew how to read nature and represent it creatively (rather than fetishistically), excelling in his understanding of proportion and perspective, especially in terms of visual creation. Indeed, his iconic *Vitruvian Man* is generally considered as emblematic of his creative and scientific understanding of the world which combined to transcend earthly limitations in a manner that Bigas Luna – at the time better known as a graphic artist – also advocates but which Leo is unable to either employ or take advantage of.

At the time of the film's production, the erosion of the power of the centralist state had opened the way for the re-emergence of previously marginalized voices, and other views from the edges. With the advent of democracy came an acknowledgement of plurality, a stark contrast to the cultural homogeneity enforced previously. The country was now free to experiment and negotiate with alternative representations of identity, which not only challenged previous restrictions but also interrogated those same artistic conventions employed for their promotion. *Bilbao* embodies both facets of this newly discovered liberty; it revels in the potential for innovative methods of representation and, in turn, with the perplexed meanderings of its protagonist, initiates an uncertain relationship between touch and meaning.

Any process of change necessarily makes visible gaps and fissures as it tries to overcome them. These are used by Bigas to create alternative meanings consonant with his acknowledgement of the collapse of preceding values and his revision of them. The resulting discourse, together with the shifts between optical and haptic visuality, open up a new space for a renegotiation of subjectivity that simultaneously destabilizes previous filmic paradigms. The 'sliding relationship' set out by Marks is indicative of the formal slippage that is an integral element of Bigas Luna's style with significant ideological implications.

Interestingly in this challenge to visual meaning, Bigas has much in common with his fellow Catalan, José Luis Guerín, whose work is the object of analysis in the final chapter of this book. Not only do they both interrogate the primacy of the visual, but also in their engagement with material culture in the cinematic space they shape an innovative approach to the construction of material objects as subjects, eliding traditional distinctions and suggesting radical revisions of previous paradigms, in line with their intensely self-reflexive approach.

Volavérunt: The Tactile Gaze and the Female Body

Despite their nuances and divergence, where theories of embodied responses to film find their common ground is inevitably in the transgressive seeping that takes place at the edges of the flesh of the world (or indeed that figure the world as flesh to follow Merleau Ponty) and the subject, to dissolve the dividing line between subject and object. This is not to suggest that ideological distinctions can be broken down and thus disregarded but rather that in a move between a cognitive and an affective encounter with the space of the film, distinctions can perhaps be highlighted, interrogated and possibly undermined. In the section that follows I refer to *Volavérunt* to demonstrate how Bigas Luna has refined his style and themes to create a more 'mainstream' and potentially less confrontational film yet which subtly delves beneath the surface of representation (literally in his examination of the paintings) in order to test the divisions – gendered, national and artistic – that a politics of vision has traditionally entailed. A frustration with a cinema screen that is out of his reach and cannot be physically apprehended leads the director to appropriate other means which invoke the tactile manipulation that he aspires to achieve. In this instance, the evocation of haptic and optic visuality (witnessed in *Bilbao*) results in a persistent interrogation of surface and depth. This is extended to other art forms and in particular the place of the still image in the moving one and the altered signification that this entails.

The containment of the female body in its representation in western art relies on a set of assumptions about the borders of this body. Sanitized female sexuality was safer when confined by the frame, where its discursive and representational inscriptions were safely contained and understood, and where the body's edges were softened by the painterly touch, a far cry from the perceived threat of the open female body. This variety of representation has as its aim the representation of a unified and coherent subject that bypasses the troubled terrain of this woman as (sexual) object. The director's sensitivity towards the symbolic value of the still and moving image allows him to delve into the roots of these meanings and consequently – through a combination of editing and mise-en-scène – open them up to reinterpretation.

It is the resistance to the containment of the subject that drives the narrative exploration of this painting. In similar terms the grotesque body as the ultimate form of resistance to regulation is explored by the concluding section of this chapter in an examination of the epicurean excesses that recur – to a greater or lesser extent – in all of these films. The boundaries between subject and object, within and without the frame – of the cinema and the painting – is granted an explicitly material dimension in its gastronomic representation. By privileging the body that consumes and the liminal sites of Goya's paintings in *Volavérunt,* this filmmaker alerts us to a further potential for intersubjectivity in this area.

Volavérunt is adapted from a novel of the same name written by the Uruguayan author Antonio Larreta and awarded the Premio Planeta in 1980 (arguably Spain's most prestigious literary accolade). The narrative takes as its premise the life of the court of the Duquesa de Alba in the late eighteenth and early nineteenth centuries. A complex web of sexual and political relationships forms the basis of the film. The most important of these (to the narrative) are that of the Prime Minister, Manuel Godoy (Jordi Mollà), and the Duquesa, Cayetana (Aitana Sanchéz-Gijón). Godoy is also committing adultery with the Queen (Cayetana's rival), while the duchess is involved with the famous painter, also resident in her court, Francisco Goya de Lucientes (Jorge Perugorría). Godoy, presented as a womanizer from the outset, also embarks upon an affair with a peasant gypsy girl, Manuela (Penélope Cruz), whom he takes to the court of the duchess to serve as a lady in waiting, so that she will be permanently (sexually) available to him. The intrigue and mystery that drives the narrative centres on the enigma of two famous paintings by Goya and the identity of their female subject and then the murder of the duchess, poisoned by the addition of toxic paints to her wine. The bodies of these women represent an insatiable sexuality in an aristocratic setting characterized by such excess, yet there is much more to their depiction than merely visual consumption by the men that surround them. Their pleasure in their own eroticism and recognition of the power it entails renders a straightforward reading of these works along the lines of gender problematic to say the least.

The shaky foundations of the objectifying cinematic gaze are traced back to a similarly objectifying gaze but this time it is the female nude in art that enables this interrogation of vision. The paintings concerned are Goya's *majas* – *La maja vestida* and *La maja desnuda* – historically controversial pieces which are famed for (allegedly) being the first paintings to depict female pubic hair. These famous oils on canvas are an enigmatic point of reference in narrative terms, the enigma surrounding the woman who modelled for the paintings.[11]

Figure 3.2. *La maja vestida,* Franciso Goya y Lucientes (c.1800)

Figure 3.3. *La maja desnuda,* Franciso Goya y Lucientes (c.1800)

The two paintings of the *maja* provide a focal point from which the film is able to engage in an examination of the problematic space that representations of the female body occupy. The title of the film is the same as one of Goya's etchings from the series *Caprichos* and in the film is also, allegedly, the name that the *duquesa* gives to her vagina. If we first insert this depiction of this woman of disputed identity within a broader history of the female nude then we begin to comprehend the ways in which an ambiguous and contested power structure is imbricated within this critical structure.

The concentration on the paintings goes further than a simple investigation of their meaning as their form and construction becomes a focal point of the film. It is in this overdetermined cinematic, historical and social space that Goya's work is able to transgress the borders of the frame. These are the borders that seek to contain the female nude in its non-threatening context. By reminding the viewer of the link between the nude and the female model this transgression unsettles the empowered gaze that contemplates the finished product. Once again the intersubjective space is preferred to the subject/object binary.

The opening title sequence of *Volavérunt* introduces us to the two paintings that provide the background to the film's narrative. They are presented to us in fragments initially with sounds that gradually are discernible as those of an enclosed public space (probably suggestive of the Prado museum where these works are displayed) reverberating heels, muted conversation and coughs, and then a mobile phone ringing, firmly situating us outside of the temporal confines of the 'main feature'. The camera frames both versions, the *vestida* and the *desnuda*, in turn as the stomach, breast, hand and hair of this unidentified historical woman is unclothed and then dissected by this cinematic lens. Bigas expertly disrobes the former as his smooth editing picks out section by section and it gradually merges with the latter version, a seamlessly effected cinematic transition that not only points to the similarities between the two paintings but also subtly suggests the camera's ability to manipulate the manner in which it chooses to display the female form. From this perspective it would be difficult to label one painting as more erotically charged than the other as the sheer fabric which contains the curves of the *maja vestida* seem to suggest more sensual possibility than the paint which depicts the bare flesh of the naked woman. Indeed the fabric clings so closely that, as the camera retreats to allow us a more complete view, flesh and fabric appear to have merged. The soundtrack complements this visual sequence as the contemporary museum sounds first merge with and then give way to more extravagant music, which appears to create its own folds and reinforce the textures of the paint through its instrumental layers.

These textural folds depicted in close-up evoke the tactility of vision that opens up the screen to an embodied engagement. The significance of this is in the nuanced treatment of the female body that it encourages. If we assume that this tactile encounter makes us think through our relationship to the body of the screen, in Jennifer M. Barker's words this is a variety of 'contact that seriously undermines the rigidity of the opposition between viewer and film, inviting us to think of them as intimately related but not identical, caught up in a relationship of intersubjectivity and co-constitution, rather than a subject and object positioned on opposite sides of the screen' (2009: 12–13). This breaks down the coherent representational politics of the original paintings and opens them up to a more democratic mode of viewing. Beugnet's criticism once more elucidates this alternative engagement. She writes:

> Whereas optic images set discrete self-standing elements of figuration in illusionistic spaces, haptic images dehierarchise perception, drawing attention back to tactile details and the material surface where figure and ground start to fuse. (2007: 66)

The framing of the paintings in this opening scene offers us a new way of looking, one that transgresses the borders of the frame (of painting and screen); not only this, the painting brings together the visual and aural symbolism of a film that concentrates on an aesthetic of layers. Paint is applied layer by layer and each new veneer becomes a part of the entire work and itself a new surface both concealing and signalling what went before. The *maja* is depicted in two ways, but the protective layer of garments which adorn her body in the clothed version do not necessarily remove the eroticism of this type of presentation of the female form. In fact, the tension between the surface and the layers beneath are indicative of the manner of cinematography which relies on veneers of sound, metaphors of make-up and paint and the construction of mise-en-scène to evoke the layers of interpretation that cause the tensions ever present in the film. This is part and parcel of Bigas Luna's provocative and decidedly ambiguous aesthetic.

The paintings occupy a similarly ambiguous position reinforcing and con-
testing the ideological formations that are explored by Bigas Luna here. Once
again it is when the construction is exposed as such that the epistemological
interrogation of the image is at its most effective. The material qualities of the
oil painting speak to this reading, and Lynda Nead also makes this comparison:
'As cultural commodities, oil paintings have been relished by critics and art
historians and the practice of applying paint to canvas has been charged with
sexual connotations. Light caresses form, shapes become voluptuous, colour
is sensuous, and the paint itself is luxuriously physical' (1992: 56). It is not only
the emphasis on surface texture in its abstract manifestation that creates a
tactile image in this scenario. The emphasis on close-up mentioned before
represents one evocation of the tactile quality of the image but it also comes
to the fore through a concentration on texture and touch as it appears diegetically: the moments in which tactile connections are made between characters in the films or the image pursues its tactility through appeal to the other
senses – the sounds of the brushing of the paint on canvas and the scratching
of the pencil on Goya's sketch pad. The glass of wine, which often features
as a link between scenes, is also framed to highlight its sensory appeal, the
shiny reflective surface of the glass and the distinctive sound of the liquid
that fills it privileged as it fills the screen and functions as a space outside the
narrative. Its position and importance in the film are prefigured in the opening sequence and titles as the camera focuses on the – subtly represented
– genitals between the closed legs of the *maja desnuda;* then the film's title
appears, the V shape in the middle of the title conveniently fitting over the
same shape of the pubis, and transforming it into a glass goblet of the same
shape.[12]

Texture as it appeals to touch, in this opening sequence, is significant in
the invitation to a specifically erotic tactility.[13] To scrutinize the female body at
such close quarters, even through the medium of the painting, has been one
element of this cineaste's work, which has led to much speculation as to its
artistic purpose and ethical justification. Such a simplistic view of this type of
representation – which assumes it carries an implicit weight of objectification
– is a limiting one. I would suggest that precisely in his fragmented method of
shooting, Bigas suggests there may be a different way of addressing the image. The assumption of a unified subject which portraiture attests – given its

Figure 3.4. A close-up of *La maja vestida* from *Volavérunt* (1999), by Bigas Luna, with the film's title superimposed on the maja's pubis

rendition of a whole figure at a specific moment in history – is thereby modified along with our assumptions. The potential of a fragmented subjectivity – enabled rather than disavowed by the cinematic camera – is liberating for the configurations of gender at work within this piece.

This female sexuality may be more liberated than the permitted variety of the eighteenth-century world of *Volavérunt* but the emphasis on a physically configured version of femininity encoded as exhibitionistic – at least initially – remains written large on this screen. Bigas succeeds in subverting the ideological assumptions that have been made about this type of display through slippage. He separates power from the gaze and in doing so unhinges the gendered dichotomy previously assumed to inhere within the apparatus of cinema. This appraisal of the way in which the visual domain of cinema is re-examined in relation to its function in these films will be examined later.

In attending to a transgressive and tactile form of vision I have attempted to some extent to remove the objectifying form of looking that lies within the parameters of the gendered gaze. Nonetheless, this is not to suggest that Bigas Luna successfully operates within a cinematic mode of gender neutrality but to say that his transgressions and infringements suggest a space outside of that confined by a sexualized gaze. Given the painterly associations of this film, the art criticism and its views on the female nude are a productive route by which to pursue this blurring of the edges that Bigas enacts. Lynda Nead is worth quoting at length in this instance:

The distinctions between inside and outside, between finite form and form without limit, need to be continuously drawn. This requirement applies to representations of the female body in high and mass culture. It extends to the way in which the categories of art and pornography are defined and maintained. In nearly every case, however, there is a point where the systems break down, where an object seems to defy classification and where the values themselves are exposed and questioned. If you know the terms of the debate then they can be played with, disrupted and this opens up the possibility for challenging and progressive representations of the female body. (1992: 11)

In *Volavérunt* Bigas Luna's treatment of the female body is problematized by its many and ambiguous relations with other factors, a strategy which offers an ideal example of its resistance to containment. The image of the woman in the paintings is interwoven with the historical narrative which, in its recreation via this filmic text, is replete with similar ambiguities. The treatment of Goya's paintings involves an unavoidable history of speculation surrounding the works of the Spanish master, speculation that provides Bigas with perfect material for a further manipulation of history. Moreover, the controversy that would have surrounded these paintings at the time of their production mirrors similar criticism of the director's own work with regards to an over-sexualized depiction of women.

A combination of this director's acute awareness of the tactile possibilities of the original painting and his ability to transport the erotics of this tactility into the film combined with the traditional connotations of the depiction of the female nude create the ideal interplay with which to question and subvert the traditional conceptions both of Spanish history and the erotic permutations of the original *maja desnuda*. Returning to Lynda Nead's quotation, 'If you know the terms of the debate then they can be played with, disrupted and this opens up the possibility for challenging and progressive representations of the female body'. This combines here the narrative possibility and the tactile gaze and superimposes them onto a painting with its own historical interpretative tensions. The female body, by means of the paintings, takes centre stage in this film, and the two female leads (both the possible subjects of the portraits) are repeatedly seen to be involved in modifications of their physicality. The relationship between art and the senses impinges on the bodies of these women as they talk about or enact various beauty treatments, and the oil paints themselves exceed their specified function as Cayetana entreats Goya to paint her face with them.

Framing of these women and the concomitant point of view of the men with whom they are sexually involved, the womanising Godoy and the enigmatic brooding artist Goya (once more Bigas proves that he is more than ready to resort to stereotypes) would initially resist any notion that they are liberated from the conventional sexism implicit in this male gaze. Nonetheless there are moments of liberation that extend those of the opening sequence to even further – frequently subtle – permutations of intersubjectivity and shifting power relations, not always embedded in the arena of visibility.

Although I am concerned here with a more holistic cinematic experience than can be achieved through the visual alone, I would not want to diminish the importance of the optical richness of this work or to claim that the symbolic latency of the visual has been superseded by the forays into a more sensorially rich mode of observation. In keeping with the musical layers and the patinas of oils on canvas, the lighting is selectively utilized with a clear focus on the choice between illumination and obscurity to mirror the narrative. The period in question lends itself to the dim yet warm light given by the candles present in many of the indoor scenes. The flickering effect of flame and the shadow effects created add visual interest, and warmth, to the image. The shiny surface of the glass which holds the poison that ends the life of the duquesa reflects these flames as the lighting lends weight to this pivotal object. During the outdoor scenes there is a preference for the muted light lent by dusk. Not only does this mirror the similarly subdued candle light – it is a liminal time of day, neither night nor day – but the failing light can conceal as much as the dying sun is able to reveal.

This challenge to conventional depictions of gender does not stop with the women in this film. Interestingly, for the domestic audience the male heroes of the tale, which represent traditional stereotypes of virility and Spanish machismo, are presented as weaker, less glamorous versions of their historical personages. Whilst their male solidarity appears strong and restates the notion of the metaphorical inscription of masculine power on the female body literally encapsulated by the painting's existence – as does their collusion with regard to it – the fragility of this social construct becomes apparent as the Queen and Cayetana reassert power through their rival political machinations. Gender cannot be considered as the sole denoter of power within the narrative, as class, wealth and social stature in general become tangled in the complex web of relations at play in the film.

Permeable Bodies: Digesting the Image

If the concern for the physical and the material has been that which most succinctly summarizes the peripheral vision of this Catalan director then it seems apposite that this chapter should conclude with a reading of another regime of physical pleasure – the comestible. The engagement with food in these films functions to reveal the wider tensions surrounding the integrity of the subject which frequently serves as a metonym for the more political issue of identity in the Spanish state. These divisions as they focus on the porosity and mutability of the somatic draw him time and again to a preoccupation with all things gastronomic. The nexus of consumption of the body and by the body as it relates to our consumption of the image acknowledges and undermines cinema's traditional dependence on the visual – and aural – mode of production and appreciation. This restates Bigas Luna's project, as I have outlined it, to unsettle the ocular regime of film in order to explore cinema's potential for multiple, embodied subjective representations and responses.

My route through his films thus far has moved from the specific contextual location of *Bilbao* within an important moment in the history of Spain to a reading of their cinematic experimentation that seeks a place for his less analysed films within a tradition of quality European cinema that goes some way to bypass problematic and limiting national classifications. To a degree my project in this final part is to reunite the specifics of the Catalan identity at work here with the embodied readings and material concerns that preoccupy this director in varying degrees throughout his own 'body' of work. This is very much in line with a tradition of Catalan culture which engages with the body as a means of resistance to the enforced hegemony of Spanish cultural practice which set itself up as the enlightened other to the less advanced Catalan tradition, a point-of-view established and reinforced by the cultural (and actual) violence committed by the Spanish state against all things Catalan during significant periods of the nineteenth and twentieth century.

Food and its consumption are foregrounded in all of his work, from an affectionate celebration of the regional variety of Spanish food to the disturbing butchering and cooking of dogs in *Caniche*. In 2009 he took part in a series for RTVE (Spanish Radio and Television) that asked selected public figures from the peninsula to talk about their fifty years of a topic of their choice. Bigas chose fifty years of Iberian icons, and paella was first on his list, a list that also included olives, ham, and chupa-chups.[14] His most recent intervention in the 'foodie' arena, and in keeping with his forays into Internet creativity, is to be found on the food blog *panvinoychocolate* (pan wine and chocolate) promoting ethical consumption and organic food.[15] This obsession goes further than simply a pleasure in food, in keeping with his visual sensibility; it works to represent the specificity of the cultural inheritance of Catalonia, both in terms of the national specificity of individual dishes and culinary practices. It locates these films within a tradition of Catalan cultural production that situates the body, and its baser functions, as a site of resistance and aesthetic possibility. This is a reading of food that reminds us of its pivotal roles in our existence and, in doing so, highlights our carnality. Relating this to an experiential reading of cinema acknowledges this sensory mode of representation and existence as a legitimate means of access to knowledge and in doing so returns us to the original contention that alternative modes of cinematic representation permit a space for marginal subjects.

As with every aspect of his work, the gastronomic for Bigas is another ambiguous arena of representation, a fertile ground that in its symbolic, physical and transgressive incarnation speaks to the possibility of becomings that the cinema embodies. Food is able to bring all of these concerns together, from its place as a marker of identity, to its analogic relationship with the capitalist commodification and consumption of the body that Bigas recognizes as an element of the visual. It also negotiates the tricky path of taste that is a recurring critical stumbling block in readings of these films, particularly in its relationship to depictions of sexual activity figured as gratuitous, sexist and excessive. This is the inevitable link between these two physical realms and what Santiago Fouz-Hernandez claims can be termed 'gastronomic eroticism' (2011: 99). If the edges that are blurred are those between subject and object in my readings of his films then perhaps there is a space to read food and sexual relationships as a further manifestation of this suggestive structure in which the distinctions that function in hegemony's favour can be eroded by these problematic material reminders of our connectedness to the world and the screen.

The Body Consumed

Initially though we must recognize the symbolic function of specific foods, the Iberian icons that Bigas referred to, dishes with an ethnic signification and a nod to his own culinary heritage. Food is culturally specific, and culinary identity provokes pride and as cultural symbol is valuable currency, nowhere more so that in Spain where food and meals are a ritual with an important social function.

The Iberian trilogy, *Huevos de oro/Golden Balls, Jamón, jamón* and *La teta i la lluna/The Tit and the Moon,* relate this alimentary consumption to popular culture's consumption of the body and to the damaging effects of the external imposition of identity on the bodies contained within the filmic space. These are probably Bigas's best-known works. Beginning in 1993 and produced at an impressive rate of one film a year, the three films traverse the historically significant geographical zone of the Crown of Aragon, an area that significantly excludes the centre of what we know today as Spain and included the paisos Catalans/Catalan countries (Catalonia, Valencia and the Balearic Islands). This triptych constitutes an ironic, and highly self-aware, intervention on the plague of stereotype, specifically gendered and national, among other things, and what is significant here is the use of food as a tool of parody, and its relation to other forms of consumption.

The body is a determining rather than determined feature, and these works represent the dissidence for which Bigas Luna has become famous as they play out their political rebellion through the bodies on screen (Keown 2008). During an early sequence of *Jamón, jamón* we are privy to an underwear publicity campaign casting. As the camera is guided along a line of male crotches, clothed only in their underwear, the grammar of the image transmits recognized codes of sexual objectification (albeit reversed as the gaze is that of an undeniably phallic female in this instance) (D'Lugo 1997: 64–65). Similarly, the food that is part of this film's narrative is carefully selected in terms of its consumption, in both physical and capitalist terms. The *jamones* of the title and the tortillas that are referred to repeatedly are examples of the symbols that 'sell' Spain and Catalonia to tourists: they are the local gastronomy vaunted by guidebooks. In this context they gain greater significance as the symbols of visceral enjoyment for a body that is being carved up for consumption in a globalized market place. They also align themselves with destructive external impositions of gender as Sylvia's breasts (Sylvia is played by a 17-year-old Penelope Cruz in this film), we are told repeatedly, taste of tortilla, and Raúl (Javier Bardem) chews raw garlic in his ham factory in order, he believes, to maintain sexual potency. This is read by Fouz-Hernández and Martínez-Expósito as globalisation's indelible imprint on the body of Spain, and they read the ending of both *Jamón, jamón* and *Golden Balls* as 'a nostalgic farewell to the *macho ibérico*' unifying gender and nationality in a clearly identifiable stereotype (2007: 27).

It is true that in *Jamón, jamón* the tortillas and hams stand for an (erroneous) imagination of a unified culinary tradition. They become representative of the Spain that is packaged and sold to tourists and in the final scene become the ultimate destructive force of the externally imposed 'national' personality; the competing forces of masculinity take the film's parodic excess to the extreme and bludgeon one another to death in the film's closing tableaux, reminiscent of Goya's painting *Duel with Cudgels* in which the weapons have been replaced with ham legs. The artistic and culinary citation continues in the second instalment of the series, this time with reference to Dalí's eggs, and the dual meaning in Spanish of *huevos* as both eggs and testicles once again links the gastronomic to a damaging construction of masculinity. Javier Bardem's body in both films is the visual representation of a crumbling national and sexual identity, in which the macho Iberian male is inscribed on this actor's body and yet in both instances proves incapable of supporting the myth that it has perpetuated.

The final instalment in the trilogy, and the only one to be set in Catalonia, engages with and ironically exaggerates the Oedipal narrative that has been employed as an underlying structure for film spectatorship. The protagonist Tete finds his position in the family usurped by his baby brother and his aggressive father, whose concern with the masculine pride of Catalonia means that he is forever shouting at Tete that he needs to 'strap on a pair'. It is through the mother's breast that this jealousy is played out and Tete goes in search of a replacement, becoming obsessed with a young Portuguese performer, Estrellita (Mathilda May) at a local holiday camp. This film restates the link between gastronomy and nationality, initiated in *Jamon, jamón:* it depicts close-ups of the preparation of *pa amb tomàquet* and the *porrones* (bread spread with tomato, and glass jugs for wine that are culinary identifiers of Catalonia) thrown by Tete's grandfather, filled in this case with milk rather than the traditional wine in a nod to Tete's continuing obsession with being able to drink from the perfect breast. Of course in this trilogy, the testing of the connections between food and national identity are tied to the larger artistic project of these three films, which invites a reading that acknowledges a critical approach to the Iberian peninsula as a pluralistic site of national and other affiliations, and criticizes its consumption through cultural production as a homogenous and 'Spanish' entity.

As I outlined earlier *Bilbao* initiates the link between physicality and the threat to the subject that comes with these inappropriate representations of food, and their link with other acts that transgress the borders of the body. It is in the testing of these divisions between mind and body that Bigas's works are at their most effective. He evokes Bakhtin's grotesque body as the ultimate form of resistance to regulation in its relation to epicurean excesses. The boundaries between subject and object, within and without the frame, are granted an explicitly material dimension in their gastronomic representation. In Rabelais and his world Bakhtin writes:

> Eating and drinking are one of the most significant manifestations of the grotesque body. The distinctive character of this body is its open unfinished nature, its interaction with the world. These traits are most fully and correctly revealed in the act of eating: the body transgresses here its own limits: it swallows, devours, rends the world apart, is enriched and grows at the world's expense. (1965: 281)

The body is posited as the disruptive element – as Bahktin elaborated – in the social order. The reason for this disruptive power lies in its openness and potential to interact with the world, and our bodily means of access to the world blurs the boundary between inside and outside, between us and the world, in a way that vision, with its dependence on distance, does not. Phenomenological readings of cinema open out the potential for an intersubjective account of its representational possibilities, of our bodies being open to the world. In this instance they enable the position of food as that difficult term, passing from object into the subject, interrogating the possibility of a separate, sanitized body on film, in fact interrogating that problematic distinction of subject and object. The transmutability of the cinematic subject/object suggested by these openings to the world becomes, in these works, a metaphor for the instability of fixed (national and other) identity. Such concern for the corporal acknowledges a move away from a purely psychological structure of viewing as we recognize our position as embodied spectators and open up the moving image to what Vivian Sobchack calls 'vision embodied – a material activity that not only sees but can be seen, that makes vision itself visible' (1992: 93).

This mode of experiential spectatorship recognizes vision as one, amongst other, sensory modes of perception in operation as we inhabit the world, and which also provide access to our comprehension of it. Sobchack writes of our access to meaning through the body we inhabit: 'Such meaning is drawn also from the perceptive capacity of the body to touch and feel, to hear, to smell, to taste, to move, to inhabit the world intentionally as a total being, a lived-body on whom, as whom, the senses describe a field and inscribe their meaning as a conscious experience' (1992: 94).

It is the combination of the intrusion of food into the order of the previously established hierarchy of the senses that evokes the dialogic element of the Bakhtinian imagination and which is extended through contemporary film theory to engage with the body, on and off screen as a site of dissonance with its own objective presence. In this reading of embodied sensuality Bigas Luna's oeuvre demonstrates that it is not just in eating that the merging of bodies troubles our notions of somatic containment; as this argument develops the sexual is allied with the gastronomic in ways that cannot help but challenge a detached mode of vision.

It is in the manner of its depiction that food stands for more than sustenance and the site of a communal activity, and in these final examples that it is humorously, and at times more seriously combined with the sexual in its attempts to proffer alternative and creative but also discomfiting depictions of the physical. A combination of extreme close-ups that dwell on and highlight the moment at which food is consumed in these works draws attention to the transgressive position that it occupies. As Bahktin acknowledges, food is a threat because of its uncleanliness; its mutability makes it undesirable. Deborah Lupton summarizes the reason for food's problematic liminal situation: 'Food intrudes into the "clean" purity of rational thought because of its organic nature. Food is unclean, a highly unstable substance; it is messy and dirty in its preparation, its disposal and its by-products; it inevitably decays, it has odour. Delicious food is only hours or days away from rotting matter, or excreta' (1996: 3).

Of course this is nowhere more true that when the source of food literally passes from one body to the other, in the act of breastfeeding. In the third instalment of the Iberian trilogy Bigas parodies the Oedipal construction of film viewing, as the young protagonist Tete observes his parents' sexual activities. He then, as a Freudian fetishist must, transposes his desire for the mother onto the desire for a breast, any breast, but one that he shares with neither his father nor his baby brother. The limits of cinematic acceptability are questioned in this scene from the film with Tete's fantasy of feeding from the ideal breast. Bigas has taken this theme even further in his Internet videos, as one labelled *mamador molar* (toothless sucker) depicts a toothless old man breastfeeding in order to make lactating women more comfortable, and in an installation work, *Ingestum,* presented at Valencia's museum of Modern Art in 2008. It is the installation which exemplifies the literal exceeding of borders, as in the space of the gallery we are forced into an immediate and unmediated relationship with the three fluids that form the basis of this exhibit, water, blood and milk. These are the fluids which traverse the body and once more invoke that unstable, mutable and porous aspect of the flesh, which joins us to the matter of the earth and which is of such great interest to this director.

This sense of (aesthetic) excess, even abjection, is reminiscent of a long Catalan tradition as is recognized by the director in his abundant references to the work of Salvador Dalí. The obsession with flies that unites these two Catalans further evokes the changing status of food – an entomological preoccupation that Bigas acknowledges stems in part from their roles in the decomposition of flesh — human, animal and vegetable.

The significance of the surreal configuration is apparent. It is the tension of failing vision, or at least in vision as an incomplete mode of sensory access to the world, a *sine qua non* of surrealist creativity which reminds us of the same suspicion of the visual realm in *Bilbao*. Gastronomy was also a prevalent theme in Dalí's art and sculptures and, as a description of his painting of himself painting a rotting fish in *Diary of a Genius* suggests (this painting clearly an inspiration for Bigas in his own piscine montage in *Bilbao*), it was the changing state of food that interested him the most, the products which represent the abject and open relationship of the body with the world, reminding us here of our own embodied status and its relationship to the image. This scene also returns us to the other element of sensory enjoyment allied with food and utilized by this director to underline his ideological and artistic project. The sensuality of his filmmaking extends to the coupling of two or several bodies and relates consumption with consummation on more than one occasion. In an early sequence from the film *Lola*, the close-up of the protagonist's mouth and fingers running with juice create a sensuous eroticism in line with the erotic excesses of the work. When she finishes she leaves the stone on a grass verge and watches as it attracts a small army of ants, again citing Dalí.

Food, like sex, in its threat to cross the borders of the body, represents that which can take on an ambiguous meaning in relation to the way in which subjectivity is represented by means of the cinematic. These films join the two as acts in which subjectivity can no longer be contained. Like eating, sex forces an interaction with the other that can articulate a new relationship between our bodies and the world. Elspeth Probyn uses Deleuze and Guattari to explain the visceral and transformative power of food and sex, arguing that 'the sensual nature of eating now constitutes a privileged optic through which to consider how identities and the relations between sex, gender and power are being renegotiated. In eating, pleasure offers itself to be problematized. As it brings our senses to life, it also forefronts the viscerality of life' (2000: 7).

The 'viscerality of life' acknowledges the transgressive reading of food that links it to sexual practice, often the more explicit, violent and degrading elements, that assault the viewer and must provoke questions about the limits of representation. This exposed and threatening element is the result of the porosity of the body – its orifices – which represent its threatening openness that Kristeva posits as menacing because it blurs the boundaries between inside and outside. Extending this liminality, Bahktin's writings on bodily functions in their relation to the carnivalesque would appear to concur with Kristeva's (1982) view of their extra-social situation, at the edges of the body and the edges of society. Bigas refuses to avoid or sanitize his depictions of the carnal, provocatively framing bodies in a way that demands attention. This was the case with the extended shots of female genitalia in *Volavérunt* and the suggestive close-ups in *Bilbao*.

Bámbola (1996) epitomizes the uncomfortable relationship that sex and food have in these films. The opening scenes are narrated by the protagonist's own voice-over, accompanying an image of her going to buy eels. Central to this initial narration is the description of the family-owned and -run trattoria, but the imagined idyll that this description hints at is immediately debased by the first image of the restaurant and of a crazed woman chopping raw goat meat with a cleaver. A blood-stained apron adds to the gore of the scene as do the insults that the woman shouts, mainly directed at Mina (Bámbola played by Valeria Marini) herself.

This exaggerated violent imagery sets the tone for a film that continues such brutality. A visual link is established between Mina and the food as her mother repeats her name during this scene and then later, after their mother's funeral when Mina and her homosexual brother, Flavio, decide to transform the trattoria into a pizzeria, Mina is shown seductively eating spaghetti lifting it to her mouth with her fingers. In one of the most explicit (and brutal) sex scenes in the film Furio, Mina's lover, wraps an eel around her neck as they have sex. The gap between the auditory and the visual and the details that render these sexual encounters (of which there are many) so disturbing are explored by Fouz-Hernández in some detail (2011).

In these brief examples from Bigas Luna's filmography the revision of previous practice emphasizes the linking of pleasure and desire and their relation to sex and food, and in two of these examples they do so humorously (*The Ages of Lulú* and *Son de mar/Sound of the Sea*). In *Sound of the Sea* Ulises (Jordi Mollà) and Martina (Leonor Watling) exchange charged glances while Ulises eats his tomato salad and Martina hangs her underwear on the washing line, visual consumption of the body exposed once more and allied with the alimentary. In his controversial adaptation of Almudena Grandes's novel *The Ages of Lulú,* a film about one woman's sexual awakening and then subsequent descent into addictive and potentially dangerous sexual practice, the first scene of seduction is allied with a young girl's hunger as the protagonist Lulú (Ainara Pérez) is shown devouring a strawberry tart, self-consciously, as her older suitor watches her. This director's love of suggestive imagery is indulged as the fruit and cream is the subject of a close-up before the camera dwells on the adolescent Lulú licking her lips in a naïve, yet ultimately successful, attempt at seduction.

All of these are ironic and playful yet they are more than this: they move beyond the destructive aspect of consumption and offer up new ways of thinking through the connections that food can forge between bodies and things. As Elspeth Probyn sets out:

> we can rethink practices of eating and sex as rhizomatic; producing bodies with 'multiple entryways and exits'. This produces fabulous bodies that are opened up, surfaces prepared for the touch of other surfaces. Bodies eating sex are thus connected rhizomatically in different permutations, and through these connections attract yet more surfaces bodies and touch (2000: 76).

This gastronomic epilogue began as an investigation into the ways in which a repressed national identity could locate a subversive and symbolic potential in a culture of food. I hope it functions to illuminate the way in which corporeality in Bigas's work is part and parcel of his wider aesthetic and political project.

There is little that Bigas Luna creates that is not suffused with irony, but I think he makes a profound ethical point about the domain of pleasure and cinema. In combining the comestible and the concupiscent he highlights the necessity, the biological imperative of both. He recognizes, in line with Linda Williams (2008), that when the cinematic moves beyond identification then we can be pleased and disgusted by the images that draw us in or repel us in some affective way. The less salubrious aspects are graphically portrayed, the sounds are magnified and the emphasis on textures and surfaces forces us into an uncomfortable relationship with these images. The possibility of an inside and an outside is central to the philosophical structure that Bigas Luna attempts to overturn in these films, and his technique is informed by theoretical approaches to cinema that recognize its affective power. If this is to propose that for Bigas Luna at least it is an ethical response to the damaging separationist politics of the Spanish state then this intersubjective movement is an enriching model through which to resist unhealthy impositions of identity from the outside. Anne Rutherford (2003) writes about this response to the moving image as 'a movement away from the self . . . a groping towards a connection, a link-up with the carnality of the idea, the affect of the body, the sensible resonances of experience'.

These experiences are always at the edges – of the body, of the frame and at the limits of taste and representative strategies. As the director himself says, 'Edges are my favourite place to work. And limits. I love to play with limits and ironies. I couldn't live without irony in my life' (Kaufman 1998). This brief post-script on the emphasis on the sensory in the link between the sexual and the gastronomic points to new regimes of desire and pleasure which do not, indeed cannot be limited to the scopic politics of distance and imagined difference. It is worth concluding with Probyn's reflection on the potential of food to offer sites at which identity can be re-evaluated in a way that I believe encapsulates Bigas Luna's cinematic sensuality: 'it does not make sense to say that eating is more important than sex or vice versa, but in this instance and others, eating sex is the catalyst for reflecting on ways of being in the world .' (2000: 75).

Notes

1.   Due to the prolific nature of Bigas Luna's filmic works this chapter at times makes brief reference to films that I do not then examine in detail or provide synoptic accounts of. My aim is to trace a particular element of his aesthetic, the embodied and intersubjective, and provide reference to other works (when available) that deal in more detail with those works to which I make reference.

2.   By 'new Spain' I mean a country that was consciously rejecting the previous years of dictatorship. This historical period is referred to as the Transition.

3.   For more on this see Smith (2000) and Allinson (2001).

4.   In his 2006 production *Yo soy la Juani/My Name is Juani* the interest in youth culture and its confusing and damaging effects resurfaces, demonstrating a new Spain with similar problems and stressing the anxiety of these repetitions and in-herited burdens.

5.   A similar type of tension that I will later explore in my examination of Guerín's documentary *En construcción/Work in Progress.*

6.   In this respect Sicily is an interesting choice of provenance for this woman. A pe-ripheral island with its unavoidable association with organized crime ensures that we make this link, as the priest that sells Maria is as corrupt as the evangelist who buys her. For a reading of this film which links it to a specific moment in the history of the United States and its ideological critique of Reagan's conservative values, see Benet (2010).

7.   Bigas Luna is not the only director from Spain who is an early commentator on the merging of television and cinema culture; it is also a frequent feature of Al-modóvar's work. See Smith (2006).

8. Pregnancy as the ultimate resistance of the female body is a recurrent trope and has been examined as the final liberation for the female lead in *Bámbola* by Fouz-Hernández.

9. This proprioceptive relationship with the film that is set out by Sobchack is taken to extremes by Bigas in the other film that was a product of his time spent in the United States, *Angustia/Anguish* (1987). This sophisticated, irreverent exploration of the horror genre won a prize for cinematography awarded by the Generalitat de Catalunya. In the special screening arranged to celebrate this award Bigas placed actors in the audience to disrupt the screening of the film, also set in a cinema auditorium, thus mimicking the on-screen action and emphasising the fragile boundary between life and screen. The sensational draws on sensation in order that there is no stable and recognisable reality in this surreal cinematic universe. It is the most explicit attack on vision that Bigas mounts in any of his films and could be read as the culmination of this exploratory sensory aesthetic. If exaggerated violence forces us into a position of alienation rather than judgment (the violence is taken to such extremes as to be viewed as parodic?) This film stages the literal violence enacted on the organ of sight and by extension the gaze.

10. A perspective adopted once again to great effect in *Sound of the Sea* (2001) where the love-making sequence is filmed by a single static camera fixed insistently on the face of Leonor Watling, obviating the intricate visuality in editing and lighting as preferred by the norm.

11. For an excellent contextualization of the paintings and their disputed provenance, see Hughes (2003: 240–243).

12. This technique calls to mind the opening credits of his 1992 film *Jamón, jamón,* in which the director superimposes his own title credit onto the genitalia of a road-side Osborne bull advertisement.

13. It is pertinent to consider, in this respect, Goya's deafness, contracted in adulthood after an illness. Although not made explicit in the film this is significant in terms of the emphasis on sensory pleasure, the luscious visuals and the recourse to touch, all of which compensate for a loss of the auditory function.

14. This video can be accessed at http://www.rtve.es/alacarta/videos/50-anos-de/50-anos-iconos-ibericos/622933/.

15. It must also be noted that in keeping with his pragmatic, commercial awareness this is also a point of sale for such products.

References

Allinson, M. 2001. *A Spanish Labyrinth: The Films of Pedro Almodóvar.* London: I. B. Tauris.

Bakhtin, M. 1965. *Rabelais and His World.* Cambridge, MA: MIT Press.

Barker, J. M. 2009. *The Tactile Eye: Touch and the Cinematic Experience.* Berkeley: University of California Press.

Benet, V. J. 2010. 'Eldorado Revisited: Spanish Filmmakers in Reagan's America'. *European Journal of American Studies Online* Speacial Issue. Retrieved 14 October 2011 from http://ejas.revues.org/8787

Beugnet, M. 2007. *Cinema and Sensation.* Edinburgh: Edinburgh University Press.

Bigas Luna, J. J., and C. Canals. 1994. *Retratos ibéricos: crónica pasional de* Jamón jamón, Huevos de oro, La teta y la luna. Barcelona: Lunwerg Editores.

Bruno, G. 2002. *Atlas of Emotion Journeys in Art, Architecture, and Film.* New York and London: Verso.

D'Lugo, M. 1997. *Guide to the Cinema of Spain.* Westport, CT: Greenwood Press.

Foucault, M. 1979. *Discipline and Punish: The Birth of the Prison.* Harmondsworth: Penguin Books.

———. 1981. *The History of Sexuality.* Harmondsworth: Penguin Books.

Fouz-Hernández, S. 2011. 'Ensnared between Pleasure and Politics: Looking for Chicas Bigas Luna, Re-viewing Bambola'. In *Spain on Screen Developments in Contemporary Spanish Cinema,* edited by A. Davies, 93–113. London: Palgrave.

Fouz-Hernández, S., and A. Martínez Expósito. 2007. *Live Flesh: The Male Body in Contemporary Spanish Cinema.* London: I. B. Tauris.

Friedman, E. H. 1999. 'Bigas Luna's "Anguish": An Eye on Discomfort'. *Confluencia* 15(1): 73–81.

Hughes, R. 2003. *Goya.* London: The Harvill Press.

Kaufman, A. 1998. 'Spanish Bad Boy Bigas Luna Sets Sail with "The Chambermaid on the Titanic"'. Retrieved 8 May, 2007 from http://www.indiewire.com/people/int_Luna_Bigas_980812.html.

Keown, D. 2008. 'The Catalan Body Politic as Aired in *La teta i la lluna*'. In *Burning Darkness: A Half Century of Spanish Cinema,* edited by J. R. Resina, 161–172. New York: State University of New York Press.

Kristeva, J. 1982. *Powers of Horror: An Essay on Abjection.* New York: Columbia University Press.

Lupton, D. 1996. *Food, the Body and the Self.* London: SAGE.

MacCormack, P. 2008. *Cinesexuality.* Aldershot, Ashgate.

Marks, L. U. 2000. *The Skin of the Film: Intercultural Cinema, Embodiment and the Senses.* Durham and London: Duke University Press.

———. 2002. *Touch: Sensuous Theory and Multisensory Media.* Minneapolis and London: University of Minnesota Press.

Nead, L. 1992. *The Female Nude: Art, Obscenity, and Sexuality.* London: Routledge.

Probyn, E. 2000. *Carnal Appetites Food Sex Identities.* London: Routledge.

Rutherford, A. 2003. 'Cinema and Embodied Affect'. *Senses of Cinema Online Film Journal* 25(March). Retrieved 18 November 2009 from http://sensesofcinema.com/2003/feature-articles/embodied_affect/

Sanabria, C. 2010. *Bigas Luna: El ojo voraz.* Barcelona: Laertes.

Smith, P. J. 2000. *Desire Unlimited: the Cinema of Pedro Almodóvar.* London: Verso.

———. 2006. *Television in Spain: From Franco to Almodóvar.* Woodbridge, Suffolk: Tamesis.

Sobchack, V. C. 1992. *The Address of the Eye: A Phenomenology of Film Experience.* Princeton, NJ: Princeton University Press.

———. 2004. *Carnal Thoughts: Embodiment and Moving Image Culture.* Berkeley: University of California Press.

Williams, L. 2008. *Screening Sex.* Durham and London: Duke University Press.

CHAPTER FOUR

José Luis Guerín
Between Reality and Fiction

In a short dossier dedicated to the state of Spanish cinema at the end of the twentieth and beginning of the twenty-first century, a 2003 edition of *Cineaste* examined a turning point for films made in Spain. Carlos Heredero noted, among other tendencies, an 'obsession with the present' in Spain's recent moving image production (2003: 33). The filmmakers I have examined thus far have established dualities only to attempt to dissolve them, and Guerín is no exception. This time the indistinction is between past and present, fiction and reality. If, as Heredero claims, there is an insistent immediacy to the recent cinematic production in Spain then Guerín's contribution would seem to remind us that the present is a continuation and response to a history of moving image practice.

This chapter explores the representational possibility of Guerín's subtle approach to filming reality and looks to this director as, perhaps, the future of the peripheral cinemas of Spain that this book has mapped. Guerín's gaze is firmly fixed on the past and the future of the cinema, and in many ways he is the director that encapsulates the difficulty of classification that inheres in the term 'Spanish cinema'. In conversation with Victor Erice in 2003 the two men commented on the lack of a cinematographic tradition in Spain which led Guerín to comment, 'Ahora mismo es imposible hablar de nacionalidades en el cine' (Currently it's impossible to talk about nationalities in cinema) (Wonenburger 2004). This is not a melancholic lament for a lost or imagined body of canonical works but rather an optimistic statement on the sophistication and quality of this country's output, able now to compete, artistically, with quality cinema concerned with the poetic capacity of the moving image and the representational tensions which it raises.

Guerín is a Catalan filmmaker whose filmography to date demonstrates a reflexive approach to the moving image that has resulted in slow and contemplative moving image texts that dwell on the nature of cinema and the creative potential of this variety of representation. His teaching on the Masters course in Creative Documentary at the University of Pompeu Fabra in Barcelona has influenced a new generation of Catalan filmmakers whose creative output is amongst the most interesting to emerge from Catalunya in recent years and has been granted screen time at events such as the 2011 Rotterdam Film Festival and special exhibitions at Harvard and in New York. Diversity of form and content and a playful attitude towards generic categories typify his works which also reveal an interest, verging on obsession, with the status of the moving image as an aesthetic form capable of affective responses and suggestive linkages, working as much in the mind and body of the spectator as on the screen itself.

As this chapter interrogates a cinematic tradition that positions itself between documentary and fiction, past and present, celluloid and other media, it becomes clear that Guerín elides the national to seek a place at the edges of the international, the margins into which quality 'art' cinema is often placed. I will analyse more closely the films he has made since 1997 in their relation to this peripheral position but it is certainly worth a brief foray into his earlier experimentations in an attempt to build a picture of the ideological and aesthetic concerns that unite his oeuvre. Making films since 1985, his first, *Los motivos de Berta* (Fantasia de pubertad), set up the intensely self-reflexive relationship, which develops in his later works, between the history of cinema and the process of transformation that it entails. In this film it comes about when one young girl's life, mainly a bucolic rural idyll, is altered by the arrival of a film crew and the subsequent shooting of the movie in this location. The young female protagonist, used to spending her days observing ants and riding her bicycle is faced with a group of enigmatic actors and film crew, and the beautiful black and white photography emphasizes her bewilderment and awe in the face of these aliens.

His subsequent production *Innisfree* (1990) marks a preference for European locations that remove him from his native land and returns once more to an engagement – more direct this time – with cinema's rich history. On this occasion he revisits the location of John Ford's 1952 film *The Quiet Man*. Here we witness the initiation of the style that re-emerges in *En construcción*, characterized by the observation of the day to day and a skill for finding interest in the ostensibly mundane.

Citing the position of cinema in the collective cultural memory of a place, in the way that *Innisfree* does, resonates with the exploration of memory and its representation that is a persistent trope of these works. Recollection of techniques that Guerín considers properly cinematic is his stated aim and this added invocation of the embedded cultural memory constructs a spectator whose involvement with the image is part of the experience of these works. This takes place explicitly through the actual revisitation of the film in *Innisfree*, but in his other works the process is subtler. Tensions between the binary divisions noted above are played out through an exploration of film as a participant in the history and reality that it purports to also represent. This participatory capacity of the moving image concludes this chapter with an investigation of spectatorship in Guerín's 2007 works, *En la ciudad de Sylvia/In the City of Sylvia*, *Unas fotos en la ciudad de Sylvia/Some Photos in the City of Sylvia* and the photographs that constituted the installation *Las mujeres que no conocemos/Women we Don't Know*.

Film as Document

When Maxim Gorky saw the Lumière brothers' film in Moscow in 1896 he observed:

> Last night I was in the Kingdom of Shadows. It is terrifying to see, but it is the movement of shadows, only of shadows . . . Suddenly something clicks, everything vanishes and a train appears on the screen. It speeds straight at you – watch out! It seems as though it will plunge into the darkness in which you sit, turning you into a ripped sack full of lacerated flesh and splintered bones, and crushing into dust and broken fragments this hall and this building, so full of women, wine, music and vice. But this, too, is just a train of shadows. (Leyda 1960: 407–408)

The excited exclamation, which warns the reader about the approaching train, perfectly encapsulates the exhilaration and involvement provoked by this nascent art form. The perceived threat to the audience which induces such a charged reaction anticipates the focus on embodied responses to cinema that are so much a part of Guerín's style. The director's choice of title for his 1997 cinematic essay *Tren de sombras/Train of Shadows* clearly takes inspiration from Gorky's evaluation of this early moving image. The style and concern of Guerín's work interweaves the concerns of early moving image practitioners and theorists on cinema's role in the recording and representation of the world around us with a concern for the inherent interest of the image, a combination that is sure to be tricky when it comes to documentary. Since this early work the term documentary has come to distinguish those moving image productions which record the world as it is from cinema that has become a form of mass entertainment, tainted perhaps with an idea that it does not engage seriously with the matters of the day that are more properly the concern of documentary. I would argue that Guerín revises this dichotomous formula in order to re-enchant the everyday, suggesting that a poetics of documentary comes through its observance of the everyday and that this too can have a responsible ethical commitment.

Documentary's complex claims to authenticity are compounded by the ontological debates surrounding cinema's status as index and its direct link to the pro-filmic event, something that the examination of *Train of Shadows* develops below. This has a tricky relationship to Spain's history in terms of its fascist past and the use of documentary to further the Francoist myth. Marsha Kinder has written an excellent study of the emergence and style of the documentary tradition in Spain, outlining its developments as it tried to break free from the shackles of this ideological legacy:

> As in other cultural contexts, the documentary or actualities was one of the first genres to emerge in Spain – one that could be used to assert the cultural distinctiveness of the nation or local region, particularly as it gained access to an advanced technology imported from the outside. The Spanish documentary genre quickly became associated with questions of local identity and the dialectics of insiders versus outsiders, issues that acquire new levels of political resonance in subsequent periods. (1997: 66)

Kinder's piece makes an excellent case for the ideological connotations of documentary that were the inevitable consequence of the Franco dictatorship's legacy of the *Noticias Documentales*.[1] She points to an emergent self-reflexivity that was the result of attempts to reclaim the cinematic document from a population used to its propagandistic capacity.

Guerín's project acknowledges and cites this rich history of documentary tradition and his aesthetic style seems a logical progression to the one described by Kinder. His approach to cinematic creativity is didactic and asserts a pronounced awareness of tradition, and in many ways the regressive tradition of documentary as closely bound to fascism (in twentieth-century Spain) enables Guerín's more creative approach. His acute awareness of the genealogy of moving images is concerned above all with their aestheticism, their lyrical potential and their narrative quality. *En construcción* presents this mediated reality at its most poetic and evocative, engaging with city and body and the fading materiality of film. *Train of Shadows* had initiated this preoccupation with materiality in its relationship to memory playing with the contrasts between a permanent version of visually captured memory and a different kind of residual memory captured by the very materiality of our sentient bodies. *In the City of Sylvia* and its discrete yet related productions *Some Photos in the City of Sylvia* and the exhibition of photographs *Women We Don't Know* move this argument towards an emerging trend, the intermedial production that demonstrates a marked preference for the construction of the image and the significance of its materiality and the shifting patterns of subjectivity evinced by this new variety of cinematic flânerie, in a mode that constructs a sentient active spectator.

The epistemology of the image is also challenged as the move from *Train of Shadows* to *En construcción* sees an engagement with the new technology of digital video, and the final three works I look at explore the intersections between photography and moving image media.

The claims to authenticity that it is assumed are irrevocably bound to mimetic representation of the pro-filmic event and, in the case of documentary, associated with a representable truth are intertwined with the debate that surrounds this digital turn. Portable, cheap technology facilitates documentary filmmaking but digital editing technology heightens a concern for the truth and veracity of this genre. The concern with a lost indexicality that is frequently invoked is assumed to be the manifestation of this technological shift.[2] The decelerated pace of these films points to their roots in photography which raises the spectre once more of the index, yet the celluloid for Guerín is not simply deictic, as worthy of the reality which it can properly record; it is also a material whose texture and tactile qualities make it worthy of visual representation itself through the digital manipulation that he has at his disposal. Thus the layers of representation are interrogated as the visibility of the world is subject to constant review in these films. He moves the debate beyond the limited conception of truth versus fiction and sees technology as revelatory and participatory and, in this, as part of reality that we live and experience in multiple ways.

Between Stasis and Motion: *Tren de sombras* (1997)

The way in which we experience the world through the visual representations that technology enables is both the subject and the stuff of these films. That is to say that the changing material conditions provide a sort of interim space between technologies that is particularly suited to Guerín's aesthetic. This transition of visual technologies from one to the next is reminiscent, although perhaps less gradual, of a similar progression from photography to film, from the static image to the dynamic version.

Inscribed within all of these films is a concern with the representability of time and the unique temporality of cinema. This works in many ways but there are two that are particularly relevant to this reading of *Train of Shadows*. The first is the historicity of the medium and its value as a container of history and, as a result of this, the anxiety surrounding the denigration of the medium, as celluloid literally disintegrates before our eyes. The second relates to the development of the medium and the way in which the moving image is uniquely placed to examine its own construction of time. Guerín highlights both of these processes through the inclusion of the photographs and apparently disintegrating film strips in *Train of Shadows,* relegating the concern with documentary and authenticity to second place as he prioritizes the affective capacity of the image to engage a spectator through this apparently attenuated pace.[3]

In 2003 Michel Ciment identified a turn towards a 'cinema of slowness, of contemplation' (2003). This debate has been taken up by a number of film critics and scholars and I don't wish to rehash these positions here.[4] But it can certainly be noted that those directors who preference a decelerated rhythm frequently do so in an attempt to make us examine the way in which time is at work in cinema.

The preoccupation with the stopping of the image – as if in its stillness we are able to extract more meaning – has been facilitated by the emergence of DVD, and the revised ontology of the moving image negotiates the confluence here of medium and the technique it appears to give rise to: since the adoption of DVD as a prolific technology in domestic film consumption some productions seem to have adopted its capacity for pause in the aesthetic of the films themselves. Laura Mulvey's work will shed more light on this onto-logical shift in the latter part of my examination of this film. For now, however, the pertinence of this type of examination lies in its preoccupation with con-templation, the image itself, our engagement with it and the assumed mean-ings inherent in these images.

Perhaps in a market where attention is held by benign and frequently pre-dictable plotlines then a slow moving Proustian investigation, such as is *Train of Shadows,* into cinematic memories, visuality and its limits – but also its vast potential – may be neither marketable nor attractive even to the most erudite of film spectators. Guerín's eulogy to celluloid and his homage to the versatil-ity of the materiality of film as it relates to cultural memory – and also in its remarkable capacity to evoke embodied experience – is a tribute to the very craft explored in this piece.

It is a difficult film to adequately describe. It begins as an elegy to the dis-appearing medium as apparently corroding celluloid is projected accompa-nied by Debussy's *L'après midi d'un faune.* The shapes that we discern are those of children playing and adults watching them, with a large house in the back-ground. Pre-titles inform us that these are the recovered family films of Gerard Fleury and that they are retrieved and replayed thanks to the collaboration of the Fleury family. Interspersed with these shots are long takes of the pres-ent day, presumably the same house and the same region. These sections are typified by a static camera and a preference for recording the comings and go-ings of the area.[5] Domestic scenes in the opening of the film are then mirrored by the interior shots of houses and gardens – devoid of human inhabitants – throughout the rest of the piece.

These staged 'historical' images set up an investigation of authenticity and acknowledge and problematize the term as it relates to memories, histories and visual media here. They become a representation by proxy for the imag-ined family life of the Fleury family. They also raise questions as to the inherent imitation that may be a part of every cinematic image and the status of the image in its permanence and transience – an apparent series of contradictions that I shall examine more fully below.

Guerín's concern in this work is with the image as both memory and archive. This is not to privilege the subjectivity of one over the – presumed

– objectivity of the other but rather to call into question the way in which both are created, and the contribution that the moving image can make to this archive, a material of memory and also an ephemeral (in the form of digital) storage bank. Marsha Kinder's excellent study has related its inherent marginality – both the subject matter and the peripheral position of this French family and the geographical locus in France – to the marginality of the director himself. There must be an evocation of the relationship between the disappearance of the nation perhaps and the disappearance of the image, its potential to fade and be destroyed. The disappearance of Gérard Fleury, which provides the narrative framework for Guerín's elaboration of his family life, makes for a spectral presence that compounds the theme of disappearance and transience which pervades the piece. Furthermore, this disappearance took place in 1930, less than a decade prior to the outbreak of World War II. The political situation in Europe, but particularly in France, was dominated by anxiety about the status of the nation and the threat posed by the loss of empire and culture. The primary concern, however, would seem to go deeper than a superficial thematic relationship between the altered significance of the nation and the fading of the celluloid. As Kinder observes, 'Perhaps the connection between the Thuit region of France makes more sense in the new macro-regional context of a transnational European cinema, where the nation is under erasure' (2003: 20).

This may indeed be part of this director's project. There is a more positive reading of this, which dwells less on the ambiguities which surround the problematic configuration of the nation in the twenty-first century and revels in the freedom of interpretation enabled by the fading image. Rather than edit out these corroded images, re-ordering them or restoring them to show only those that remain in good condition, Guerín takes pleasure, and invites the spectator to do likewise, in the new shapes, textures and narratives which are the product of this degradation.

He intersperses these 'original' images with long slow takes in the present and refuses to cloud the image with unnecessary dialogue or narrative explanation. The commentary on the nation's place in this sequence of images is therefore enhanced and altered by a process of suggestion and connotative interpretation. The nation is a concept that might fade but in its fading takes on a new form which has at its centre a new type of freedom, distancing itself from the ties that previously bound it. Choosing marginal subjects for study, as he also does in *En construcción,* provides a further comment on the power of cinema to create and make visible and on the transmission of experience, rather than the didactic form of documentary, opening a new interpretive space at the edges.

The disappearing image is made visible by its reinsertion in this new context and the white patches that mar the clarity of these opening images are imbued with a dual function as they open the film. Choosing to present these indistinct and shadowy images on screen before any explanation or coherent image sequencing evinces this dual function and significance. We will later realize that these are imitations of the result of corrosion of old films, but at this moment, though, they are abstract shapes evoking rich colours and textures in the manner of an abstract art form, imbued with the added interest of movement by virtue of the medium in which they are included.

They are complex in that they must on the one hand be considered as index and on the other hand, in their abstraction, they are available to further layers of interpretation and as an image with their own inherent visual interest. Given their inherently abstract form, they are of greater significance to the art of cinema, where semiotics is a troubled method by which to delve for meaning, and the beauty of the image can sometimes be as important as its ideological import. They are a visual representation of the destruction of the passing of time and as such reminders of the complex temporal logic at work in cinema. More than this they are also contradictory images, which at once represent transience and the impermanence of being and yet in this form are immortalized in their cinematic incarnation.[6] They embody a tension between the Bazinian conception of cinema's capacity to freeze time, a tendency that runs the risk of fetishizing the moment, and its apparently contradictory potential to transform reality, through the literally changing medium of the film but also through the divergent temporalities that are ushered in through this mode of address.

Guerín constructs within this film, a dialogue between past and present, old and new, and between what it is that constitutes the image and what is left out, as gaps and elisions.[7] These blotches and blurrings at the beginning are thus metonymic of his aesthetic project. When we view the sequences of footage of the Fleury family it becomes apparent that these strange shapes are what is not there, the fragments that age has destroyed, yet they create a unique aesthetic which is richly suggestive of the same process at work in cultural memory and the ideological project which must always bubble under the surface in the production of cinematic time and space.

It is perhaps more than coincidental that the year in which *Train of Shadows* was released coincided with the first marketing of digitally formatted films. Layering of sound and image draws attention to the way in which stillness can be made dynamic and meaning comes to reside in images thanks to the way in which they are (technologically) manipulated and then viewed. The relationship between photography and the moving image is made explicit by Guerín's choice of long contemplative takes in the latter section of the film effected in the present day, imitating the muted colours of the sepia in the first half of the piece. The employment of a static camera allies these images with the family portraits which, in their recording by the present day cinema camera, reveal the process by which this same camera takes a series of stills and imbues them with movement due to the technology which it has at its disposal.

The first part of the film which projects the footage of the Fleury family investigates the nostalgic function of cinema and its voyeuristic potential in so much as it has the ability to make the private public. As a commentary on the creation of history and memory and the public or private nature of both, the destroyed images are an example of the fragility of records, and they call into question the ability to preserve and recount history. The use of these images draws attention to the historicity of the gaze celluloid 'bore within it and produced for its spectator, a respect for the resistances and thereness of historicity, for that which leaks out and cannot be contained within the notion of semiosis. Its promise is that of touching the real' (Doane 2007: 146–148).

Guerín's precision and attention to detail in this film force us to consider the relationship between the index and the authentic, and the way in which these relate to the scrutiny of history. As the camera trains its lens on a maid in an upstairs room she waves coquettishly and then closes the window and retreats before the camera removes its gaze. The awareness of the camera's presence, which has an effect on any documentary's unstaged quality, is here revealed, as is the feature of exposition and concealment mirrored by the closing window.

The segments of family life depicted here play a part in a personal history as well as a wider history of cinema. The sequence in which Guerín constructs this montage and the choice of the inter-titles guide our viewing and initially make us aware of the intimacy of the scenes we are watching, as though we were prying on a happy family life. The use of inter-titles acknowledges the history of silent cinema and its place (in its time) in the history of cinematic innovation:

> *Tren* marshals a diverse series of layered contexts and complex recon-structions for recuperating and reinterpreting scant filmic remnants ravaged by decay, and shows how this found footage can be recontextualized within several regimes of knowledge to generate very different kinds of meaning about the mysterious disappearance of the auteur, the cultural and historical specificity of this particular region of France, the materiality and fragility of the film medium, the respective values of film preservation and historical representation, the history of European silent cinema, the nature of memory and history, and the permeability of boundaries between genres and all other bordered domains. (Kinder 2003: 17)

Laura Mulvey's investigation of stillness in cinema takes the form of a reflection on the ontology of the image and the manner in which this is affected by the way in which it has been created and what it consequently represents. This informs my reading of Guerín as they are both ultimately concerned with the way in which the image itself and the technology behind it invite a certain type of engagement with this image. Returning to Marsha Kinder, this type of encounter comes about as a result of the challenging structure of the piece:

> In fact *Train of Shadows* is one of several experimental non-linear European films from the 1990s that enable us to imagine new modes of interactive spectatorship – through expanded forms of montage, database, structures and simulations of randomness, a combination that generates new narrative pleasures. (2003: 21)

Both Kinder and Mulvey suggest that there is something inherent in the construction of the film that necessitates a more active spectatorship in order that we may properly interact with these images. Mulvey makes recourse to Barthes and his assertion that film cannot engage him in the way that photography can precisely because in its movement it is 'elusive'. New technology makes cinema's roots in stillness explicit and, for Mulvey, this creates an illusive return to the image that apparently embodies time and therefore articulates its own mortality (2006: 66). I would take this further, arguing that Guerín enriches the image through his recourse to further sensory pleasure and that it is in the invocation of both memory and experience, triggered by the image but drawing on other sensory and experiential modes of relationship to the cinematic, that the sophistication of this director's work is to be found.

The interconnectedness of the elements in this early film locates the significant tropes that are foregrounded and extended in the section on *En construcción*. The focus on that documentary and its perhaps slightly weightier treatment in this chapter is testament to its place as a nexus of ideological import with regards to alternative depictions of the edge and the periphery initiated by *Train of Shadows*, in particular the sensory and the experiential in relation to the changing nature of the cinematic and the emphasis on uniting and interpreting the various temporal structures that this mode of filmmaking explores.

Cinema's Past, Present and Future

The process of film preservation and the evidence of the effect of decay on the physical entity of the film itself allows for the invocation of a direct physical interaction with the film's material. This physical alteration of the celluloid strips changes their appearance on the screen and alters the surface textures and the graininess that we see when we view these images. Like the shadow of the title, the projection is a mark of an actual material and moving presence. The links then, between the shadow and the body which it projects, and the image and the film from which it derives, are synergetic, actual and persistent at the same time as imaginary and fleeting.

A further physical interaction with the material of film is its ordering and cutting which, transforming the original recording into a sequential narrative, alters the form and content in a way which has been extensively examined for its ideological import. Editing is a process of stopping and starting, of selecting sequences of images that then become a moving sequence. The process of editing is the epitome of the image in the process of becoming. It is also a further temporal layer in the complex folds of the film.

Controlling the rhythm of the sequences of images, as well as disrupting their temporal and linear progression, creates a new type of engagement. The image selection in documentary has a heightened power in that, along with editing, it becomes the main means by which a director can influence the shape that the film takes. Guerín's long static camera shots appear to resist an overbearing method of control. Shortly after the switch is made from "old" images to the present day in the film, there is a shot of a café taken from across the road at eye level which lasts for over a minute during which time there is no dialogue or extra diegetic sound. This type of shot is a precursor to many similar ones in *En construcción*. It also sets up a distinct rhythm to this piece; movement and stillness are used to control the dynamism of each scene.

The static camera emphasizes the moving world that is being recorded. On many occasions movement occurs only when people, animals and vehicles enter and leave the frame. The body's motility is highlighted by this technique and the camera becomes the disinterested observer. The pace of this section adds a further – and distinctly marked – contrast to the pace of the initial section. The ostensibly speeded up version of the "old" film races the spectator through a much more rapid succession of images, less open to prolonged contemplation due to this sometimes dizzying speed.[8] The indistinction and reduced quality of the images adds to this effect of disorientation. In contrast the ponderous takes in the present draw us into the spaces of the recording through eye-level camera work and diegetic sound.

Apart from the representation of history in the reconstructed footage that forms the first part of the film, the manipulation of the film's progression also alludes to a unique filmic temporality. The reconstruction of the Fleury family footage has already motioned in the theme of memory, history, the passing of time and film's ability to alter these notions. At times Guerín's piece appears to teeter not only on the boundary of fiction and document, past and present, but also between complicated conceits that surround a cinematic construction of temporality and the way in which it can be understood and represented. The way in which subjectivity is defined within a certain understanding of time means that these cinematic investigations affect the subject's place within this type of cinema.

This new type of subjectivity drives the investigation. Guerín offers moments for contemplation of the image that are apparently out of time. One such moment is evidenced part way through the piece in the final section of the 'old' footage where Guerín skilfully combines a sequence of images that carefully contain details through which the main themes come to the fore.

The medium long shot is of three trees taken with a static camera. Little by little figures walk into the shot from right to left appearing as little more than silhouettes because of the muted, grey lighting. Visually they echo both the train – albeit in a human form – and the shadows of the title. All of the following shots contain either trains or shadows. After the trees and the silhouettes comes a repetition of a recording of a man carrying what appear to be a briefcase and an umbrella, running through a sloping cornfield. This shot is played five times, each time slightly differently. At the end of each shot one or two young boys join the man. In each of these differing shots a steam train passes – from left to right – in the background.

As is so often the case with this director the importance of the scene lies in the way in which the image is constructed and its persistent residual ambiguity or potentiality. A probing investigation into the uncertainties of cinematic representations of history inevitably takes into account the way in which time is represented by this medium. The passing of time and the immortalisation of events on the screen provoke questions of authenticity and point of view – whose history is this and by whom is it represented? Guerín blurs the divi-

Figure 4.1. Found footage? People and trees in *Tren de sombras* (1997), by José Luis Guerín. Courtesy of Pere Portabella - Films 59 y Grup Cinema Art, S.L.

sion between the 'then' of the screen and the 'now' of the viewing time by calling into question the stability of the image and the reliability of it as historical
document. He does not do this with the intention of undermining the validity
of cinematic accounts of history but rather intends that the latent versatility of
cinema should be explored when such representations are embarked upon.

Cinema as a Creative Archive

As Mary Anne Doane investigates the phenomena of cinematic temporality
she examines the idea of contingency in relation to the subject's relation to
the historical image:

> Film seems to respond to the dilemma of the representability of time
> with an easy affirmation. The indexicality of the cinematic sign appears
> as the guarantee of its status as a record of temporality outside itself – a
> pure time or duration which would not be that of its own functioning.
> This is what imbues cinematic time with historicity. Because it seems
> to function first and foremost as a record of what happens in front of
> the camera, the cinema emerges from and contributes to the archival
> impulse of the nineteenth century. In it, images are stored, time itself is
> stored. (2002: 23)

Guerín, as we have already examined, has undermined the security of the
relationship between index and meaning, and now he moves this into an interrogation of the idea of the record. Doane's examination here of course refers
to the nineteenth-century notion of the cinema as a means of storing time.
The relevance of this to the way in which Guerín chooses to work is that it is
precisely in deconstructing these notions that he is able to acknowledge the
beauty of traditional cinematic form and, at the same time, call it into question
by the subtle reformulation of the traditional image.

So many elements of this piece refer to the difficulty of temporal specificity and elect instead for freedom of movement between two time frames. As
with the fluidity of the tactile and the visual epitomized by *En construcción*,
Train of Shadows constitutes a formal and narrative betrayal of recognized
temporal structures in order to allow a space for the subject to move between

times and question the way in which they are to be formed by the creation of the moving image.

The sequence of shots which frame a collection of doors and windows, entries and exits, places of movement across boundaries, visually represents that same movement between temporal structures that cinema enables. Guerín's cinematic intentions are rich and varied but at this point we return once more to the driving force behind both of these cinematic essays; the enabling function of cinema as a vehicle for new ways of contemplation. The unfinished element of the film is the means by which we are forced to engage with these works in different ways. In these sequences of frames within frames the soundtrack creates further elisions, mirroring the visual gaps on screen; sporadic inclusion of classical music at apparently random points during this sequence disrupts the conventional function of music in film as the interruptions of music call into question the cohesive unification of sound and image, and the layers involved in the completion of the image are again peeled back.

The final shot of a frame is that of a mirror and a clock. Precisely at the moment where the possibility of an accurate reflection of time may be pos-

Figure 4.2. Clock and mirror in *Tren de sombras* (1997), by José Luis Guerín. Courtesy of Pere Portabella – Films 59 y Grup Cinema Art, S.L.

sible, the image underlines a playful side to the excessive self-reflexivity of this author. The same humour and minute observance of details (also clearly present throughout *En construcción*) results in an extended contemplation of a lone sheep in a garden. As the sheep stands next to a children's play house staring into the camera and then looking into the door of the house, the awareness of our own relationship to this image is underlined and humorously debunked.

As with the rest of the piece a mobile camera is dismissed in preference for the static recording that accentuates the mobility of the subject and the constructedness of the image. A long shot taken from behind a washing line of hanging white laundry observes as (presumably) the same sheep wanders through the garden, at some distance from the washing line. The sheets on the line function as stage curtains, allowing this ovine protagonist to enter a miniaturized frame within that frame and leave it by disappearing behind another sheet. There is a sentimental humour in this contemplation as once more this director demonstrates a preference for those marginal subjects that are not usually permitted such extended screen time.

We are repeatedly surprised by detail, by the peripheral making its presence felt in unlikely ways. Establishing this technique, as I have observed, involves overt scrutiny of the cinematic apparatus and a concomitant on-screen revelation of its mechanisms. Nonetheless, rather than diminishing the exotic beauty of the image, these meticulously selected fragments of aged films elucidate cinema's continued attraction as they threaten to disappear behind the blotches that dissimulate the ravages of time. It is precisely these marks that arouse the curiosity in the capacity of the image to conceal as much as it reveals. Desire functions through these images by tantalising with part images and inviting a curious spectator to engage with this partial image and in so doing implicates them as a further layer of meaning in the intersubjective spaces of these films. This in turn both undermines, but also relegates as less important, the capacity of cinema to accurately relate historiographical detail and highlights its capacity to reorder and reimagine the archive, which is of particular import of course in those cases of marginalisation where history has not been written. History is an elliptical narrative which acknowledges that its own omissions, particularly memory and personal histories, are better served by the creative narrative capacity of this kind of cinema, at least Guerín would appear to believe.

At roughly the mid-point of *Train of Shadows* there is a sequence in which Guerín returns to the 'old' footage, but this time overlays the images of the film with the sound of a projector. Previous to this the young girl on a swing looks intently into the camera challenging with a prolonged gaze which is obscured in fragments by the blotches that overlay these images. Temporal ruptures within the film work against a fluid and linear imagining of narrative here in order to suggest the episodic structure of memory. The time and space of this film that breaks and then rejoins with itself, thanks to the process of filming, as such cannot be seen to follow any linear progression nor any logical spatial journey.[9]

Of course recollecting, replaying and revisiting moments in the past is the function of memory. Guerín is a filmmaker who prefers these horizontal structures that privilege the ambiguity of different realms of cultural knowledge and specifically in this piece the multi-layered temporality that necessarily invokes the difficulty of concrete representations of memory and history. To highlight the skilful editing at work here or to refer to the juxtapositions of times and spaces employed to create meaning to criticize established structures of meaning does little more than extend Eisenstein's theories of montage. Whilst the 'collisions' between shots that Eisenstein referred to are certainly in evidence there is a greater reliance on gaps and suggestion, evoking several possible interpretations as they move between several different temporalities.

Train of Shadows is littered with motifs that remind us of the passing of time – the clocks and the deliberately recorded signs of the seasonal passing (many shots of the outside and of trees with leaves in their varying seasonal stages.) Yet the existence of the reconstructed archive images are the epitome of the way in which time can be halted, slowed down and revisited. The use of decelerated images that might evoke the photographic image illustrates how these developing technologies partake in discussions about history and the archive. This is aptly explained by Lutz Koepnick in relation to photography and memory:

The most essential question is therefore not how different technological inventions *cause* different representations of temporality, but how we place certain images – digital or analogue – in larger narratives of history and memory; how we make use of both their formal inventory and exhibition in order to connect different pasts and presents; how we rely on different strategies of naming, description and inscription, of discursive en-framing, in order to infuse them with temporal texture or pass them off as souvenirs of frozen time; and last but not least, how we engage with older myths of reference, objectivity and truth in order to define the relationships between image-makers, photographic subjects, and viewers as relationships of either asymmetrical authority or mutual recognition. (2004: 101)

In this sense the still photographs (and the almost static cinematic images that resemble photographic images) are objects, which partake in the texture of time in these films. Objects are a crucial element of this cineaste's work and his interest in them is twofold. The filmed object becomes an example of the transformative capacity of film, contemplation via the camera adding a new signification to an apparently quotidian event. The Proustian bent of *Train of Shadows* arises from its excavation of personal memory and the fractured yet creative rendition of individual scenes from this recorded memory.

The trees that provide a visual anchor in the scene I mention above are an example of the Proustian object and its use as a trigger for speculation in the field of personal memory. Nonetheless, whilst the evocation of Proust's narrator's memory relies on its phenomenological function invoked by a sensory experience, Guerín's memories are not shared but imagined and are not personal but form part of a cinematic representation, a recreated reality. In that sense the objects as framed by Guerín must be assumed to have a universal appeal which is able to transcend the specificity of the taste of Proust's *madeleine* and its propensity to bring to mind only a specific and highly personal childhood memory.

One effect of this alternative engagement (in opposition to mere contemplation of objects) is a move away from the negative connotations of objectivity that reside in its cinematic usage. As if to reflect the fluidity between other apparently oppositional elements, already outlined, this amorphousness between subject and object reinscribes the photographs and films with a subjective space and gaze that permits them the dual function in this context, as material artifacts that are fading and changing and as representations of a people and a past. This is the image and object status of the photograph that interests Elizabeth Edwards, who states, 'the photograph has always existed not merely as an image but in relation to the human body, tactile in experienced time, objects functioning within everyday practice' (2009: 228).

In fact, this newly positive function of the object is epitomized by the protagonist/photographer, Gérard Fleury, and thus the subject of *Tren* who becomes Guerín's filmed object in his re-ordering and re-editing of these photographs and their modern additions. It is the flexibility of cinema's temporal structure that allows this type of transience between subject and object and thus enables a redefinition of centre and periphery. The choice of the everyday things and the emphasis on the transformative power of cinema upon these everyday objects sits at the heart of the cinematic project as perceived at its inception and returns us to the investigation of cinema's earliest documentary project. Paolo Cherchi Usai's work on the material status of film and its integration into the digital age theorizes the project that Guerín makes visual in this piece. As Cherchi Usai explains:

> Travel, leisure, hilarious or notable occurrences are at the origins of the moving image. More precisely, moving images arise out of an intent to transform into an object whatever is forgettable and therefore doomed to decay and oblivion. The impermanence of these events finds its empirical counterpart in the moving image and determines its status as an artifact. (2001: 65)

The marginality of this project to a tradition of cinema in Spain is located primarily and most apparently through the choice of subject matter and geographical location, as Kinder has examined. There are also links between the creation of memory from traces and objects which is metonymic of a similar process of recuperation currently taking place in Spain and which I examine more fully elsewhere.[10]

With this in mind genre is an important feature of this style of filmmaking. I have broadly assumed that the works I look at here can fit within the category of documentary. Kinder has explored manipulation of generic convention throughout *Train of Shadows* and Guerín's resulting success at side-lining the importance of its habitual restrictions. The director himself has discussed the constraints of screenplay and dialogue – more readily associated with fiction – to the finished cinematic product, referring inevitably to the imperative of narrative progression:

> En la mayoría de las películas de ahora, si hay pensamiento se circunscribe únicamente al guión, que ejerce un despotismo cruel. Se piensa

en el guión y después el rodaje y el montaje se ejecutan metódica-
mente, como algo ya previsto. No se deja nada al azar. (In most contemporary films if there is thought it is limited to the script, which can
exert a tyrannical sway. Thinking is done in the script and then filming
and editing are carried out methodically, as though preordained. Nothing is left to chance.)[11] (Wonenburger 2004)

Both *Train of Shadows* and *En construcción* elicit a combination of the freedom which this lack of a script and screenplay entails and revel in documentary as a means of explicitly problematizing the way in which historical events
can be recorded. Guerín's place as a marginal filmmaker situated in a Catalan,
Spanish and European tradition, with all of the prevailing conditions of this
heterogeneous identity, allows him precisely to exploit these shifting certainties and shaky definitions. Such a strategy is expressed by Bill Nichols who
sums up this aesthetic of productive gaps and elisions perfectly and moves us
neatly into an exploration of the engagement with the documentary image in
En construcción:

Traditionally, the word documentary has suggested fullness and completion, knowledge and fact, explanations of the social world and its mo-
tivating mechanisms. More recently, though, documentary has come to
suggest incompleteness and uncertainty, recollection and impression,
images of personal worlds and their subjective construction. (1994: 1)

The screen image and its lack of clarity in *Train of Shadows* reflect the obfus-
cation of clarity and meaning that this work at the boundary of fiction and
nonfiction and between the past and present gives rise to. In the following
section the temporality finds itself inscribed within a space that exceeds the
visual grasp of the documentary image.

At the Margins of the City in *En construcción* (2001)

Films of the city have a long history. From the early city symphonies and Ver-
tov's *Man with a Movie Camera* (1929) there has been an understanding that
the modernity of the urban environment was eminently suitable for depiction

by a similarly modern art form. The city, like the cinema, privileges the visual. It encourages its own consumption through visual means whilst offering its streets as a place of performance. Yet this interest, as Benjamin speculates, goes beyond mere pleasure for the eye; it is the lived experience of these cities that continues to fascinate: 'Wherever asphalt workers hang their coats on iron railings, that's their hall; and the gateway that leads from the row of court-yards into the open is the entrance into the chambers of the city' (1929: 262). The two films that are the focus of discussion for the remainder of this chapter move into these urban environments and to a degree interrogate the more traditional representations of the urban. They engage with the inhabitation that privileges motility and contact. In the latter film, *In the City of Sylvia,* this investigation into the possibilities of cinematic dynamism has come to inflect the possibility that the medium itself may be made dynamic as the cinema, in the form of installation, literally breaks free from the confines of the frame.

Examination of urban space has typically focussed on contact, even con-tamination, which typifies our inability to escape the urban milieu. Nonethe-less, in Benjamin's articulation of this truth about the inhabited city he also stresses the immanent democracy of space therein. Guerín exploits the lim-inality of this area and the camera's ability to adopt a position of cohabitation rather than solely observation to explore the tactile potential of this environ-ment, emphasising the lived bodily experience of these documentary subjects. The edge here is doubly marked: Barcelona itself is a peripheral location and here we have a peripheral neighbourhood in Barcelona. But Guerín locates the positive potential of this edge in its inevitable contact with a new space. Trapped between the old and the new, the inside and the outside, the inhabit-ants of this area are dislocated and marginalized but in a combination of a sen-sory, inclusive and democratic vision of life in Barcelona; in his documentary the clear-cut division is problematized through a combination of innovative filmic technique, underlining the unique physicality of this experience as well as the very tangible contours of the urban environment.

With a distinctively fluid cinematography and observance of the minute details of every day life Guerín invites a new impression of the significance of Barcelona's infamous *barrio chino* through a repeated confluence and meld-ing which emerges by means of a filmic language which, I will suggest, can be read as haptic in quality. As was suggested in the case of Bigas Luna, the formal properties which invite this type of reading have as their basis a refusal to delimit strict boundaries between city and body as the intimacy they share becomes a central focus of the film.

An ideological project subtends the director's concentration on the horizontal democracy of a city that resists external, vertical attempts to impose meaning. On a more aesthetical level, the ability of cinema to represent these alternative modes of being within this context centres on the relationship of the body to the city.

To return to the earlier debate on slow cinema and the creation of narrative within documentary, a genre that presumably relies on the accurate depiction of events rather than the external imposition of meaning, we witness in this instance how Guerín acknowledges this in his treatment of narrative within the diegesis. Anticipation of a denouement, or a significant event that will propel the action is resisted – indeed inverted – as long takes emphasize contemplation and reflection as opposed to action. Indeed, the editing makes deliberate use of temporal ellipses as little by little the building of the cinematic sequence mirrors the construction of the buildings depicted. Significantly, the omnipresent clock on the Banco de Bilbao in the Plaça de Catalunya serves as a graphic reminder of chronological time in its relentless passing. The subject's powerlessness in the face of temporal flux resonates with the wider concerns of the work and its empathy with its impotent dwellers in the face of this development. This echoes the preoccupation as manifested in *Train of Shadows* with the complex temporalities of cinema.

Cinematic Flânerie in the *Raval*

Guerín limits his scope to this small neighbourhood in the city of Barcelona with its own particular historical and ideological significance. *El chino*, a densely populated urban area, and the section of *El Raval* closest to the port, is significant for its transient population, its openness to outside influences and its multicultural population.[12] The director evokes a neighbourhood inscribed with multiple ideological meanings, a conflicting site that has been variously appropriated to serve political ends. The area is thus a microcosm of Barcelona itself whose construction was as much ideological as it was architectural as, from the Restoration onwards, the *bourgeoisie conquérante* exerted its hegemony in urbanistic terms not only by exacting political control over the working class areas but also by imbuing 'their' metropolis with a Catalan sensibility in their own image and likeness.[13]

Spectatorship in this film is severely compromised and afforded a foundation as shaky as the crumbling buildings which are depicted throughout as, once again, vision maintains an uncertain relationship with understanding and Guerín posits new ways to transmit the experience of life in this *barrio* of this city.

Joan Ramon Resina has shown himself sensitive to Guerín's questioning of the fundamentals of such orthodox means of depiction and asserts poignantly that this film is 'an extended metaphor on the instability of the visible' (2008: 257). The implications are, of course, significant. If the visible is unstable then our appreciation of film which has traditionally been bonded to this very realm is evidently to be severely compromised.

> Guerín's tribute to a lost dwelling through an extended view of its deconstruction is also an allegory of the fading of the transcendental subjectivity that used to guarantee the lucidity and cohesion of the image-world from its position behind the camera. Now the classic subject, no longer secure in the pre-empirical categories of time and space, disintegrates and ceases to ground the image. (2008: 257)

It is productive to illustrate this dialectic with reference to the distinction between *voyeur* and *flâneur* as posited by De Certeau in the context of the city. For this commentator, the only way to see the city was to remove oneself from it: literally to rise above its contaminating influences to a place where 'one's body is no longer clasped by the streets' (1984: 92). Within the city there is little opportunity for individuality: at least no hope of the separation necessary in order to begin to comprehend the conurbation of which the inhabitants are an integral part. Cinema, however, with its supposed privileged viewing condition exemplified by the possibilities of the elevated, distanced perspective is able to render this superior detachment denied the voyeur. In fact, it is a primary position, which is repeated throughout this film.

However, De Certeau appears to predict Guerín's critical revision of the artificiality or untenability of the conventional totalising vision and illustrates this with reference to his *flâneur*. The loss of vision is not, however, entirely negative as it also opens up new and varied means of appreciation, even appropriation, of the urban text. In this case, a more satisfactory relationship between city and subject involves a seeping, an exchange and an interdependence taking place at the edges and which is part of a transient relationship, which seems to fall very much into line with the Catalan's cinematic depiction:[14]

> The ordinary practitioners of the city live 'down below', below the thresholds at which visibility begins. They walk – an elementary form of this experience of the city; they are walkers, *Wandersmänner, whose bodies follow the thicks and thins of an urban 'text'* they write without being able to read it. These practitioners make use of spaces that cannot be seen; their knowledge of them is as blind as that of lovers in each other's arms. (Certeau 1984: 93) [emphasis mine]

The image of 'lovers in each other's arms' anticipates a remarkably similar recent exploration of haptic visuality by Laura Marks. She employs the same metaphor to evoke the tactile potential of film in relation to experience saying, 'it is hard to look closely at a lover's skin with optical vision' (2002: 3). Marks acknowledges the importance of the visual but believes it to be most effective in its complementary relationship with the sensual. *Flânerie* demands a more dynamic, sensorial engagement with the physical space of the city than can be experienced through sight. And Guerín's subjects are certainly *flâneurs* in their city, more specifically in their *barrio*.

Moving through Time and Space

The opening of this film with its traditional situating shot, taken from black and white archive footage, entices us with its voyeuristic potential. As in *Train of Shadows* this engagement with the physical history of a cinematic past alerts us to the meta-cinematic references that pervade both texts. Subsequent cuts lower our perspective so that we are suddenly looking up at these chimneys and down once more to the upper echelons of a street, as if looking at the scene from a balcony: an observation of the people who inhabit the street below (a technique which Guerín mimics in much of his own filming). Finally we are lowered, with the camera, into the throes of the crowds milling around this notorious district. The streets are full of people coming and going, entering and leaving bars. Prostitutes and their clients leave cheap hotels and the area is presented as being full of life and movement.

At this point the camera is still relatively static, allowing us the expected distance between spectator and filmic subject. However, the final sequence of this archive footage assumes the position of one of these city dwellers as it begins to move amongst them following a lone and apparently inebriated sailor through the city streets. A cut jolts us out of the past and into the present with an eye-level camera contemplating an already crumbling wall. Graffitied with a cluster of detached eyes, this wall is a motif of traditional filmic practice, symbolic of our readiness to accept superficial visual representation, detaching our eye from the rest of our body. This is a symbolic refusal to grant the separation between these eyes and the city: they have become part of it and this is emblematic of the film's attempt to construct an aesthetic that can represent this lived experience.

Guerín's formal approach negotiates the intersections between a highly stylized approach and an adherence to traditional (or at least established experimental) forms of depiction and a more innovative approach to the ethical and empathetic dimensions of this variety of documentary. This is felt most acutely in those works which observe, or even intrude into, the lives of their subjects, raising ethical questions yet which shy away from explanation and in this extended observation must take care to acknowledge and yet avoid the traditional concerns surrounding the voyeuristic nature of film viewing. Bill Nichols locates a number of ethical concerns surrounding the objectification of the documentary subject and the authenticity of the events represented:

> The act of representation no longer seems as clear-cut as it once did. The issues of specificity and corporeality bring to a focus tensions within the domain of representation. They sharpen questions of magnitude posed by the felt tension between representation and represented. (1994: 2)

A tendency to trust in the indexical image, the 'truth' recorded, is problematic so Guerín opts to embrace this paradox. His approach is deliberately elliptical, and our access to filmed reality will always be partial, mediated and at a temporal and spatial remove. The peripheral position of the inhabitants of *El chino*, at the margins of a changing physical and social reality is aptly expressed by the poetic fluidity of this cinematic technique. The ethics of representation cannot be avoided but he points to new methods of depiction, which highlight the innate problems of representation.

The camera adopts a similarly marginal position to that of the social actors; there are frequent close-ups and long takes of building materials emphasising their surface texture and the physical imposition of this environment. Shots of communal meals eaten in the open air in the midst of the building site both emphasize the universality of experience whilst highlighting its distinct physicality. The city is ingested as body and city once more merge.

The proximity of the camera to the bodies it portrays – a technique which pervades the essay – affords the spectator a privileged view which apprehends the lived physical reality of the situation. As the camera, which is necessarily the stand-in in this space for our physical presence, moves closer to its subjects the ability to focus is removed and we relate to this intimacy within the filmic space in new ways.

In a clear return to Benjamin – as one of the earliest exponents of the primacy of touch in the city dweller's experience – tactility is repeatedly privileged by the Catalan cineaste in his mediation of the experience of these construction workers through their manual labour: 'Buildings are appropriated in a twofold manner: by use and by perception – or rather by touch and by sight . . . on the tactile side there is no counterpart to contemplation on the optical side' (1999: 233).

Two of the film's central subjects are a teenage couple made homeless during the course of filming. As Juani, the young girl, puts on her make-up before she goes out to work (as a prostitute) the invasive and intimate style of filming unsettles any illusion of critical distance. A discomfiting combination of extreme close-ups and long takes increase the sensation of entrapment in which the spectator is implicated. The camera repeatedly adopts the position of its human subjects and, as a result, frequently suffers from obstructed points of view as barriers are erected to demarcate prohibited areas. Space is regulated from afar, forcing these people out. The majority of shots are taken from behind railings or through windows: there is no conventional privileging here of the cinematic eye but rather a deliberate frustration with the limits of our perspective.

Interspersed with the shots of the building site and the remaining residents struggling to come to terms with their displacement are, poignantly, full screen shots of placards displaying the architects' plans and artists' impressions of the area as envisaged officially. These sketches portray Haussman-style boulevards flanked by Mediterranean palm trees. When the camera pans out, to the right and below the sign are nothing but piles of rubble. This visual aside effectively underlines the actual construction at work as well as the construction of Guerín's piece.

As with the fusion which takes place between city and body so the visual is enhanced by the tactile, smoothly fulfilling expectations of a more wholesome sensory experience. Reciprocity as the basis of contact with the environment is symbolically utilized as a two-way relationship which has external ramifications, implicating us within the space of the film.

En construcción offers an emphasis on tactile pleasure by drawing attention to the physicality of the task of construction. In one long sequence we watch a joiner and his son work together on the staircase for the new building, wherein visual pleasure is achieved through the repeatedly drawn zigzag lines on the stairwell. Here, the precision of the measuring combined with the diegetic sound of pencil scraping against material intensifies the sensory experience. Indeed, the shape, visually and aurally depicted, becomes a motif in the film, recurring in the shots of the gantries used for work on the higher levels.

In a later scene, a shot from on top of scaffolding contemplates the snow falling on the neighbourhood and also on the heads of the immigrant workers. The contrast of black amongst white offers an intensely lyrical experience with clear ideological connotations. However, the sequence also evokes once more the sensory experience of this construction work itself. As the snow piles up on the head of the black worker the lengthy contemplation highlights the visual beauty and the sensory potential of the image. The juxtaposition of outside and inside – the exterior construction work on what will eventually become the interior of the finished dwellings – underscores the transience of the image to which Resina refers.

As if to reiterate the peripheral situation of the work the majority of the film takes place outside, or brings the outside in, as shots from within buildings are framed with windows taking prominence. This is especially significant when, towards the end of the film, the flats now nearing completion are shown to prospective inhabitants. As these families of professional people and upwardly mobile young couples are foregrounded by the ever-observant camera the work of construction continues alongside and behind them.

These scenes appear almost choreographed in the seamless 'dance' executed by the workers as they continue their finishing of the apartments yet are ignored by these prospective owners. The proximity to the neighbour's balconies and the intrusion of the outside is inescapable. One family mentions their concern that their neighbours shouldn't be allowed to hang washing out on the front of the building. As a refreshing counterpoint, we witness a pastiche of Romeo and Juliet as a young builder courts a girl hanging clothes out on a balcony. These working people conduct their lives at the edges, at these traditional points of observation where change takes place and is observed. And collisions between old and new, evinced by this juxtaposition of convention and the marginal, are most acutely felt in this ideological remodelling of space crystallized by the gesture of a young mother who holds her baby up to the window to peer outside.

This element of the film overlaps with a further sensory characteristic of cinema, one much more readily aligned with the tradition of the cinematic experience, the aural domain. Observation of cities is often as much auditory as it is visual, something best appreciated at those margins where one is privy to both its sights and its sounds. Lefebvre muses on the aural experience of cities and specifically what he designates their 'rhythms'. Perspectives from a window privilege the notion of a marginal space, which traverses the inside/outside division in relation to our attempts to apprehend the experience:

> In order to hold this fleeting object, which is not exactly an object, one must be at the same time both inside and out. A balcony is perfect for the street and it is this placing in perspective (of the street) that we owe this marvellous invention of balconies and terraces from which we also dominate the passers-by. (1991: 219)

Just as the gaze within the film which, in its alliance with the subjects it films – and its proximity to them – is more internal than external, so sounds are shared with the subjects who experienced them firsthand. Unusually – even for the documentary mode – most of the sound is insistently synchronous and diegetic; and there are long sequences in which there is no speech but we are acutely aware of the construction site and its rhythm. Despite the numerous oppositions played out in this area, inside and outside, old and new, Guerín resists the temptation to comply with these schisms, preferring the temporal coexistence of the construction period rather than the clear-cut before-and-after dichotomy.

Time in the City

These temporal layers and their interrelationship with the space and physical presence of the inhabitants are most succinctly demonstrated by the recording of the discovery of the Roman burial site. This scene creates a visual résumé of many of the themes of the whole piece. The nature of a diverse history of a people is explored as we are privy to discussions as to the origins of these bones. Concern as to whether they are Roman or Spanish is prevalent. The manner of shooting here is also significant. As with the rest of the film there is unmediated representation of sound and vision: they are recorded synchronously without voice-over or interview. The sounds of the city are captured alongside the visual commentary.

A more harmonious viewing experience is thus ensured which reinforces the involved, experiential method of filming and promotes a sensorial immersion in the space of the film. Guerín also chooses to record only the faces and conversations of the crowd that have gathered to observe these unearthed bones. The camera aligns itself with its subjects and frustrates our point of view just as theirs is frustrated. It is reminiscent of the style of filming which confined us to obstructed points of view and restricted perspectives in the earlier sequences which observed Juani and Ivan and their own equally frustrating and constrained situation. Although analysis of Guerín's engagement with the politics of exclusion and inclusion at work in the gentrification of this area is not of major concern here, the formal properties of this sequence make an implicit comment on this aspect. This depiction of diversity is contrasted to the uniformity of the new flats and the imposition of homogenous social and cultural codes. The multicultural nature previously constitutive of *El Raval* is now a distinctly temporary phenomenon; the immigrants working on the properties will be surplus to requirements once they are completed.

The democracy of a city that is open to inhabitation by whoever chooses to roam its streets, as described by Benjamin, is exemplified in this depiction of the burial site. A tension is exposed in this democracy in its opposition to the attempted regeneration that seeks to structure the streets of this city by means of economic and social stratification that is forcing these people out. As various groups of people discuss the archaeological discovery in their preferred language, ethnic, cultural and linguistic diversity is prevalent. In this sense the camera does appear to simply record: the director demonstrates no linguistic preference but simply pans along the lines of people listening to their comments. Sign language, Spanish, Arabic and Catalan are some of the languages perceived in this scene. The long takes and mobile camera emphasize the relaxed ambience within this community as well as drawing the spectator into the scene and highlighting our feeling of participation in a film that resists the external imposition of uniformity thanks to its democratic aesthetic.[15]

The physical disruption to the work caused by the discovery of this burial site is afforded a metaphorical significance by Guerín as his subtle visual commentary acknowledges the importance of the history of space and people and their interconnection. It is not insignificant that historical sediments resurface to compromise the realisation of a new architectural abstract space. These planners are reminded that their attempts to empty out space and inscribe it with new meaning are not possible, mainly due to the physical imprints of the inhabitants, both past and present. Lefebvre's analysis of this topic informs a reading of this urban environment, used here as a filmic subject rather than solely a backdrop:

> Traditional historiography assumes that thought can perform cross-sections upon time, arresting its flow without too much difficulty; its analyses thus tend to fragment and segment temporality. In the history of space as such, on the other hand, the historical and diachronic realms and the generative past are forever leaving their inscriptions upon the writing-tablet, so to speak, of space. (1991: 110)

This element is expertly alluded to in the scene which depicts Howard Hawks's classic *Land of the Pharaohs* (1955) being shown on the television in the bar. Once again we view this significantly and frustratingly from outside the door, receiving only a partial view. The notion of building for ideological purposes as regards the pyramids of ancient Egypt haunts this similarly ideological construction in the present, performed by these same North African workers as though it were a similar burial chamber. The monumental nature of construction in its ideological manifestation evoked by these images recalls the similarly elitist bourgeois project of the *noucentista* and *modernista* movements, which underpinned the ideals of Catalan conservatism, as well as the re-construction of this *barrio* imposed by the Town Hall. Resina points to the cynicism with which these ideological notions are treated by estate agents whose feigned interest in history is little more than a sales tool and the uncovered cemetery becomes 'a supplement that promoters are quick to commodify' (2008: 270).

Presenting his work as an unmediated encounter with reality, Guerín exemplifies his stylistic endeavour to open this transient peripheral space to the full reality of existence. Cinema works alongside the city and the body to re-evaluate the connotations of the body as it inhabits this space and to embrace the possibility of representations of subjectivity which are not limited by cinema's previously assumed reliance on visuality. In portraying the potentiality of such mutually enriching relationships we, as spectators, are encouraged to view the possibilities for positive reciprocity in other areas of the film. Of course the protagonists of this work are trapped in a development that carries on around them apparently disregarding their presence. Nonetheless, in the final analysis the unconventional methodology of this director with its innovative editing, discomfiting liminality and unsuspected lyricism may yet be seen to grant them a sense of empowerment external to this apparent exclusion. A partial release from the repressive contingencies of their existence, no doubt, but a release nonetheless as Joan Ramon Resina surmises pertinently:

> None of these characters are at home in their world, no matter how insistently Guerín's camera homes in on them. All of them are in transit ... All of them are uprooted, estranged, out-of-the-ordinary for as long as this film lasts. Theirs is, ironically, a metaphoric fate that embraces and sucks us into the frame that turns them from marginal figures into real presences with a measure of power over our perceptions. (2008: 264)

The marginality of transient characters becomes the central tenet of Guerín's subsequent film, and its associated productions. This time the ideological import of working within a documentary medium has been removed to a degree, although the political marginality of a site with conflicting identities is more than alluded to in the location of Strasbourg, the Alsacienne regional identity, which reflects a mix of French and German language and tradition.

Images of the Past, Present and Future in *En la ciudad de Sylvia, Unas fotos en la ciudad de Sylvia and Las mujeres que no conocemos*

The affective capacity of the cinematic image in time and space is re-imagined by Guerín's foray into installation here. If *Train of Shadows* explored time and *En construcción* moved that temporal dimension through space, then here the two are further enmeshed. Cinema's mobility can be viewed in various ways. There is the obvious dynamism of the screen action, as the images that literally move before our eyes, and there is the motion of the celluloid through the projector itself, which then reproduces that movement on the screen. There is also a degree of nomadism in the foundations of cinema that has been attended to in its historiographical dimensions by Giuiliana Bruno and Anne Friedberg (Bruno 1993; Friedberg 1993). They link this topographical rendering of movement and the moving image to the confluence of movement and the cinematic in the city. For Friedberg it provides a model by which to explain the new and virtual gaze, which can enable temporal and spatial wandering but which becomes viable because of the consumerist space of the shopping mall.

The trilogy, as I have labeled it for the sake of convenience and because of the interrelatedness of the three works, consists of a feature length film, *En la ciudad de Sylvia/In Sylvia's City*, released in 2007, and two compilations of still images, *Las mujeres que no concocemos/Women we don't know* which was exhibited in the Spanish pavilion at the 2007 Venice biennale, and a DVD, *Unas fotos en la Ciudad de Sylvia/Some Photos in Sylvia's City*. The DVD is silent and composed entirely of black and white images with explicatory intertitles, written by Guerin, explaining the premise of the production itself and also the later fictional production *In the City of Sylvia*. Although this DVD was not necessarily intended to accompany the film, *In the City of Sylvia,* and is a beautifully constructed piece in its own right, I believe that to read these three pieces together cast light on the process of image making and meaning making which preoccupy Guerín.[16]

In these three works, Guerín extends his musing on the experience of the properly cinematic and its changing nature. In so far as this spectatorship is active, it depends on our experiential understanding of the image; it is a means of viewing, which necessarily functions at the locus of past, present and future, speaking to memory, experience and the imaginative projections enabled by cinema. In moving these works into the gallery there is an obvious degree of motility to the spectatorship, which is mirrored by the active eponymous protagonist of the Sylvia 'trilogy'.

Guerín evokes Deleuze's work on cinema in a remark about the conceptual and actual work on *En construcción*, and cinema's legacy to contemporary filmic production not as replica or copy – which runs the risk of reducing a rich tradition to stereotype – but as 'a way of thinking' (Guerín 2003). I have already looked in some detail at the formal techniques that encourage us to ally ourselves to the camera's frustrated and partial and yet properly experiential gaze. In these works each image, especially when stilled and repeated across the different media, recalls cinema's past while invoking a present moment of becoming and unfurling imaginings of its future. This is the way in which the 'thinking' evoked by Guerín can be considered Deleuzian in its relation to time.

The purely optical image, designated by Deleuze, is that image which can be momentarily disconnected from narrative, a moment of contemplation or as Ronald Bogue summarizes, 'purely optical situations disconnected from the common-sense coordinates of their standard usages and practices' (2003: 109). These situations must, however, relate to the images with which they are associated. I would argue that Guerín draws our attention to these moments of pure looking as we move through the images of various women that pass before his lens in Madrid and Strasbourg during the creation of these works.

Looking and Walking in Sylvia's City

The main feature, *In the City of Sylvia,* provides the poetic exposition of the affective memory of a moment (the protagonist's first meeting with Sylvia several years previously). The narrative premise is slight and not, perhaps, instantly absorbing. A young man in Strasbourg observes the young women that inhabit the city's streets, walking, in cafés, or waiting for or travelling on trams. Initially we are unsure as to why. The dreamer (Javier Lafitte), as Guerín's young protagonist is known, carries a sketchbook in which he draws, in pencil, the faces of these women and the first part of the film consists mainly of these sketches and observations, when the camera oscillates between the point of view of the young man and the people that he watches. Playing on the limited capacity of the gaze to reveal, these shots are often spatially less than coherent, with foreground middle and background populated by different faces, and the object of his gaze is frequently made deliberately opaque.[17] It's a visual strategy that draws us into a film that, as yet, is a mystery to us. The narrative is constructed through the use of the image. As David Bordwell concurs, 'And a search for story plays a part here. We're primed for some action to start, and we browse through these shots looking for anything that might initiate it' (2007).

This method of filming, along with the young man's sketches, appear to make visible this splitting of the present into simultaneous past and future that Deleuze refers to in Cinema 2:

> The past is constituted not after the present that it was but at the same time, time has to split itself in two at each moment as present and past, which differ from each other in nature, or, what amounts to the same thing, it has to split the present into two heterogeneous directions, one of which is launched towards the future while the other falls into the past. (1989: 79)

This temporal splitting is elaborated by the static images (documentary photographs and production stills), exhibited in both the exhibition (*Women we don't know*) and the DVD (*Some Photos in the City of Sylvia*) as they extend and comment upon this 'main' text (*In the City of Sylvia*), testing the borders that separate them (and other boundaries too) as they perform cinema's complex relationship with time. The layers of images encompassed by the three productions reinforce the status of the image as affective memory object in and of itself and extend a Deleuzian contemplation of reality as a nexus of images. Temporal layers work in each production and across the three works (the time of recording, the suggested past of the director and the 'dreamer' who becomes his fictional stand-in, and the pre-film time of the DVD which sets itself up almost as a 'research trip' for the main event).

The active and ideal spectator here is, I believe, constructed by Guerín through his representation of cinema under construction and as an immersive/interactive art form. This is what draws the past and the future into the present; for Guerín the integrity of the image depends on this capacity for temporal layering that creates the ellipses where meaning, or simply affect and interpretation in the instant of viewing, come to reside. These stratified

Figure 4.3. The dreamer in Strasbourg in *En la ciudad de Sylvia* (2007), by José Luis Guerín. Permission granted by Eddie Saeta.

images enable alternative forms of engagement which oscillate between attention and distraction that Elizabeth Cowie exemplifies in her writings on documentary installation:

> It is the viewing subject who authors the work's time in a process of memory and identification in her attention and encounter, with the attendant anxieties and jubilation.... Cinema and the gallery thus each represent specific possibilities of encountering the materiality of time and image in time-based works; and each can focus the question of the subjectivity of our encounter as a movement of attention and distraction. (2009: 129)

These three productions perform this temporal splitting, and the work of memory and identification referred to by Cowie, by projecting many images of women in Strasbourg with barely perceptible differences and long static camera shots in which the women pursued by the mobile camera enter and leave the frame (in *In the City of Sylvia*). They perform their separate pasts at each moment of their viewing that Deleuze refers to, engaging the spectator's understanding of the time and space of these different media forms. This cinematic replaying and recycling enables the relationship to each present moment with its own past, an image in the process of becoming. Through the use

of black and white images and the silent films with on-screen textual explication, these productions also reiterate the history of cinema initiated in *Train
of Shadows*. Stillness is the means by which this history is revealed. As Mulvey
remarks, 'Stillness may evoke a "before" for the moving image as filmstrip, as
a reference back to photography or to its own original moment of registration
... [and] this underlying stillness provides cinema with a secret, with a hidden
past that might or might not find its way to the surface' (2006: 67).

The dialectical relationship exposed and informed by viewing these two
works alongside one another epitomizes the use of the image as memory; furthermore it establishes the spectral presence of the director across all three
works, as he reveals, in *Some Photos in the City of Sylvia,* that the quest to find
the woman who inspired these works was initially his. He met her twenty-two
years previously on what he calls a 'literary pilgrimage' to Strasbourg, following
in the footsteps of Goethe. This elision between director and the subjective
camera's gaze in all three works inevitably calls to mind the problematic notion
of the pursuit of the female that is a recurring trope of this trilogy. Indeed in
two reviews of the film in *The Guardian* newspaper the word stalker was used
in relation to the young man's pursuit of this woman – or rather the pursuit of
a memory of this woman.

I would return to the motility that was cited at the outset, and its relation
to the same dynamism inherent in the urban that was, to a degree, explored
by *En construcción*. These women are the active inhabitants of this urban space
and we witness their involvement in a democratic inhabitation of it. In these
images, to make visible is not to objectify; rather to make visible is to open up to
interpretation and engagement, to demand a reinterpretation and constant revision of the image according to the moment in which it is viewed. Like his previous films, this film and these photographs are extended musings on the gaze
which invite us to critique the way in which we look. To read these women as
the objectified bodies of a male gaze would be to ignore the multiple inscriptions of meaning at play in the variously encoded temporalities with which
Guerín works. The slowing down and extending of each image challenges us
not only to be active but also to resist a voyeuristic contemplation. We are
made uncomfortable by the postures of the women, particularly by the views
of them in many postures in the photographic exhibition, but this prolonged
contemplation does not disavow the presence of the spectator; it rather makes
his/her presence a necessary element in the construction of the image.

Images as Ghosts and Memories

This engagement with the image as a spectral reminder of other images is perhaps most explicit in the photographic exhibition *Women We Don't Know*. Interestingly this is subtitled *Film en 24 cuadros*.[18] In this installation Guerín instigates a relationship between the still and moving image – encapsulated in its title – that goes some way to reverse the expectations of both, slowing down the film and adding movement to the photographs. The incorporation of still images, projected in sequence, and then their apparent opposites, static shots in the film, provides a reflexive contemplation on the cinematic edit, pointing to what it is that is lost between frames. This is a temporal and spatial gap and in its exposure by Guerín it becomes an elliptical space for contemplation, allowing the films to become the mode of thought that he claims he desires.

The installation begins with photographs taken of a girl at Alfonso Martín metro station in Madrid. Guerín's authorial intervention (the inter-titles that are the film's only verbal element) explains that – contrary to his wishes – the

Figure 4.4. Woman behind a scratched window in *Las mujeres que no conocemos* (2007), by José Luis Guerín. Permission to use generously granted by José Luis Guerin.

auto focus function of his camera foregrounded the scratched glass of the train window rather than the face of the woman that Guerín had selected as the subject of the image. Nonetheless, the result is an image which reminds us of our selective vision and the power of the author and editor. It also has the effect of producing an aesthetically pleasing and complex image, forcing our gaze to move to the surface texture and relegating the human protagonist to opaque and shadowy background.

In these photographs, intersecting spatial and temporal planes hint at the backwards and forwards mental journey in which the dreamer partakes during the film, and an object or image functions as a link to the past and converts itself into a renewed interest in his future quest, the pursuit of Sylvia, in a sort of 'coming-to-know' of this enigmatic female subject, albeit one that resists the neat teleology of conventional narrative.

This is exemplified in an early sequence from *In the City of Sylvia*: the young *dreamer* is shown sitting on his hotel bed, and the static camera remains in thrall to his every move for over a minute and a half, an eternity in contemporary and commercial film terms. During this extended take he barely shifts his body, occasionally effecting a slight movement to the pencil he holds and towards the end of the take, almost imperceptibly, moving his lips. The interest stems from a sensorial immersion in a beautifully constructed cinematic image, a skill Guerín had honed in his previous productions. I previously drew on Cowie's writing on documentary installations in galleries. Guerín's filmic technique and, of course, the installation images speak to this immersion of the type defined here by Cowie: 'The immersive is always a very active sensory engagement and one which is never merely responsive or habitual; for it is always open to a becoming other, to a newness, as immersion gives way – as it always must – to reflection' (2009: 128).

In this respect the construction of narrative not only depends on the editing process, in which the intimation of death and loss slips between each frame, but also on the active role of the spectator. The DVD production is an example of new technology exposing the potential of the former aesthetic practices of photography and cinema (filmed on digital video, the feature on 16mm blown up to 35mm). He has moved beyond the contemplation of the inherent aesthetic interest of the changing medium that he examined in *Train of Shadows*; Guerín's contribution to the debate on changing media is not to lament the loss of the index but to explore the expanded potential of the new.

The spectral presence of photography and the ghostly presence of the editor's cut that are evidenced in these works also has a thematic presence in the works when read in combination –that of pursuit. This is exemplified by the composition of the images and the selection of several consecutive images. They also pursue the ghost of the woman whose name unites these works, and who herself becomes a ghost.

As much as he seeks the elusive feminine persona of the title, Guerín also seeks to represent the possibility of cinema to observe, preserve, project and imagine in a post-cinematic era. Despite their different qualities, the three components of this trilogy have in common a concern with the way in which we connect with images in time, whether they are still, moving or something in between (the still photographs that are made to move in the video of stills). This is a connectedness that is frequently represented by disjunction and not narrative linearity in the way we might expect it.

It may seem paradoxical to suggest that these three works make a comment on the post-cinematic as they simultaneously illustrate its beginnings, but Guerín's technique, in particular its call for what I've chosen to call an active spectator, speaks to an interactive variety of viewing that has much in common with contemporary digital works. In choosing these three modes of representation he creates an intersubjective space in which contact is privileged and no one means of encounter prioritized so that our apprehension of each individual piece is informed by and informs our relationship with the other two. Thus, the photographic exhibition is imbued with movement due to its extra-textual discourse with the film, and the video of photographic stills appears to add to our knowledge of both the exhibition (including as it does some of the same images) as it provides a meta-narrative to the feature film.

It is fitting to end with this obsession with ghosts and spectral presences – an unremitting feature of all of Guerín's work and which articulates, for me, the peripheral nature of his work. It is haunted by a national cinematic tradition that has yet to be coherently and competently addressed. Whilst it is easy to make a case for the universality of a cinema not bound by nationality, I return here to the central if at times unwritten concern of this project, what Jaume Martí Olivella terms 'the fractured experience of Catalan cinema' (2011: 187), which is identifiable precisely through the shifting signifiers, the playful generic conceits and the elliptical structure of these films. Of course the ghost of the girl that the dreamer seeks and the projection of a love that might have been (which appears to be Guerín's implication) mark the film with a fragility of reference that evokes this phantasmagoric feature.

Notes

1. These were the Francoist newsreels shown in cinemas before the main picture and, although presented as news, were spurious, propagandistic accounts of the successes of the Franco regime and the country's economic prosperity.

2. For an excellent analysis and précis of these various theoretical conceptions of the index, see Trifonova (2011).

3. This is not the time to delve into the rich theoretical literature on the generic limits of fiction and non-fiction/documentary film (even the terms are sometimes contested). Where generic blurring occurs they strengthen my argument on the testing of boundaries more generally but for Guerín, I believe, the intention is not to mislead or produce specific effects via the juxtaposition of 'reality' and 'fiction' but rather to explore what cinema can do, its potential for representation that exceeds the limits of commercial, standard practice.

4. Perhaps most notably Nick James and Jonathan Romney in *Sight and Sound* and then Stephen Shaviro who took the view that it was a gratuitous tendency employed in order to mark films as quality or to ensure a place in the festival circuit that appeared to privilege this particular style.

5. For an excellent critique and synopsis of this film, see Hughes (2009).

6. Bill Morrison is another director whose work plays with the potential of degraded celluloid images, making new and beautiful works from these changed images his films: *Decasia* (2002) and *Light Is Calling* (2004) are poignant and beautiful examples of this.

7. This creates the same kind of slippage between image and meaning that we have seen creatively employed by Medem and Bigas Luna.

8. The apparently speeded-up effect observed in this instance is an acknowledged result of old film being badly projected rather than its actually being too fast (or too many frames per second).

9. Despite their very different approaches to narrative, this style reminds us of Medem's preference for abstracted time and space.

10. See Loxham (2011, 2012).

11. Translation mine.

12. For a further examination of the historical and ideological significance of the area see Ealham (2005).

13. See Mackay (1985).

14. In this regard it is useful to consider the mobility inherent in the practice of *flânerie* as distinct from voyeurism and the implications on subjectivity raised by Anne

Friedberg in her excellent volume, where she states, 'Like the panopticon system, *flânerie* relied on the visual register – but with a converse instrumentalism, emphasizing mobility and fluid subjectivity rather than restraint and interpellated reform' (1993: 16).

15. The sociolinguistic situation in Barcelona is highly complex and it is recognized that such assertions should be treated as necessarily speculative. For more information, see Boix and Vila i Moreno (1998).

16. I didn't see the photographic exhibition but there is also a DVD production of these images, projected in a similar way to their projection at the exhibition; therefore some of my comments in this feature will be speculative and concerned with the images and their sequences rather than the experience of the installation in situ.

17. I would argue that it is this technique by which Guerín refutes accusations that this project is little more than a misogynistic extension of the objectifying male gaze.

18. These photographs were projected onto gallery walls and as they progressed and changed it was often possible to see sequential images changing as the previous images and those which would soon take their place were given a lengthier projection on another wall. I have only seen the still image and a DVD version of this so will limit myself here to discussion of the significance of this choice of image and style of exhibition and not address specific affective responses to the spatial and experiential facet of this piece.

References

Benjamin, W. 1929. 'The Return of the Flâneur'. *Walter Benjamin Selected Writings*. Cambridge, MA, and London: Belknap Press.

———. 1999. *Illuminations*. London: Pimlico.

Bogue, R. 2003. *Deleuze on Cinema*. New York and London: Routledge.

Boix, E., and F. X. Vila i Moreno. 1998. *Sociolingüística de la llengua catalana*. Barcelona: Editorial Ariel.

Bordwell, D. 2007. 'Three Nights of a Dreamer'. Observations on Film Art. Retrieved 10 November 2009 from http://www.davidbordwell.net/blog/2007/11/05/three-nights-of-a-dreamer/

Bruno, G. 1993. *Streetwalking on a Ruined Map: Cultural Theory and the City Films of Elvira Notari*. Princeton, NJ: Princeton University Press.

Certeau, M. 1984. *The Practice of Everyday Life*. Berkeley: University of California Press.

Cherchi Usai, P. 2001. *The Death of Cinema: History, Cultural Memory and the Digital Dark Age*. London: British Film Institute.

Ciment, M. 2003. 'The State of Cinema'. Address given at 46th San Francisco International Film Festival. San Francisco. Retrieved 15 October 2010 from unspokencinema.blogspot.com.au/2006/10/state-of-cinema-m-ciment.html.

Cowie, E. 2009. 'On Documentary Sounds and Images in the Gallery'. *Screen* 50(1): 124–134.

Deleuze, G. 1989. *Cinema 2: The Time Image.* London: Continuum.

Doane, M. A. 2002. *The Emergence of Cinematic Time Modernity, Contingency, the Archive.* Cambridge, MA, and London: Harvard University Press.

———. 2007. 'The Indexical and the Concept of Medium Specificity'. *Differences* 18(1): 128–152.

Ealham, C. 2005. 'An "Imagined Geography": Ideology, Urban Space and Protest in the Creation of Barcelona's "Chinatown", c.1835–1936'. *International Review of Social History* 50:373–397.

Edwards, E. 2009. 'Photographs as Objects of Memory'. *The Object Reader,* edited by F. Candin and R. Guins, 221–236. Oxford and New York: Routledge.

Friedberg, A. 1993. *Window Shopping: Cinema and the Postmodern.* Berkeley and Los Angeles: University of California Press.

Guerín, J. L. 2003. 'Work in Progress'. *Rouge.* Retrieved 13 February 2005 from http://www.rouge.com.au/4/work_progress.html.

Heredero, C. F. 2003. 'New Creators for the New Millennium: Transforming the Directing Scene in Spain'. *Cineaste* 29(1): 32–37.

Hughes, D. 2009. 'Tren de sombras'. *Senses of Cinema Online Film Journal,* 50 (April). Retrieved 23 April 2012 from http://sensesofcinema.com/2009/cteq/tren-de-sombras/

Kinder, M. 1997. 'Documenting the National'. *Refiguring Spain: Cinema/Media/Representation,* edited by M. Kinder, 65–98. Durham and London: Duke University Press.

———. 2003. 'Uncanny Visions of History: Two Experimental Documentaries from Transnational Spain, *Asaltar los cielos* and *Tren de sombras'. Film Quarterly* 56(3): 12–24.

Koepnick, L. 2004. 'Photographs and Memories'. *South Central Review* 21(1): 94–129.

Lefebvre, H. 1991. *The Production of Space.* Oxford: Basil Blackwell.

Leyda, J. 1960. *Kino: A History of the Russian and Soviet Film.* London: Allen and Unwin.

Loxham, A. 2011. 'Objects of Memory in Contemporary Catalan Documentaries'. *Senses of Cinema Online Film Journal* 60 (November). Retrieved 19 February 2012 from http://sensesofcinema.com/2011/feature-articles/objects-of-memory-in-contemporary-catalan-documentaries-materiality-and-mortality/

———. 2012. 'Subjective Pasts and the Imaginative Power of the Image in *Bucarest, la memoria perduda* and *Nedar'.* In *The Noughties in the Hispanic and Lusophone World,* edited by K. Bacon and N. Thornton, 130–141. Newcastle Upon Tyne: Cambridge Scholars Publishing.

Mackay, D. 1985. *Modern Architecture in Barcelona.* Sheffield: Anglo Catalan Society Occasional Publications.

Marks, L. U. 2002. *Touch: Sensuous Theory and Multisensory Media.* Minneapolis and London: University of Minnesota Press.

Martí Olivella, J. 2011. 'Catalan Cinema'. In *A Companion to Catalan Culture,* edited by D. Keown, 185–205. Woodbridge, Suffolk: Tamesis.

Mulvey, L. 2006. *Death 24x a Second Stillness and the Moving Image.* London: Reaktion Books Ltd.

Nichols, B. 1994. *Blurred Boundaries: Questions of Meaning in Contemporary Culture.* Bloomington, Indianapolis: Indiana University Press.

Resina, J. R. 2008. 'The Construction of the Cinematic Image: *En construcción* (José Luis Guerin, 2001)'. In *Burning Darkness: Half a Century of Spanish Cinema,* edited by J. R. Resina 255–276. New York: State University of New York Press.

Trifonova, T. 2011. 'The Twilight of the Index.' *Cinema: Journal of Philosophy and the Moving Image.* Retrieved 27 January 2012 from http://cjpmi.ifl.pt/2-trifonova.

Wonenburger, C. 2003. 'Las complicidad de dos miradas insobornables.' Presented at *El documental: la realidad y sus simulacros* Seminar. Retrieved 12 December 2005 from www.trendesombras.com/la-complicidad-de-dos-miradas-insobornables

Looking Forward to the Past

> Spain is like no other country in the world. Many of its films bear testimony to this truth, for the films are the expression of an individualism that is deeply rooted in cultural, one might even venture to say racial, pride. Whether we take the historical epics of the 1940s or the zany comedies of Pedro Almodóvar, all are merely the varying facets of an unmistakeable national identity. And, also for better or worse, those men and women behind the Spanish lens have been and will continue to be inexorably bound by that identity.
>
> —P. Besas, *Behind the Spanish Lens*

When Peter Besas closed his 1985 book with these words the nationality and national identity of Spanish cinema was if not the primary object of interest for scholars of Hispanic culture then at least an assumed unifying factor and untroubled point of departure for analysis. This book seeks to loosen these inexorable binds not only from the history of Spanish cinema but also from the theoretical trends that have enclosed this history within paradigms of nation and identity that left little space for emergent dissident visions. Of course there is a tradition of dissidence but this was located against a background of authoritarianism that formulated a binary division of official and other cinema and absorbed production into one of these two main categories.

Besas's prediction is contested on two levels by the work of Julio Medem, José Juan Bigas Luna and José Luis Guerín. Primarily, they all remove themselves deliberately, subtly and at times daringly from the Spanish identity that Besas claimed cineastes would be forever 'bound' by. Furthermore, the bind of national identity already discarded, they have cast off the shackles of other types of identity and located a new aesthetic idiom that cuts across critical trends within both Hispanic studies and in the broader arena of visual culture.

In terms of the present study this has meant that Spanish cultural criticism has at times taken second place to the theory of cinema and its aesthetic appeal. This approach has produced a series of discrete and specific studies on each director and a selection of his films. Each of these discrete elements is unified by the engagement with a new approach to cinema which demonstrates a sophisticated engagement with a broad range of philosophical trends that seek to extend the mediations on spatial practice, embodied vision, film's materiality and its alternative sites of display.

The manner in which the construction of the narrative inflects the construction of the cinematic image in order to blur the distinction between subject and object, spectator and image is identified as a recurring theme in all of the works under scrutiny here. A self-reflexive style of creation dwells on the specificity and suitability of cinema to this particular project. During the final editing of this book the sad news of Bigas Luna's death was announced, and in the days that followed a plethora of tributes made mention of his outstanding talent and secured his place as an innovative and adventurous director. French newspaper *Le Monde* called him the cineaste of Iberian excess, perfectly capturing his inclusive approach to the identity of the peninsula and his eccentric style that pushed everything to the limits. This awareness of what cinema can do, of its scope to challenge, debunk and criticize at the same time as it expands our experience of the everyday is a tendency that I have explored by thinking with all of the works contained within this book. A final look at Bigas Luna seeks to engage with the ways in which this cinema is moving forward, proudly positioning itself as a universal art form from Spain.

The opening sequence of Bigas Luna's 2006 offering *Yo soy la Juani/My Name is Juani* – and indeed the ninety minutes for which the piece runs – sums up the complex situation of the cinematic output that I have examined and engaged with over the course of this book. The credits roll at the opening of the film to an electronic synthesized beat; the harsh tonalities preferred by Bigas in his 1978 feature *Bilbao* are reincarnated here in a particularly twenty-first-century style. Their visual accompaniment resembles a 'skin' of the type that Windows Media Player electronically selects to accompany tracks as they are played on a personal computer (along with the portable MP3 player, the computer appears to be the current medium of choice for the appreciation of new music). The pink and white electronically produced visual is another highly stylized nod to the colour scheme of the piece, imitating the colours and styles of the teenage world that the film seeks to inhabit. Soon the digital visual becomes human, yet no less generic, as a teenager armed with a can of spray paint decorates an outdoor wall, in a speeded up sequence whose acceleration is matched by the pace of the accompanying soundtrack.

That technology and its development should become the obsession of a talented director is no surprise, given the advances made in this medium during the length of his working life. What is different about the latest piece is that the technology becomes the claustrophobia-inducing method of control for its group of young protagonists. It would be impossible to conclude a reading of Bigas Luna by locating any overarching and unifying theme throughout his cinematic work; this is where its interest lies. Nonetheless, recalling *Bilbao* and the enormous potential granted to the technology of the image therein a contrast appears in this latest work, and it is in the space in between that the new style of 'Spanish' cinema has emerged and continues to emerge. In his *Variety* review of *My Name is Juani* Jonathan Holland focuses on the shiny surface of the attractive packaging and criticizes the director for doing the same, stating, 'Like the culture it is scrutinizing, pic emphasizes style over substance. While sympathizing with the kids' existential difficulties – poor jobs, little money, no prospects, a ruthless society – it fails to help viewers empathize with the kids themselves' (2006).

The evaluation of style over substance misses, I believe, the major preoccupation of this 'veteran Catalan director' as Holland calls him in the same piece. It is in the power of the image and its recycling and reformulation that Bigas, along with Medem and Guerín, have all found their distinct voice within the cinematic tradition of Spain.

Criticism of *My Name is Juani* focuses on a weak screenplay that distances us from the characters and reduces any possibility of empathy with them and their plight. Empathy and social realism are not, I propose, Bigas's aim in this instance. His heightened sensibility of the plastic arts engenders a compelling engagement with the power and significance of each image. The profusion of images in this film replicates the plethora of screens, which have become our means of communication and a way of mediating our existence. Computer games, mobile phones, music videos, point of sale cash registers and MP3 players present us with images of varying sizes and differing degrees of quality.

Empathy suggests an understanding based on human contact: the screen has replaced this contact and Bigas's examination may not be intended as a political comment on the lack of communication within youth culture but it is a musing on the unique power of the image and its place on the big screen. This is not a concern unique to directors working in Spain and the Spanish language but it does typify the tendency of these three directors to render the universal specific. The communicative power of cinema and its relationship with a process of subjectivisation, which exceeds the binary spectator–screen dynamic, focuses here on the disenfranchised Spanish youth of Tarragona, a new marginal subject for Bigas.

The subversive potential of on-screen representations of physicality that were located in Chapter Two are elaborated upon in this piece. The estrangement that this multiplicity of screens represents to these young protagonists acts to alienate them from their own bodies. In line with the concentration on surface as a site for intersubjective interaction the body has become another surface and as such another subject. It thus offers itself as a site for alteration and projection. Clothes, make-up and jewellery are time worn modes of bodily embellishment and the more permanent adornments, represented by tattoos and plastic surgery, are a way of destabilizing fixed representations of identity.

One of the major avenues for enquiry throughout this book has been the way in which cinema is able to interrogate authenticity and agency in order to put forward a more fluid politics of identity or subjectivity. The bodily modifications in *My Name is Juani* epitomize the desire of these teenagers to express an authentic, self-claimed identity but the direction exposes them as ineffectual and alienating as the promise of independence is undermined by their superficial attempts at self improvement and their frustrated method of interaction with the world.

As the eponymous protagonist (played by Verónica Echegui) lives her life through a series of screens she marks these screens with her presence as they mark her body with their manipulated versions of reality. This film dwells on the negative effect of such a mediated existence as even the abuse that Vane (Laya Martí), Juani's friend, suffers at the hands of her boyfriend has to be filmed by a home movie camera in order that it can be digested as another of a sequence of images with which we are confronted. Is the twenty-first century's exploitation of Vane's body on the cinema screen so vastly different from Goya's depiction of his *majas*?

How does this help to draw together a heterogeneous reading of peripheral identity and these three directors? This study began as an attempt to demonstrate the specific cinematic qualities of these pieces and their acknowledged peripherality in terms of an alternative national cinema. Of course such a simplistic vision has been proved neither useful nor relevant. If any one conclusion can be drawn it is that the peripheries of Spain are moving into the mainstream of Europe and that a global cineliteracy brings a new means of interpretation for these films, one that I have employed in order to shed light on their awareness of the cinematic and its extraordinary creative potential. The emphasis on perspective that is drawn on time and again in examination distances itself from focal points and ocular-centric discourse that surrounds and drives the debate as to cinema's ideological bias. In other words the identity (national or otherwise) of cinema will always depend on the location of the scrutiny or from where we are looking.

The matter of perspective has been crucial to this discussion, it is clear that the peripheral has both metaphoric and ideological resonance throughout this study. In an article proposing the scant evidence of Spanish nationalism against which to define a peripheral opposite, Hamilton M. Stapell suggests an alternative construction of national identity which accords with the artistic definition of it formulated by these three directors: 'Spanish identity after the end of the dictatorship might be understood as a group of overlapping circles of collective identity, produced through the process of constant contestation and negotiation, and not simply as binary or "dual" identity specific to some regions' (2007: 182).

The spatial freedom that was also a model for the topological formulation of the gaze in Chapter Two might hint at the subjective construction of actual, imaginative, cinematic and metaphorical spaces and, in doing so admit the competing territorial dimension as a productive site for the negotiation of subjectivity. Perhaps the only way to construct this (cinematic) map of the new Europe is to do so by letting the films place themselves on an alternative cartographic and cinematic depiction of reality, one which privileges encounters, reciprocity and image as a function of imagination.

The problem of space and place is one that Medem grapples with and ultimately solves by allowing his cinema to emerge in that space which is found at the intersection of actual place with imagined and virtual space. The camera then emerges at those cinematic sites which are the new spaces of a nascent filmic language that has moved us beyond the need to differentiate between the real and the hyperreal or the Real and the Imaginary. What is left is the space of a new variety of cinematic articulation, which is enriched by its association with a Spanish tradition but which can more usefully be located in a heterogeneous European current. Once the tensions surrounding this spatial example were grappled with in Medem's work, then the way was opened to situate the gaze in multiple different edge spaces. In fact, to remove the gaze – or at least demote it – is an acknowledgement of other notions of cinematic appreciation.

The narrative and formal properties of the pieces in question reveal a marked preference for the prioritisation of the subject in the process of becoming rather than as already established (be it the diegetic protagonist or the ostensively passive spectator) with a stable notion of identity, peripheral or otherwise. Moreover, these subjectivities as explored on screen are distinctly shaped by their relationship to, or place within, the sequence of cinematic images, and the history of the moving image more broadly. These images can transcend language – and subsequently identity as contained by language – and as such are informed by the performative function of language that plays with and extends the possibility of creative identities.

Actuality for these three directors is not reducible to the world as consumed on screen but it is involved in a two-way relationship in which the altered and enhanced world of the screen – and the image as projected onto that screen – adds to reality and renders our means of experiencing it as both dependent on, but also enriched by, the filmic projection. Power and the gaze have structured our comprehension of mechanisms of visual culture for some time, and what has emerged in the course of this scrutiny of these directors is that it might be playfully rethought in order to suggest a more flexible approach to power. Laura Marks claims, 'Spectatorship defined this way is less a matter of aligning oneself with an all-powerful gaze or perish, and more a matter of trying on various viewing positions, not untraumatically, but not entirely destructively' (2002: 76).

The cinematic takes its own place within reality not as the mirror for it but as an integral and mutable part of it. This must be the unifying feature of the works thus far. This is not to stress that their creativity and imagination removes these films from an engagement with an historical or current reality or that the emphasis on imagination is devoid of ideological commitment. Bigas's Transition statement made through *Bilbao* demonstrates that the opposite is true and that this innovation is useful precisely because of its ability to review reality. A concentration on new forms of cinematic engagement seems to have led implicitly to the status of cinema as a tool of representation not just of the marginal and the peripheral, as established, but also as a discourse through which to examine reality, memory and the past in all its fluidity. This has literally become the case for Guerín whose recent works have moved from the traditional cinematic auditorium to gallery exhibition spaces in the travelling exhibition *Todas las cartas/Totes les cartes/All the Letters*. This cinema situates itself at the intersection between temporal reality and collective and personal memory. When memory and cinema intersect to tackle contemporary political and ideological issues, this concentration on the body and its full gamut of sensory perception has been adopted to full effect by these – and other European – filmmakers.

The future of Spain's cinematic production seems committed to this variety of excavation of memory and the senses. It is a project concerned with the actuality of Europe and the camera's ability to expose the minutiae of life in smaller (peripheral) places in order to comment on the notion of inhabitation of this new European society. This conclusion is visually encompassed by an image from Bigas Luna's final part of his Iberian triptych, *The Tit and the Moon,* in a scene depicting the ten-year-old Tete's imaginations about his future. As he looks at the moon and imagines walking on it one day, he claims that he will replace the shabby old American flag with two new ones, the stars of Europe alongside the stripes of Catalonia. An ironic but prophetic musing on the nature of European cinema perhaps?

All these films function to provide references to other times and other spaces through affective and connotative relationships, moving away from the ossifying notion of the camera as fixing these subjects and objects in posterity and reflecting a notion of reality as both provisional and enduring but most importantly as lived. I have made little distinction between fiction and nonfiction throughout this book; in fact it was a further critical distinction that has been re-thought through Guerín's highly sophisticated hybrid works but also in Medem's political documentary *Basque Ball* in which the imperative to discover the truth foreshadowed, even obscured, the film's potential to question the possibility that such a quest might be possible or even ethical.

The mainstream success of both Bigas Luna and Medem is testimony to the fact than any marginalisation I refer to in relation to them is largely aesthetic and national. Guerín, on the other hand, is still positioned at the edge of the commercial mainstream, although the festival circuit seems to have embraced him wholeheartedly and as such became the subject of his 2010 film *Guest*. What has been possible through this study is to note the conditions of possibility for further scholarship in this area using these three directors as an example of the aesthetic engagement with a new subject position: the assumption of an independent subjectivity for cinema from the Spanish state.

Medem, Bigas Luna and Guerín engage with the technology of the moving image to expand its representational potential. An alternative theoretical approach that employed Lacan through to haptic and phenomenological enquiry by no means attempts to provide a definitive schema through which to analyse such a disparate group of texts. Rather I hope I have found a way of moving through and thinking with these thick, textural works – films that stubbornly defy a gaze and a cinematic language that defines, represents and reduces the other to an object of vision, and instead inhabit a new site of richly intersubjective perception.

References

Besas, P. 1985. *Behind the Spanish Lens: Spanish Cinema under Fascism and Democracy.* Denver: Arden Press.

Holland, J. 2006. 'My Name is Juani'. *Variety* 405(2): 61.

Marks, L. U. 2002. *Touch: Sensuous Theory and Multisensory Media.* Minneapolis and London: University of Minnesota Press.

Stapell, H. M. 2007. 'Reconsidering Spanish Nationalism, Regionalism, and the Centre-Periphery Model in the Post-Francoist Period'. *International Journal of Iberian Studies* 20: 171–185.

Filmography

Allen, W. 2008. *Vicky, Cristina Barcelona*.

Almodóvar, P. 1995. *La flor de mi secreto/The Flower of My Secret*.

———. 1997. *Carne trémula/Live Flesh*.

———. 1998. *Todo sobre mi madre/All about My Mother*.

Amenábar, A. 2001. *Los otros/The Others*.

Bigas Luna, J. J. 1976. *Tatuaje/Tattoo*.

———. 1978. *Bilbao*.

———. 1981. *Renacer/Reborn*.

———. 1983. *Caniche*.

———. 1986. *Lola*.

———. 1987. *Angustia/Anguish*.

———. 1990. *Las edades de Lulú/The Ages of Lulú*.

———. 1992. *Jamón, jamón*.

———. 1993. *Huevos de oro/Golden Balls*.

———. 1994. *La teta i la lluna/The Tit and the Moon*.

———. 1996. *Bámbola*.

———. 1997. *La femme de chambre du Titanic/ The Chamber Maid of the Titanic*.

———. 1999. *Volavérunt*.

———. 2001. *Son de mar/Sound of the Sea*.

———. 2006. *Yo soy La Juani/My Name is Juani*.

———. 2010. *Di Di Hollywood*.

Buñuel, L. 1929. *Un chien andalou*.

———. 1933. *Tierra sin pan/Land Without Bread*.

Godard, J. L. 1998. *Histoires du cinema*.

Guerín, J. L. 1984. *Los motivos de Berta*.

———. 1990. *Innisfree*.

———. 1997. *Tren de sombras/Train of Shadows*.

———. 2001. *En construcción/Work In Progress*.

———. 2007. *En la ciudad de Sylvia/In Sylvia's City*.

———. 2010. *Guest*.

Hawks, H. 1955. *Land of the Pharaohs*.

Medem, J. 1992. *Vacas/Cows*.

———. 1993. *La ardilla roja/The Red Squirrel*.

———. 1996. *Tierra/Earth*.

———. 1998. *Los amantes del círculo polar/Lovers of the Arctic Circle*.

———. 2001. *Lucía y el sexo/Sex and Lucía*.

———. 2003. *La pelota vasca/Basque Ball*.

———. 2007. *Caótica Ana/Chaotic Ana*.

———. 2010. *Habitación en Roma/Room in Rome*.
Morales, G. 2010. *Los ojos de Julia*.
Morrison, B. 2002. *Decasia*.
———. 2004. *Light Is Calling*.
Pons, V. 1978. *Ocaña: Retrat intermittent/Ocaña: Intermittent Portrait*.
Toro, G. del 2001. *El espinazo del Diablo/The Devil's Backbone*.

Index